Soul Samples

The Devil's strategy for our times is to trivialize human existence and to isolate us from one another while creating the delusion that the reasons are time pressures, work demands, or economic anxieties.

Philip G. Zimbardo, Ph.D.
"The Age of Indifference,"
Psychology Today,
Aug. 1980, pp. 71-76

Soul Samples

Personal Explorations in Reincarnation and UFO Experiences

By R. Leo Sprinkle, Ph.D

Granite Publishing
Columbus, North Carolina

Library of Congress Cataloging-in-Publication Data
Sprinkle, R. Leo, b-1930
Soul Samples : personal explorations in reincarnation and UFO experiences
by R. Leo Sprinkle

p. cm. -- (New Millennium Library; v. 7)
includes bibliographical references and index.
ISBN 1-893183-0 5-X (perfect bound)
1. Human-alien encounters--Psychological aspects.
2. Reincarnation therapy--Miscellanea.
I. Title. II. Series
BF2050.S67 1999
001.942--dc21   99-26143
CIP

Volume VII
The New Millennium Library

Cover Artwork: Eric Sprinkle
Manuscript editors: Brian Crissey, Amy Owen Demmon, Shirley Parrish

Printed in the United States of America.

Address all inquiries to:
Granite Publishing, LLC
Post Office Box 1429,
Columbus, NC 28722 U.S.A.
828-894-3088

Granite Publishing, LLC., is committed
recycled or tree-free paper.

Dedication

This book and its message is dedicated to Marilyn Joan (Nelson) Sprinkle who has served patiently and pleasantly, wisely and well, in so many ways, including: advisor, beadologist, business person, comic, companion, consultant, critic, community volunteer, friend, goad, gourmet, guide, home-builder, housekeeper, listener, music teacher, neighbor, office manager, partner, philosopher, pundit, sexual plaything, reincarnation soulmate, and workshop leader. I appreciate, beyond words, our creative co-dependence!

Marilyn, I like you; I lust you; I love you!

I thank you for our mutual efforts and explorations, especially your willingness to experience suffering and joy, body/mind/soul, by inviting to join us and share with us their talents: Nelson Rex Sprinkle, Eric Evan Sprinkle, Matthew David Sprinkle, Kristen Martha (Sprinkle) Shelstad.

Acknowledgments

Many persons have provided support and assistance in the writing of this book.

My thanks to sons Nelson Sprinkle and Eric Sprinkle, for their creative artwork that introduces each chapter and demonstrates—once more—that a picture is worth a thousand professional words.

Appreciation is expressed for the encouragement given by good friends, including Ann Brooke, C.B. Scott Jones, Ph.D., Ida Kannenberg, Lucille McNames, Cindy Rostohar, and Bob Teets.

Special appreciation is expressed for the assistance from Diana Goldman for her editorial insights and for typing the initial draft; Shirley Parrish for her counsel and competence, and retyping (and retyping) the manuscript; Lynne Pendley, Ph.D., and Darrell Pendley, Ph.D., for several computer printouts, occasional nagging nudges, and many a loving Waytogos.

Dr. R. Leo Sprinkle

Table of Contents

List of Appendices

List of Figures & Tables

Figures

Tables

Prologue

The late afternoon sun shone brightly, but the winter wind was stiff and cold. I struggled to maintain a slow pace, as I jogged along a street toward the top of a low hill. Huffing and puffing, sweating and groaning, I anticipated the moment that I could turn a corner and look over the snow-covered town of Laramie, Wyoming.

It was January 28, 1993. I reflected on the recent national events of the past week. I wondered if the Clinton administration would be able to produce changes, e.g., in campaign financial reform, crime control, judicial procedures, and public health care. I wondered if the rise of democratic aspirations among nations of the planet would be reflected in a decrease of the military powers and an increase in the cooperative interactions among segments of the international community.

But, primarily, I was anguished and frustrated in my own perspective about my personal and professional situation. I had left the University of Wyoming in 1989 when I was only fifty-nine years old. I assumed that—in one year—I could heal myself, body/mind/soul. Now, three and a half years later, I was healthier, body/mind/soul, yet I had only a fistful of notes to show for a major objective: a book about my experiences and explorations into ESP, reincarnation, and UFO encounters. Huffing and puffing, I continued to jog, but in my frustration I almost sobbed with self-pity and self-anger. I mentally asked my inner self, "What's wrong? Why can't I write the manuscript? I know how to write! Hell! I've written articles, chapters, entries in encyclopedias, etc. And I've written letters—every week, every month, every year—for more than three decades—to thousands and thousands of people. Why can't I write this damned manuscript?"

Then suddenly, three events occurred simultaneously, plus one more: insight! First, the street circled back toward town and, rather than struggling uphill, I began to move downhill. Second, I now was jogging, not against the wind, but with the wind. Third, I was asking myself the important question "To whom do I wish to address my comments? To whom am I writing?" *Insight*: I became aware, once again, of what I had learned years ago; I recognized, with new understanding, that I had been two-faced. I had been talking to clients and students with one "face," and talking to scientists and professors with the other "face."

Sobbing and laughing, I continued to jog downhill and downwind. Giddy and giggling, I savored the moment. I recalled a conversation in 1975 with a University of Wyoming staff member, who reviewed my manuscript, "Self-Improvement Program Handbook." He asked, "Leo, are you writing to professors or to students?" I knew that he had asked the important question, but I didn't know the answer! I did, however, respond by cutting the manuscript in half. I duplicated copies of the one-hundred-page handbook and distributed them to participants who wished to learn self-hypnosis procedures and techniques for stress management.

Once more, when faced with a choice between helping students and playing the professional game, (See "Sticks or Shticks?" on page 7) I chose to help students. The consequences, both positive and negative, were inevitable; I accepted those consequences and came to appreciate their significance for my personal and professional life.

However, the insight of that sunny and windy afternoon in January of 1993 was this: I no longer must choose between two groups of readers! I no longer need to worry about my comments to students and/or my comments to professors. Now, I can write to colleagues—true colleagues—persons who share my enthusiasm for new science and who are neither desperate to absorb nor desperate to avoid my comments, persons who are willing to consider what I have to offer.

I laughed out loud and shouted with glee; I rejoiced in my new-found freedom. I celebrated my new sense of science and my new sense of self! At that moment, I knew that I would write—not for some fearful professors and not for some eager students—but for other compassionate, courageous, and curious colleagues who are also seeking a spiritual path of love and light.

I recalled the profound comment by Brian O'Leary, Ph.D., former professor of physics at major universities and former astronaut-in-training, who has written *Exploring Inner and Outer Space*, *The Second Coming of Science*, and *Miracle in the Void*. Dr. O'Leary has been asked that all-too-common question, "What do your colleagues think of your interests in parapsychology and ufology?" He has responded, "I have new colleagues, and they are pleased with my interests and activities in New Science."

After jogging, cooling down, stretching, and showering, I dressed and enjoyed the "glow." I knew that the manuscript would be written. I didn't know if it would be published, and I didn't know if any published book would be financially successful.

Yet I knew, deep within, that I had learned a powerful life lesson. I knew that I had moved from being a "rescuer" toward being a "guide" in my role with others around me. No longer was I anxiously trying to please every obsessive left-brained reader, and no longer was I trying to please every compulsive right-brained reader. Now, I could write to some persons who were both rational and emotional in their intellectual response.

I recognized, and accepted, the probability that I could be accused by domineering rationalists of being self-centered—perhaps self-serving—by focusing only on my own psychic and UFO experiences. I recognized, and accepted, the probability that I could be accused by submissive emotionalists of discounting—perhaps demeaning—their anguish by writing about the need for suffering, as well as joy, in understanding UFO activity and the evolution of humanity.

However, I also knew that there are many good souls, with an intellectual and emotional strength, who are sincere in their search for a satisfactory and satisfying theory about the purpose of UFO activity.

Objective. The objective of this book is to offer one person's views of the journey of the soul, the significance of UFO activity, and the role of the individual person in human evolution. My intent is to offer my own perspective so that others, if they choose, can compare their philosophy with my own philosophy. Thus, I share with any reader these personal events that have helped me to learn and to love myself, others, and life itself, to become aware, to accept, and to acknowledge the interactions of humans, ETs (extraterrestrials) and higher beings.

Some years ago, in a profound and hilarious interview, Keith Thompson and I were discussing his thesis that the UFO phenomenon "covers its own tracks" (see his book, *Aliens and Angels*). In a generous comment, Keith encapsulated my efforts. "Leo," he said, "when other investigators were chasing lights in the sky and gathering soil samples, you were helping UFO experiencers and gathering *soul* samples!"

Soul samples! The words were like a magnet to my mind. Suddenly, I knew that the explorations of possible past lives and UFO encounters could be strung in various ways, by various theories. The task for me was to arrange them according to my own insights, then other writers and observers could arrange these according to their insights. Perhaps, as more samples are gathered, a useful theory can be developed.

Outline. This book is divided into four parts; these divisions are somewhat arbitrary because these experiences as outlined did not occur separately. However, the division does provide some organization of events that helps the writer (and, I hope, the reader) to sort through the progression of ideas, emotions, choices, and decisions.

Further, the outline is presented as a rough example of a marvelous model (see "A Model Chapter" on page 157) by Carl Gustave Jung, M.D. Jung described four psychological functions: feeling, intuiting, sensing, and thinking.[1] He considered two of these functions (sensing and intuiting) to be methods by which we humans obtain information. He considered two of these functions (thinking and feeling) to be methods by which we humans evaluate information.

The model can be presented as a circle with each function as an aspect of the circle:

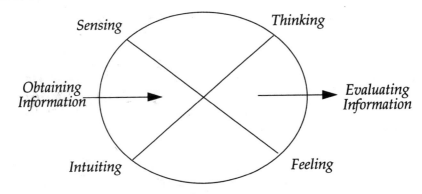

Sensing

Thinking

Obtaining Information

Evaluating Information

Intuiting

Feeling

FIGURE 1. *Jung's Model of Four Psychological Functions*

Jung noted that in various cultures there may be different social values and differing institutional influences by which these functions are cultivated and expressed.

For example, in some societies, intuiting (rather than sensing) may be emphasized as a method of gaining information; feeling (rather than thinking) may be emphasized as a method of evaluating information.

In the U.S., with a tradition of male dominance and a theory of materialistic science, the emphasis has been on sensing (not intuiting) as the approved method of gathering information, and thinking (not feeling) as the approved method of evaluating information. However, according to many observers that tradition is changing. A new focus is now occurring: a new/old age of science *and* spirituality, technology *and* ethics, masculine science *and* feminine science, god *and* goddess, blade *and* chalice, empirical science *and* experiential science, hierarchy *and* network, etc.

If so, then Jung's model offers more meaning as a dynamic, rather than static, description of individual human process and—perhaps?—a prescription for human interactions.

Thus, the reader should be aware of my bias. Yes! Now the new/old age is dawning. Yes! Each psychological function is worthy of scientific exploration and public expression. I wish to work with other persons in a social climate

1. Jung, 1933.

that promotes, in various ways, our own personal styles of intuiting/sensing/feeling/thinking.

Parts of the Book. The four parts of *Soul Samples* are arranged to emphasize each function: Part One emphasizes my sensing of **UFO experiences** (UFOEs). Part Two emphasizes my intuiting of **Possible Other Lives** (POLs). Part Three emphasizes my thinking about some studies of UFOEs and POLs. Part Four emphasizes my feeling about a possible synthesis of reincarnation and UFO activity.

Part One presents my personal and professional background and the events that caused me to view myself as a UFOEr—a UFO experiencer—as well as a UFO researcher. Part Two describes my experiences as a psychologist, which led me to become a past life therapist and a researcher of POLs. Part Three offers a brief summary of some studies on the personality characteristics of UFOErs and the reactions of clients who explore their POLs. Part Four provides a personal perspective of a possible social synthesis of reincarnation and UFO activity.

If one person reads this book, I am satisfied. If several persons read it and understand its message, I am pleased. If many persons read it, understand the message, and use the message to explore self and others, I am blessed.

PART ONE

Personal Analysis of UFOEs

To insist that the only reality are phenomena that can be submitted to the paradigm of classical science is itself a religion.

—*Dietrick E. Thomson*
Sr. Ed., *Science News*,
115, No. 2, Jan. 13, 1979.

Introduction

Some philosophers have claimed that the focuses of science and religion are different. In general, science deals with the question, "What can we know?" In general, religion deals with the question "What can we believe?"

Throughout my lifetime, I have struggled with the differences—and the similarities—of these related questions. The younger philosopher attempts to separate these questions; the older philosopher strives to integrate them.

The Ideal or the Moral Scientist?

The AAAS (American Association for the Advancement of Science) is considered to be the basic community of U.S. scientists. I became a life member in 1967 because of my interest in the philosophy of science and because of my bias that ESP and UFO phenomena are worthy of scientific study. (I hoped that by joining I could elevate both my bias and the AAAS. Hah!)

In 1979, I was pleased when the AAAS approved the Parapsychology Association as a division of AAAS. Yet I was disappointed later when the American Psychological Association (APA) rejected, several times, the proposal that a division of parapsychology (or transpersonal psychology) be added to the list of approximately fifty APA divisions. Does the condition indicate that APA is more or less scientific than the AAAS?

In 1990, the AAAS journal, Science, published a brief summary of a document that summarizes the guidelines that are meant to promote the "highest ethical standards," but not meant to become "prescriptive" as "rules."[1] According to these guidelines, the ideal scientist is a good mentor and teacher, knows the importance of maintaining primary data and making them accessible to colleagues, publishes just "the right amount"—neither too much nor too little, is listed as an author of a paper only if he or she actually did

---

1. "Guidelines for the Conduct of Research" (The Ideal Scientist Described, 27 July 1990, 249, #4967, p. 355)

3

some of the work, never abuses peer review by taking a colleague's idea as his or her own, and, finally, if the ideal scientist is a physician, he or she carefully follows all the existing guidelines that are in place for the protection of patients.

My reading of the *Science* article gave me both pleasure and displeasure. I was pleased that my motives would fit within the guidelines. Yet I was bothered by the omission of additional guidelines. I viewed the guidelines as pertaining to the "moral" or the traditional conventional scientist, yet it seemed to me that the "ideal" scientist is one who also is willing to study difficult or unpopular phenomena; one who uses courage and compassion, as well as curiosity, to advance knowledge, thereby contributing not only to scientific understanding, but also to human welfare. I continue to differentiate between social morality and personal ethics.

Thus, Part One not only describes my personal and professional background, but also provides examples of experience that caused me to choose between what I perceived to be the social road of the conventional "moral" traveler and the personal path of the "ethical" explorer.

Sticks or Shticks?

No one is exempt from talking nonsense.
The only misfortune is to do so solemnly.

—*Michel de Montaigne*
French Author

This beginning chapter provides the reader with a summary of my personal development, including the events that led to my "shticks" (special traits) or my patterns of activity: the double duty of being both a UFO experiencer (UFOEr) and a UFO researcher.

ER: Earliest Recollection

According to those who were there, (and for the benefit of any reader who is an astrologer), I was born at 10:30 A.M., August 31, 1930, in Rocky Ford, Colorado. Although I was not aware of the notion that my basic spiritual path—or life-style—already was established, I did become aware early on that my life-style as a psychologist was firmly established at a rather young age. My earliest recollection is as follows:

I remember an early spring day, when rain water flooded the dirt floor basement of our house. The outside door of the basement was open. My brothers and I could see the muddy water that covered the lower steps of the basement stairs. Bob, the oldest brother, had an idea for a game: Who can pick up the most sticks (tree twigs) from the yard, run down the steps, and throw the sticks into the water?

My youngest brother Gene and I were eager to play—and win—the game. However, Bob (about six-and-a-half years old) had the advantage, Gene (about three years old) had the disadvantage, and Leo (about four-and-a-half years old)—was the "average" player in the game.

I remember my attempt to keep up with Bob when he first ran down the steps. He threw his handful of sticks into the water, turned, and ran back up the steps. I was close behind Bob, but Gene was crawling down the steps. As I turned, Gene and I collided. He fell face down into the muddy water. Angry and fearful, I yelled to Bob, but he had disappeared over the top of the stairs. I knew that the water was too deep for me to jump into and pull Gene to safety.

I climbed the stairs as quickly as I could, and running to the kitchen, I called to Mom. She rushed outside, down the steps, waded into the water, and lifted Gene to safety. I remember my relief when I saw Gene, kicking and coughing, but alive and well.

Analysis of the ER (Earliest Recollection). Alfred Adler, M.D., colleague of Sigmund Freud, M.D., and Carl Jung, M.D., used the ERs of his patients to assist them in their psychoanalysis. Adler argued, with examples, that the ER of each person provided him or her with an interpretation of life-style or self-attitudes.[1] The ER can be used to understand the person's relationships with others and the basic attitude toward life as being threatening, supportive, satisfying, etc.[2] Any interpretation of my ER, and thus my life-style, probably would include an analysis of the following "retelling" of the story:

Leo is eager to compete, and win, especially in relation to older brother, Bob. However, Leo views himself as "average" in development and ability, so he must work very hard in order to experience success. Yet, there is an additional difficulty: Leo also must deal with the plight of younger brother, Gene, before he continues with the game. He is not able to persuade Bob to help him save Gene, who has been harmed by the rivalry or extreme competition. Thus, Leo must find a way to save Gene. Younger sister Faye is an infant who is unable to help. Dad, Rex, is at work and away from home. Thus, Mom, Annas, is the only person who can help. Leo asks and receives help from Mom, and Leo is pleased at the outcome of the situation when Gene is saved.

Interpretation of ER. Any reader who is educated in academic psychology and/or experienced in human behavior now has the means (if he/she is interested in such matters) to understand little Leo's personal development and to predict the choices that he shall make along his life's path.

Adler argued that we "forget" other early memories, and we focus on that specific memory that teaches us a lesson: the lesson of what life is all about and what we can expect from ourselves and others around us.

And what did little Leo learn? My current interpretation of my life-style is as follows: Leo is eager to play, and succeed, at the game of professional science. He wishes to be recognized by other professional persons as a capable

---

1. Adler 1931, 1958, pp. 71-92.
2. For further study, see Bruhn, 1989.

and competent contributor to a better understanding of human behavior, especially in regard to the relationships between persons. However, Leo regards himself as an "average" player, who experiences difficulty in keeping up with the "real" scientists, the traditional scientists, who are following established rules of science. They are busy picking up "sticks" (engaging in experimental activities), and throwing the sticks into the water (contributing books and theories about science). Further, Leo is aware that the competitive nature of the current game of science has become harmful to the "little persons," especially UFO contactees. These persons are struggling to deal with their UFO and ESP experiences, yet they are not receiving assistance from traditional scientists and conventional psychologists.

Leo attempts to gain the attention of Older Brothers, the traditional conventional scientists, but they are busy with their games of achievement within a masculine, authoritarian culture; they cannot understand—they cannot hear!—a cry of distress from Leo!

So, Leo seeks assistance from "ancient" science: the feminine, maternal, and spiritual philosophy from which modern masculine materialist science has emerged. Leo becomes involved in hypnotherapy, parapsychology, past-life theory, etc. In his compassion for his friends and/or clients, who have fallen into the murky waters of psychic phenomena and UFO encounters, Leo tries to communicate his concerns to other professional persons. However, some of his colleagues, who are older and more sophisticated, have decided that Leo himself has fallen into the waters—probably after pushing his clients into these weird experiences! In effect, their attitude is: "Leo, you caused these events, so you must deal with them, but these are neither professional nor scientific problems. These are personal problems; deal with them yourself. We have our game of Science to play."

And how did little Leo deal with his concerns? Let us look at some other early memories and compare them with our "key": Leo's pattern of double duty, or his attempt to play the conventional, competitive game as well as the caring, compassionate game.

Childhood Experiences

As a child, I was very shy and very quiet. When relatives or friends came to visit, I often hid behind a chair, until I was coaxed by my parents to come out and talk with the visitors. My parents were loving, but strict: "Spare the rod and spoil the child." If we children neglected our chores, or forgot to replace tools, etc., the razor strap would sing its song and we would do our dance.

Our two-story house was rather small, and without modern plumbing; there was an "out house" for our toilet, and a cistern and kitchen hand pump for our water. On Saturday night, bathing was brief. The ritual was conducted in an old iron tub that was placed on the kitchen floor. We were a poor family, but we ate good food. We had a cow, pigs, chickens, and many fruits and vegetables. Our basement cellar was lined with jars and jars of tasty food. In the 1930s, the economic depression was severe; our hard-working mother sometimes worried that there were patches on our jeans, but our clothes were clean! Our father first worked as a butcher, then barber (some wags said that there was no difference), and later, as a life-insurance salesman. Dad was athletic, hard-working, social, energetic, and ambitious, but in the 1940s, during World War II, the level of insurance sales went down. He became a bookkeeper in the local sugar beet factory, and Mom worked as an assistant to the chemists who analyzed the sugar content of the sugar beets.

Thus, my brothers and sister and I were expected to do many of the daily and weekly chores: milk the cow, feed the cow and pigs and chickens, clean the barn, gather the eggs, clean the house, help with the washing of clothes as well as the cooking, and washing and drying of the dishes.

In those days, children were "seen" but not "heard," according to many families. Our parents had similar expectations, but they allowed us to talk and tell jokes during the meal. If there was a squabble, or mischief, we were reprimanded. If we did not obey quickly, we would be warned. If we disobeyed, we would be "spanked." (In those days, it was called "discipline"; in the 1990s, some persons would describe the whippings as "child abuse.") The razor strap was a magical motivator, and we preferred to see it on the wall rather than in our father's hand.

As a small child, I wondered about the reasons for a recurrent nightmare. (As I grew older, and became a professional psychologist, I thought that I knew the answer. But did I?) The nightmare, which occurred perhaps a dozen times while I was five and six years old, can be described as follows:

Recurring Nightmare. I am alone, with a feeling of impending terror; I am in the boys' bedroom. In my mind's eye, I see a man climbing the stairs; I "know" that when he arrives at the top step he will turn toward me. Then, suddenly, he is transformed into a giant crab! I am frightened, but I can hardly cry out.

Finally, my mother comes with a broom and chases the giant crab away. I am greatly relieved as I awaken, shaking and shuddering, from the nightmare.

There were other strange events, which occurred when I was about ten years old. I awoke several times with a bloody nose and strange but vague memories of frightening figures. As I grew older, I rationalized the bloody-nose events as a result of my collision with brother Gene during a game of hide-and-seek. His head hit my nose, which bled profusely and often. However, I was bothered by the (undercurrent) memory that the blood on my pajamas and pillow had occurred before Gene and I had collided!?

A Hissy Fit. Another early recollection seemed even more strange because I behaved in such an unusual manner. As a boy, not only was I shy and quiet, but I also was deferent and obedient to my parents. Yet on one occasion, I had a "hissy fit," as my mother described it.

After a big snowfall (in 1940 or '41, when I was ten or eleven years old) we were preparing to walk to school. Our parents told us to take some old socks and pull them over our shoes, so that we could wade through the snow-drifts. I remember both Mom and Dad kneeling on either side of me, while I was stamping my feet, and crying, in rage and terror! For some unknown reason, I did not wish to wear those old socks over my shoes! They insisted! So, the socks were placed over my shoes and my pant legs tucked into the socks. I ran from the house, sobbing and screaming; finally, while walking through a field near the school building, I grabbed the socks, tore them from my shoes, and threw the socks into a drainage ditch. I wanted no one to see me with those old socks over my shoes and ankles.

Years later, as a graduate student in psychology, I rationalized my memories of those events in a manner that was almost satisfactory. I told myself: "Well, of course! As a child, you were worried about what other school kids thought about you. You didn't wish to be known as a poor kid, with no boots or overshoes, so you reacted with anxiety and anger when your parents forced you to wear old socks over your shoes!"

That explanation made sense to me, and I connected that memory with the earlier memory of the recurrent nightmare. That, too, was explainable by my childhood attitude about my Dad: I had been afraid of him! Thus, I fantasized him in my dream, coming up the stairs, and turning into a big crab! Of course! (Later, I learned that his Zodiac sign was Cancer, the Crab!) Thus, I had called on my image of a caring mom to help chase away the threatening dad! Praise be to the Oedipal Complex and Sigmund Freud!

Arithmetic and Astronomy. However, one memory of childhood made no sense to me, even as an adult and as a psychologist. It was not until 1980, when I was fifty years old, that I came to understand the following conscious memory.

I was ten years old; I was in the fifth grade, Washington School, Rocky Ford, Colorado. It was a dull and dreary afternoon. My shoulders slumped. Our teacher, Mrs. Sickenberger (a great name for boorish, boyish jokes!) reminded us of the importance of learning our arithmetic lesson, positioning the template form over our notebook paper, and completing—accurately—the problems.

Then, she gave us an extra incentive: "Class, if you finish your assignment before the end of the period, you can go to the library and read any book that you wish to read." I was inspired! I leaned over my desk and I worked as quickly as I could. I soon finished the arithmetic problems. I handed my answer sheet and form to the teacher. Then, as quickly as possible—without running!—I walked to the library room, knowing the book that I wished to read: a big black book on *science*! I could hardly wait to read it.

Inside the library room, I pulled the book from the shelf. I sat down, opened the book; and there! In the first chapter on astronomy, there was a photograph on a lower right hand page. The photograph, according to the caption, showed a group of stars in this part of our galaxy. Instantly, the photograph came alive! I gasped! The stars in the photograph seemed to be moving toward me! My mind seemed to swirl; my vision was fixed on the moving stars. I felt dizzy and confused, yet also exhilarated. Somehow, I seemed to be experiencing—again—something that I had experienced before.

Although I had no way to explain that strange event, the memory of that afternoon lingered with me; it was a reminder that my inner mind had mysteries to explore, someday. Meanwhile, after the fifth grade, I changed in several ways: from a shy boy, who was criticized by teacher and father for my poor posture, to a more social and confident boy. I improved my classroom achievement; I began to play basketball and other sports, and I took an interest in class activities.

In the eighth grade, I confided in a teacher that I might grow up to be a lawyer, maybe a statesman, and maybe even to become president! (Abraham Lincoln was my idol and, most of all, I admired his honesty.) Thank goodness, my teacher listened without laughing at me.

Honest Abe or Nervous Neurotic? One cold morning, with pitchfork in hand, I was cleaning our little shed of cow manure. I was in a hurry, so that I could walk to school without being tardy. (I had an eight-year record of no absences and not being tardy.) Suddenly, I knocked out the shed window with the pitchfork handle. I groaned, knowing that the offense was punishable by the fearsome razor strap. But I also knew that it would be best to confess now than later. I went to the house, into the bathroom—by then, we had indoor plumbing and a coal-oil stove—where my father was shaving. Keeping one eye on the razor strap, and the other eye on his quick hand, I told Dad what had happened. He thanked me for being honest. He shook my hand and told me that if I would always let him know when "something was wrong," then he wouldn't spank me anymore.

Tears came to my eyes. I was so pleased that he trusted me and treated me as if I were a man. I promised to keep my part of the bargain.

Years later, as I learned more about the effects of "morality," I recognized that I had been overcommitted in my response. What did it mean for me to tell my dad if "something was wrong"? Are we talking about individual errors? Family? Society? Humankind? God?

At that time, I became a little neurotic (or a big neurotic in a little body!). Not only did I do my chores and homework in a diligent fashion, but also I picked up scraps of paper on the sidewalk, etc. Years later, I recognized that I not only worried about my ability to keep my promise, but I also worried about his ability to keep his promise. (He did!) For my part, I was a good Boy Scout, a good member of Sunday school class, and a nice, awkward lad who was delightful in the eyes of teachers and disgusting in the eyes of other boys. Nevertheless, the confidence in my relationship with Dad, and the support in my studies from Mom, provided me with a sense of destiny as well as a duty. I knew, before I entered high school, that I wished to earn a scholarship for college. I didn't know if I wished to study law, or science, or religion. My emerging interest in religion stemmed from two (unrelated?) events.

Church Camp. When I was fifteen or sixteen years of age, I attended a church camp for Methodist youth near Colorado Springs. Palmer Lake was a beautiful area of grass, trees, and water. I was enthralled with a week of new friends, Bible classes, and my "Green Cathedral": a few minutes each day of individual prayer or meditation, next to a bush or tree. At the end of the week, a visiting minister spoke quietly and eloquently about the purpose of life and he encouraged any girl or boy to step forward and dedicate her or his life to serving God and others.

I knew that I didn't wish to become a preacher, but I did feel an undeniable urge to come forward. With tears in my eyes, and with a deep sense of awe within me, I stood with several others and committed my life to spiritual service. I wasn't certain of my plans, but I felt a powerful source of energy that was radiating within me. I "knew," somehow, that if I maintained a path of integrity and service, I would be rewarded inwardly if not outwardly. (Later, in a college course on the Psychology of Religion, I read a book by William James, *The Varieties of Religious Experiences*. I then recognized that I had experienced a garden variety of spiritual emergence. At the time, however, I described the event as being "reborn," a religious rebirth, a turning point in my life.) It was such a powerful experience that I asked my friend, who had arranged a blind date for me, to offer my apology to the girl: I wished to be alone in order to deal with my emerging thoughts and feelings.

Church Conference. Another important event occurred in 1947 when I was a junior in high school. I faced a dilemma: to attend a Methodist youth conference in Detroit, or to miss an important boys basketball game? Which activity was more important?

I decided to travel by bus to the conference, with other youth from the region. It was a marvelous opportunity for a country hick to share stereotypes about kids from the east, west, north, and south, as well as an opportunity to listen to some excellent speakers. I was impressed with the scholarly and compassionate presentation by Dr. Overstreet; but, some of my friends viewed him as somewhat dull and very mystical. They were excited about the next speaker, whom I viewed as a pulpit-pounding, Bible-thumping voice, who raged about the Devil and how modern society had become evil! At one point, he yelled out to all of us about a specific example of evil, from his own experience. My memory of his story goes like this:

"Yes, boys and girls, with my own eyes, I have seen the sins of our society! Just this morning, as my friends and I were walking to a restaurant for lunch, we saw a man lying in the gutter. No one (his voice became louder), *no one* was paying attention to this man! *No one* was looking to see if he was dead, or ill, or drunk! *And do you know what?* (Screaming!) When we came out of the restaurant, that same poor man was still in the gutter!"

I laughed out loud! Several youth, all around me, looked at me in disdain. One of my friends, with shock and shame in his voice, whispered, "Leo! You shouldn't laugh at that poor man in the gutter!" I said nothing, but I wished that I had the courage to state, "I'm not laughing at the man who was lying in the gutter. I am laughing at the man who is standing before us. Why didn't he attend to the man in the gutter, or ask someone to check on the man in the gutter?"

The irony (or hypocrisy?) of the story seemed to be lost on my youthful friends—as well as the speaker. I resolved that, someday, if I were in a position to assist others, then I would wish to be more like the quiet voice of the professor than the shouting voice of the pulpit-pounder.

Yet, my lack of courage to speak out was of concern to me. Then, in 1948, as a high school senior, I had an opportunity to learn that particular lesson.

A Strike-Out or a Base Hit?

One sunny autumn morning, I walked into the classroom for our senior U.S. History course. Other students were excited and whispering to each other about a "strike." One of the ringleaders approached me. "O.K., Sprinkle, everybody knows that you're a goody-goody, but don't screw up this deal! We're studying labor union history, so we're all gonna go on strike! Everybody has agreed, so whadda ya say?"

Slowly, I shook my head. "I don't think that this is a good idea." He retorted, "Aw! Come on! Everybody has promised to go along with it! Whadda ya say?"

"Well," I said, "if everybody has agreed to go along with the plan, then I will too."

We settled into our desks. When our teacher (and track coach), Mr. Nus, reminded us about the class examination, we all took out a sheet of notebook paper. Mr. Nus walked his 6'5" frame around the room while we wrote our answers to his questions. Then, when we were told to turn in our answer sheets, I took out another sheet of paper; I wrote my name and date; then, in large letters, I wrote the word "*Strike!*" I handed in my paper along with those of my classmates.

Of course, because of our weird behavior, Mr. Nus had suspected something was wrong. He told us to remain seated while he left the room. One student, watching the teacher, said that Mr. Nus was going to the office of the principal. Another student quickly scanned the papers on the teacher's desk in order to see who had followed the plan. Soon, Mr. Nus returned and he reprimanded us for our actions. He announced that anyone who turned in a blank sheet of paper would receive a double UU (unsatisfactory) or two failing grades for the test.

Later we learned that only four of the two dozen students had gone on "strike": Two quiet, shy females, another quiet guy, and myself!

It was a valuable lesson for me. The loud ringleaders were unable to act on their own plan. Many years later, at a reunion of our seventy-five-member class of 1948, I thanked the other attendees. I thanked them for that opportunity to learn that I can make my own decisions without the common concern about what others will think about me.

A Budding Psychologist

From then on, the lessons came quickly and thickly. I attended the University of Colorado-Boulder on an academic scholarship, and with a job in the kitchen of a women's residence hall. I started as a hasher, then dishwasher, pot and pan washer, and finally as an assistant cook. I worked thirty-five hours a week with a crew of young men and women who also were students with academic and/or athletic scholarships.

I knew that I wished to become a counselor of some kind, but because our high school had only begun the hiring of a part-time guidance counselor, I did not know the duties for that position. So, I chose a "distributed major": psychology, sociology, history, and education. I was interested in science, but I decided to prepare myself for becoming a high school history teacher in case I was not successful in becoming a psychologist. Ideally, I hoped that I could find some answers to questions like these: What is the nature of the human mind? Where did humanity originate? How do individuals learn? Why do people act differently in groups than when they are alone? Where is humanity headed in the future?

I soon learned that I would not find many answers to these questions. The faculty of the Department of Psychology were involved in "science," not "philosophy." With stopwatches and charts, we were rigorous little scientists, who timed the responses of our "subjects" to various tasks.

I did sign up for one experiment in hypnosis; the graduate student was interesting, but I was disappointed. I relaxed deeply, but I was able to hear everything that was going on around me; thus, I decided that my participation was a failure, and I doubted the existence of "hypnosis." I developed a skeptical, somewhat cynical, view of human behavior and human nature. I was well on my way to developing a materialistic, empirical philosophy of science.

General Semantics and Flying Saucers. Then, one day in 1949, when I was a university sophomore, I was exposed to an experience that blasted open my rigid philosophy of science and my dogmatic notions of reality.

A fellow student and co-worker, Joe Waggoner, told me of a lecture on general semantics by a visiting speaker. After work, we changed from our "whites" to our jeans and T-shirts and we walked to Hellums Hall, the Arts and Science building, for the presentation. It was an excellent lecture, just what I had hoped for; I was pleased to hear a scholarly presentation on a theory that might explain why different scientists disagree over their observations about the nature of reality.

As Joe and I came out of Hellums Hall, we were playing a little game; we asked ourselves questions, and gave ourselves answers along these lines: "What do you see over there?" "I see a tree." "How do you describe this tree?" "Well, I claim to see a trunk, branches, twigs, and leaves." "Is this description on the first level of reality or the second level of reality?" etc.

Just then, we saw something moving over Hellums Hall. We continued our game: "What do you see there?" We both gawked and gasped.

I perceived a silver gray object, apparently elliptical in shape, moving from south to north over the A & S Building, and then over the campus toward a grove of trees. I could not determine how large it was, or how far away it was. (Later, as we reviewed the experience, we estimated the apparent size of the object as that of a fingernail at arm's length. However, if it were the size of an airplane, it would be moving faster than jet airplanes moved in those days.) Along the rim of the metal (?) object, I perceived a small flashing light. I couldn't determine if the pulsating light was a reflection from the setting sun, or whether the small light was from an internal source of light. The visual effect was that of a rotating edge, or rim, of the object. Then, the object disappeared behind some trees.

Not a Flying Saucer. Both Joe and I were mystified; we talked about what we had seen, but we couldn't explain the puzzling event. Certainly, it was not a "flying saucer"! In 1949, only "kooks" claimed to see flying saucers! We weren't kooks! We were serious students, even aspiring scholars! We tried, in our imagination, and in our conversation, to turn the object into an airplane, a balloon, a helicopter, etc. Finally, in desperation for an explanation, we agreed: The object probably was an experimental aircraft of the U.S. Army or U.S. Air Force!

Later, I refused to talk to anyone else about the experience. In fact, I didn't wish to think about the sighting, because the experience had shattered my sense of science and my view of reality. I tried to concentrate on my studies, but I went through a mild depressive episode. I lost my academic scholarship for a brief period. I stopped my usual routine of "introspection," a nightly routine of relaxing and reviewing daily events and then planning for the next day's activities. (In high school, I called the routine "prayer," but in college, I knew that it was best to call it "introspection." When I learned that "introspection" was not "scientific," I discontinued the practice. Finally, in graduate school, I called it "meditation," and I regained the results of comfort and well-being that the practice provides.)

Gradually, I was able to regain a sense of self-confidence, but I had lost confidence in Western science. I prepared myself to become a history teacher, in case I was not successful in becoming a scientist and psychologist.

Marilyn J. Nelson

Then, the best event in my life occurred! I met (again?) Marilyn Joan Nelson, of Gurley, Nebraska. During the summer of 1951, on the campus of the University of Colorado-Boulder, Marilyn and I were introduced to each other by her brother, John D. Nelson. John and I worked in the same residence hall kitchen, and he knew of my interest in writing down some ballads that I had composed with my little ukuléle guitar. He told me that his sister was in music school and perhaps she might be willing to help me by recording the notes of the melodies.

When I met Marilyn, I recognized her from an earlier event. In 1950, I was walking across campus toward my room in Baker Hall. Just ahead, I saw long blonde hair and a rust-colored coat. As I walked past the young woman, I looked at her lovely face, with sunshine glowing on the crown of her head. I had a strong urge to speak, but I didn't know what to say. I hurried on past her, but the memory of her beauty lingered with me.

As Marilyn and I talked, she agreed to transpose my songs from voice to music sheet. I watched her as she leaned over the piano board; I wondered if she considered my songs to be silly or too sentimental. I thanked her for her skill and her effort. (Later, Marilyn laughed when she told me about her thoughts of that initial project; she thought to herself, "After all of that work, he didn't offer to buy me a cup of coffee!") I was so smitten that I could barely muster my usual rural awkwardness.

During that summer, I gathered my courage and occasionally asked her for a date. Our first date was to view the movie, Cyrano de Bergerac, with José Ferrar. As we walked back to the campus, I held her hand, and I was both frightened and exhilarated by the emotions that rocked within me.

At the end of the summer session, we corresponded; then, at the beginning of fall semester, we were together every evening. Three months after we met, we were engaged to be married. Seven months later, we were married, June 7, 1952. I was joyful, yet apprehensive, about my prospects for supporting a wife. I completed my bachelor's degree, August 1952. While waiting for military draft notice, I worked at odd jobs: skinning deer hides, digging a well, selling children's books, etc.

I entered the U.S. Army at Camp Crowder, Missouri, completed basic training at Camp Chaffee, Arkansas. After becoming honor student Number One in leadership school, I was sent to Germany for artillery training. (My friends and I, who were married men, were sent to Germany. My unmarried friends were sent to Korea.) Once again, I was honor student Number One, NCO Academy, Munich. A general pinned on my PFC (Private First Class) stripe.

The commanding officer was impressed with my work, and I often obtained a pass to leave the barracks and stay overnight with Marilyn in our small room (until I had the gall to loan a book on army rules and regulations to a prisoner, an African-American soldier; thereafter, I experienced difficulty in obtaining overnight passes).

Misery or Magic?

Marilyn was with me in Germany for a year. We had many opportunities to travel, whenever I could arrange a leave of absence from military duties. We traveled (third-class rail, of course, with friendly people who stared at my army uniform and Marilyn's strange shoes) to Italy, Austria, France, and—by boat and/or airplane—to England and Scandinavia.

One journey was important as a lesson in love: Marilyn and I rode all night on a train to France; I was tired from a very busy schedule, including guard duty. When we arrived in Paris, I was ready to nap, but Marilyn insisted that we explore the city. The bus driver was disdainful of Americans who could not speak French. We got off too soon and had to walk a long way to reach the Eiffel Tower. I was crabby about French people and impatient with Marilyn. Suddenly, I recognized my silliness. I thought to myself, "Why am I complaining? I'm with my lovely wife; there are flowers; it is April in Paris! Enjoy!" We hugged and kissed! Ahh, such bliss!

When I completed my tour of duty, we returned to the U.S. in 1954, so that I could enroll in the University of Colorado Master of Personnel Service program: psychology, sociology, education, and business.

It was a rather unruly period of student activities on campus, including panty raids and some dynamite blasts. I served as a residence hall director, with two undergraduate assistants, for two hundred young men. My leadership skills were tested quite often!

I kept a small sign posted on the apartment door so that—at 3:00 AM, when some student pounded on the door—I could remind myself of the aphorism by U.S. psychiatrist, Harry Stack Sullivan, M.D., "Nothing makes living difficult except other people, and one's own inadequacies for dealing with them."

Some of my friends, laughing at the sign, provided me with advice: "Just leave off that last part, Leo: nothing makes living difficult except other people, *period!*" I would smile, nod my head, and then say, "However, if I add that last phrase, then I have something to go on. I don't have much control over others, but I can learn how to deal more effectively with others."

Another Multiple Witness UFO Sighting!

The main event that captured my attention—and redirected my professional interests—was another UFO sighting in the summer of 1956.

Marilyn had been encouraging me to read books about the topics of ESP and UFO reports, but I would not listen to her. I already knew that she is brighter than I am. (I had seen her and my academic test scores when I served as a graduate assistant in the testing center.) However, I had wished to be viewed not only as a graduate student, but also as a scientist! I knew that interest in ESP and UFO phenomena was not scientific!

I could no longer be the scoffer that I was before my 1949 UFO sighting; however, I was a skeptic, and I rejected her suggestion that I read books about these unusual phenomena. (Old proverb: We become what we resist.)

In the summer of 1956, one late afternoon, just after sunset, Marilyn and I were returning from Denver. As our car topped a hill overlooking Boulder, we both noticed a bright orange-red light above the Flat Irons (Rocky Mountain foothills). We both remarked on the beauty of that evening star, or planet. Then suddenly, the light began to move.

I stopped the car. We got out and continued to watch the light, or object, as it continued to move. (Later, Marilyn recalled the initial movement as "back-and-forth," like a pendulum. I recalled the initial movement as back-and-forth, with a dipping motion, like the pattern of a falling leaf.) As Marilyn and I stood there, watching the strange light, we could view it as hovering between us and the Flat Irons. (Thus, I knew that it was no evening star or planet!) During the next few minutes, the object or light hovered, moved, hovered, moved, etc. There was no sound that I could associate with the light. However, I could hear car horns, and I could see car headlights being turned on in the gathering darkness.

I knew that I was witnessing something that was extraordinary, but I hardly knew how to describe it—much less explain it. Gradually, the light disappeared to the north.

As Marilyn and I talked about our perceptions, I tried to rationalize the experience. But I knew that the experience could not be a sighting of an airplane, a balloon, or a helicopter. The object, or light, was large, like the size of a helicopter, if it were hovering over the city as I perceived it to be. However, if it were hovering next to the Flat Irons, then the UFO would have been huge, like a university building!

I consoled myself: "Well, at least there will be some news about this unusual sighting on radio and in the newspaper. Surely, there are other people who are watching this extraordinary event."

Alas! Next morning, there was no public information about the incident: no newspaper notice and no radio announcement. Slowly, the awareness of the significance of the event permeated my inner being. I had learned two important lessons: one, I knew that I must investigate UFO phenomena, and two, I knew that it would be a lonely task.

Director of Wildlife

With Master's degree in hand, and with our worldly possessions in an old cattle trailer, Marilyn and I drove our little car to Columbia, Missouri. I had accepted a position as instructor/counselor in a women's college, Stephens College. At $4,200 a year, we could begin our family and enjoy a new life.

At Stephens College, I learned several lessons. I learned about my sexist attitudes, as well as my dogma about the kinds of curricula that can be established for higher education. I came to understand, and accept, the principles that women—and men—can be interested in a variety of occupations, can be interested in both science and religion, and can integrate their personal and professional behaviors.

I was admitted as a candidate for the degree Doctor of Philosophy, in counseling psychology, at the University of Missouri-Columbia. During a transition time at Stephens College, I served as (temporary) director of student life, which included supervision of student government and student-union activities. Some graduate students at the University of Missouri called me "Director of Wild Life," because of their views about the escapades of some of the Stephens Susies! Despite my lack of interest in ESP, I learned that coincidences can occur, and I learned that some persons have the ability to create coincidences and to confirm their view of reality.

One day, two friends (fellow sufferers in the University of Missouri doctoral program) were walking with me as we left that campus and approached Stephens College campus. My friends, unmarried males, were begging for information. The conversation was animated. "Come, on Leo, tell us! Is it true that there is hanky-panky going on between Stephens students and professors?" I shrugged my shoulders and replied, "Not that I know of." "Ahh! Come on!" they insisted. "You can tell us! Is it true?" I emphasized, "Not that I know of."

Just at that moment, a lovely young woman walked toward us. I recognized her as the wife of a friend of mine who was a fellow instructor at Stephens College. He and I often played tennis on weekends, and sometimes she would sit with their infant child and watch us as we struggled, sweating, in the hot muggy air. I looked at her and said hello. She did a "double-take," then she smiled in recognition as she said, "Oh, hi, Leo! I didn't recognize you with your clothes on!" My two friends gagged and chortled in glee! What a moment for their reality-testing!

Doctor of Philosophy

In all of my academic endeavors, like most students, I had experienced both joy and suffering. I enjoyed the acquisition of new skills and new knowledge, but I experienced stress in my conflicts about the purpose of certain coursework.

As doctoral students, we sometimes questioned the importance of the role of scientist versus the role of practitioner: Are we being prepared for competition or cooperation? For rivalry or compassion? For establishing ourselves as experts or applying ourselves as helpers?

And, of course, our (nonverbal) questions were answered (nonverbally) by our professors: Yes! You are being prepared to be expert helpers. You are being prepared to be both scientist and practitioner.

Ubiquitous! Ubiquitous! One morning, on the campus of the University of Missouri-Columbia, I learned a valuable lesson about learning. I was a student in Dr. David Premack's class, and I was contemplating his research studies on "positive reinforcement." I wondered to myself, "If positive reinforcement is more effective than negative reinforcement, then why use negative reinforcement?"

I was reminded of my reaction to the overuse of the Devil as a concept in the theology of some Christians. If the love of God is more powerful than the hate of the Devil, then why not focus on the more powerful effect?

Just ahead of me on the crowded sidewalk were three male students. The tall young man in the middle was ambling along, almost shouting as he turned left and right between his buddies, apparently expressing his anger at some professor. He yelled, "Ubiquitous! Ubiquitous! If he says that word one more time, I'm gonna look it up!"

I almost gagged as I stifled my laughter. I thought to myself "Wow! The power of education!" Then, as I contemplated what I had experienced, I sensed that something important had happened. I wasn't certain of the conscious recognition.

Only later, when I was reading some channeled information about "joy and suffering" was I able to integrate my "sensing" and my "thinking" about the importance of suffering and negative reinforcement.

In response to the question, why is there so much suffering in the course of human learning, came the answer: because so few persons are willing to learn through joy! I recognized, once more, that I could decide for myself what is "joy" and what is "suffering."

Was it joyful or miserable for me to complete advanced courses in theory of personality, counseling theory, and practicum counseling with a variety of clients? Once again, I recognized an old familiar pattern: double duty. I wished to be a counselor and adviser for students, but I also wished to be a professor of psychology. I knew that, someday, I would serve on the faculty of a university, and also assist students in a university counseling center.

But I also knew that—somehow—I was preparing to become a UFO investigator. My friend, Steve Fiore, taught humanities courses at Stephens College. He and his wife, Ginger, showed Marilyn and me his collection of

UFO books including those by Frank Edwards and Donald Keyhoe. By 1961, when I finished the doctoral degree, I was familiar with the strange claims about UFO phenomena. I was a doctor of philosophy, a counseling psychologist, yet I knew that an important task before me was to investigate the strange claims of UFO reports.

UFO Investigator or
UFO Experiencer?

I do not seek to follow in the footsteps of the men of old;
I seek the things they sought.

—Basho
Japanese Poet

"Leo! Be careful! You can't be a UFO investigator and be a real scientist! If you become a UFO investigator, you will lose any reputation that you might earn later on."

These words, or words to this effect, were spoken to me by well-meaning colleagues at the University of North Dakota-Grand Forks (UND).

When I graduated from the University of Missouri-Columbia (UM-C), with a Doctor of Philosophy degree in 1961, I had three choices: a teaching position at the University of Illinois-Urbana, a counseling position at the University of Texas-Austin, and a teaching-counseling position at UND.

Some of my friends urged me to accept an offer from one of the more "prestigious" institutions. However, the dual tasks (of course!) of professing and counseling were appealing to me. Marilyn and I, and sons Nelson and Eric, were able to adapt to the cold weather, and we enjoyed the good people of North Dakota.

NICAP. One of my first unofficial acts was to search the files of the UND library for a microfilm record of a Fargo newspaper. And lo! I found the information: an article about the report of a "dogfight" between a UFO and a pilot in the North Dakota Army-Airforce National Guard. I had read of the incident in a book by Major Donald Keyhoe (retired U.S. Marine officer, and one of the founders of NICAP, National Investigations Committee on Aerial Phenomena).

I was excited to learn that the newspaper account of the incident was retold accurately by Major Keyhoe. (I thought to myself, in skeptical fashion, "OK! The newspaper article may be wrong, but the author reported it accurately in his book!")

I wrote to NICAP Headquarters in Washington, DC, for information about membership. I joined NICAP, and sometimes sent $20.00 as a contribution for special projects.

APRO. Then I joined APRO (Aerial Phenomena Research Organization), headed by Jim and Coral Lorenzen of Tucson, Arizona. They asked me to serve as a consultant, along with Frank B. Salisbury, Ph.D., professor of plant physiology, and James A. Harder, Ph.D., professor of engineering, University of California-Berkeley. I enjoyed association with them, both personally and professionally.

A Lesson in Humility

I learned two lessons in humility at UND: one from my friend and colleague, Roger Myers, Ph.D., and one from the other professors in psychology. The department of psychology was composed of thirteen male members. Each was bright, well trained, and competitive. There was a strong push to publish peer-reviewed articles in scientific journals and to prepare the department for approval by the APA (American Psychological Association). I enjoyed the intellectual sparring in formal departmental meetings, as well as the informal discussions in the faculty club. I learned, however, that my intellectual abilities and levels of knowledge were not as high as those of many departmental faculty.

Roger Myers and I never quarreled, but we enjoyed philosophical and professional arguments about science and psychotherapy in order to display our wit and fund of information. I soon learned that Roger (who received his Ph.D. from Ohio State University) was brighter and more articulate than I. If I argued, for example, that religious experiences should be included in any comprehensive theory of personality, he could provide several reasons to dismiss, or at least to doubt, my contention. I learned to "die on home soil" by arguing for my own personal belief, rather than to speak on behalf of other academic psychologists.

Another Lesson in Humility

I learned another lesson in humility, 1962-63, during an important departmental meeting. The meeting was called by the UND president in order to deal with the schism that had developed between the "old" model of experimental and clinical psychology, and the "new" model of counseling and guidance. The controversy became so heated that President Starcher asked the departmental head, Ralph Kolstoe, Ph.D., and the head of the guidance institute, Paul Munger, Ph.D., to present their views on whether there should be one department or two departments.

The night before the meeting was very difficult for me. I did not know how I should vote. I fantasized my vote as the "swing vote": six professors might vote to maintain the status quo; six might vote to split the department; thus, my vote might decide the outcome. I could sympathize with the "older" colleagues, and also I could sympathize with the "younger" colleagues, but I did not know which option was better for the department and the university. Finally, in order to sleep, I decided that I would go to the meeting, listen to the arguments, and then decide.

Next morning, as the meeting proceeded, President Starcher oriented us to the purpose of the meeting. He was very articulate, a professor of mathematics, and a keen judge of character. He asked Dr. Kolstoe to state his position. (Ralph was a true professor; students liked his enthusiasm about the science of behavior, but they joked about his proclivity toward details: "Dr. Kolstoe is a professor who, if you ask him what time it is, will give you a history of watchmaking!") Dr. Kolstoe stated his position with—surprise!—only a few brief comments. Dr. Starcher then asked Dr. Munger to state his position. Briefly, the position was as follows: the guidance institute brings approximately $225,000 each year to UND; if the proposal to split the department is not approved, the director shall go to another university and take the institute funds with him.

President Starcher then summarized the two arguments, pointed out the advantages and disadvantages of each position, and concluded that the financial weight of the institute was decisive: there would be two departments. I learned a valuable lesson about politics: When money talks, people listen! And I learned something about my own influence in certain controversies: it don't make no difference!

Also, I learned that my own position of Mr. In-Between was not entirely honest. I had wished to be accepted and respected by those who were traditional, as well as those who were innovative, in their views. I longed to be regarded as rigorous and skilled in scientific methodology, but I also wished to be compassionate and helpful to students. Some of the professors assumed that one is either tough minded or tender hearted.

Robert Rosenthal, Ph.D. Yet, one professor, Dr. Robert Rosenthal, seemed to be tough minded in regard to data and tender minded in regard to persons. I liked his approach, and I enjoyed my participation in several of his studies on the effects of experimenter bias. I regained some professional confidence from his results: everyone is biased. The scientific task is to be aware and to account for the effects of bias in one's own observations.

Initial UFO Study

In my wish to learn more about UFO phenomena, I recognized that I had few skills to offer in the study of physical effects of UFO activity. So, I decided to study the characteristics of persons who were involved in UFO organizations.

I began with the help of Richard Hall, NICAP, and a small grant ($278.00) from SPSSI (Society for the Study of Social Issues, APA). I conducted a survey study of approximately 250 members of NICAP. (See Chapter 7.) I concluded that the scores of NICAP members were distributed normally—compared to UND professors and graduate students in psychology—in regard to the levels of "open-minded" and "close-minded" scores of the *Rokeach Dogmatism Scale*.

Another Study

I discontinued another survey: ratings by faculty on various topics for scientific investigation, and whether the acceptable evidence could be "anecdotal," "expert opinion," "empirical," and/or "laboratory" experimental evidence. The study was not completed because some of the professors refused to complete the survey form. (One professor, who expected his rats to participate in his studies, became frustrated when he recognized that the "laboratory" rating could not be used to deal with all of the listed topics, e.g., "evidence for extraterrestrial life."

I decided that a better source of information about UFO reports would be the witnesses themselves. (Part of my motive was scientific curiosity, but part of my motive was personal anxiety: I was worried about the kind of characters with whom I was associated!)

Psychotic or Neurotic?

In the 1940s and 1950s, some professional persons claimed that UFO witnesses—especially those of us who claimed multiple sightings—were "crazy." As a psychologist, I was intrigued by these claims, but as a "multiple sighting" UFO witness, I was skeptical of those claims!

In 1963, I began a study of UFO contactees and their responses to personality inventories. I had written to several psychiatrists and psychologists; I had asked them if they had noticed any association of psychic phenomena and UFO phenomena. Only one scientist had replied, Jule Eisenbud, M.D, a Denver psychiatrist and psychoanalyst and well-known scholar of parapsychology. Dr. Eisenbud was doubtful about a connection between ESP and UFO activity; however, he expressed an interest. Later, he contributed essays on the topics of UFO phenomena and pyschical research.

A Study of UFO Contactees

In 1964, when I joined the faculty at the University of Wyoming-Laramie, I continued with the survey of UFO contactees. (See Appendix A: UFO Report Form.)

I had assumed that, in one year, I could obtain the background information and personality inventory scores of 100 participants. Then, I could compare their ESP experiences and UFO experiences with their pattern of response to personality inventories. Actually, it took four years (1964-1968) to obtain information from 82 participants. The results indicated that a majority of participants were "normal" in their responses to personality inventories; further, their vocational interest scores were more like those of professional persons than technical/outdoor persons. (See Appendix B.)

I was unable to publish the results in a psychology journal, so, in 1976, the results finally were published as a chapter in a book by Jim and Coral Lorenzen, *Encounters with UFO Occupants*.[1]

In 1968, I "knew" that most UFO contactees were "normal"; however, I also knew that other professional psychologists did not hold that view. So, I decided that I would engage in a long-range study of UFO contactees. Each year, I spent many hours and hundreds of dollars to conduct the survey.

In 1973, the University of Wyoming Graduate Faculty Research Committee provided a small grant ($275.00) to support the study. I corresponded, each year, with hundreds and hundreds of persons and I continued to learn more about their views of psychic phenomena and UFO experiences.

NBC-TV Programs

In 1966, I had the opportunity to participate in two NBC television programs. One program, called *UFOs: Fact or Fantasy?*, featured a panel of six men, including J. Allen Hynek, Ph.D., professor of astronomy, Northwestern University; James A. Harder, Ph.D., Frank B. Salisbury, Ph.D., and myself. The two "stars" were Howard Menzel, Ph.D., professor of astronomy, Harvard University; and John Fuller, investigative reporter and author of *The Interrupted Journey*, the story of Betty and Barney Hill.

At one point in the presentation, Dr. Menzel was yelling, "Shut up! Shut up! I don't have to stand for this inquisition!" He was complaining about the quiet but persistent questions from John Fuller, who—in response to Dr. Menzel's claim that two policemen who confirmed the report of a UFO witness were suffering from "mass hysteria"—was asking questions about the names, ages, addresses, etc., of those same policemen. John Fuller did not ask if "mass hysteria" is a well-known meteorological phenomenon; he merely asked the kinds of questions that he had asked, as a reporter, when he interviewed the

---

1. Lorenzen and Lorenzen, 1967.

two policemen. Apparently, Dr. Menzel was not used to being needled; certainly he was not used to his considerable authority being doubted! However, he had not interviewed the policemen; John Fuller had done so. I wondered who had behaved in a more scientific manner, the reporter, or the professor of astronomy?

Betty and Barney Hill. Later, in 1966, I had the opportunity to participate in a panel of writers and scientists who were interviewing Mr. and Mrs. Barney Hill. (Barney and Betty were husband and wife, living in Portsmouth, NH; he was a postal worker; she, a social worker. Their UFO experience occurred September 19, 1961, on a drive back from Canada. In 1964, the story of their work with Boston psychiatrist, Benjamin Simon, M.D., was revealed.)

During the TV program, I found myself in my usual dilemma. I wished to be respected by the "experts" (Jim McDonald, Ph.D., professor of atmospheric sciences, University of Arizona; Carl Sagan, Ph.D., professor of astronomy, Princeton University; and New York science writers); yet, I also felt compassion for Mr. and Mrs. Hill as I "resonated" to their feelings.

During a break in the program, I was confronted in a hallway by one of the science writers. Obviously, he was upset by my sympathetic comments with this misguided couple. He stated, "You're a psychologist! (Oops! Here comes another lesson!) You know that people *see* what they wish to *see*!"

His was a tall and commanding presence. I deferred to his authority, and I agreed, "Yes, you're right. I believe that people see what they wish to see. However, I also believe that people do *not* see what they do *not* wish to see." He reacted with a grimace and he terminated the conversation.

Later in the program, I learned the lesson, once more, that "everybody is a psychologist." At one moment, Carl Sagan, Ph.D., was expressing his doubts about the claims of UFO abductions and medical examinations by UFO occupants. He stated, in effect, "Mrs. Hill, you said that, during the hypnosis sessions with Dr. Benjamin Simon, you remembered a long needle being placed in your navel by one of your examiners?" She nodded and replied, "Yes." Waving his hand, and demonstrating his considerable charm, Dr. Sagan smiled. "Now, Mrs. Hill, we're all amateur psychologists here...."

Suddenly, he halted; he looked over at me, and he apologized. I smiled and replied, "That's all right. My colleagues think of me as an amateur psychologist."

UFO Abductees

The TV interview with Betty and Barney Hill was a turning point for me. Not only did I recognize their experiences as worthy of further investigation by a variety of scientists, I also recognized that my professional training (1965) in hypnotic procedures could be helpful in my own UFO research.

Jim Harder and Coral Lorenzen encouraged my interest in providing hypnosis procedures with UFO witnesses. Dr. Harder had talked with Leslie LeCron, a California psychologist and author of a 1964 book, *Self Hypnotism*. Jim developed a short questionnaire for using the pendulum technique (Chevreul Pendulum).

In 1967, I worked with a Denver UFO witness, and with Mr. and Mrs. Trenholm, Boulder, Colorado. The results were as dramatic as those of my first UFO abduction case. The first investigation was with a University of Wyoming student who came to the counseling center for assistance with troubling dreams and "loss-of-time" experience. She and her boyfriend had driven to a "lover's lane" area, east of Laramie; later, she was puzzled about the events of that night and sought hypnotherapy to explore her memories. She was able to recall a weird figure, with scaly skin and strange eyes, who mentally communicated with her about the purpose of the examination of her mind and body. She felt that a device, like a small "spool," had been placed in her head.

I encouraged her to seek an X-ray examination at the student health services, but she told me later that her mother would not give permission for that procedure. The young woman was bright, articulate, and able to discuss objectively her experience and the related psychic effects. Here, in a live counseling session, was a demonstration of what I could expect—on the basis of many questionnaire results—from other persons from all over the U.S. and several foreign nations. I was pleased that she was willing to talk and proud that I was willing to listen! I continue to wonder if her "future visions" shall be realized. We shall see!?!

U.S. House Committee. From then on, my professional activities intensified. I participated, by mail, in a panel of "experts" who testified before a Committee on Science and Astronautics, U.S. House of Representatives.[2] I provided comments on the question of whether public information and governmental research should be conducted on the topic of UFO reports.

Condon Committee. In 1968, I participated as a consultant to the Condon Committee, University of Colorado-Boulder. I was invited to assist the committee in an interview with Herbert L. Schirmer, a police-patrolman of Ashland, Nebraska, who described his strange UFO experience. I enjoyed my associations with Jim Ahrens; David Saunders, Ph.D.; Roy Craig, Ph.D.; et al. However, my brief meeting with E.U. Condon, Ph.D., was puzzling; I somehow intuited that he was aware of "something," but he had no intention of discussing with me what he knew.

Later, in correspondence with me, Dr. Condon showed the same propensity, or I experienced the same ambivalent reaction. On the one hand, he warned what might happen to me and to the University of Wyoming if I

---

2. Sprinkle, 1968.

revealed information about my interview with Herb Schirmer; on the other hand he told me of (teased me with?) a comment about ESP/PK[3] and Sirhan Sirhan! Of course, with my pattern of chasing the "real" scientists and assisting the "true" contactees, I resolved my dilemma by talking to the university attorney (to learn if there was any objection), and then writing a paper about my work with the Condon Committee. The paper appeared as part of a chapter in the 1976 book by Jim and Coral Lorenzen, *Encounters with UFO Occupants.*[4]

UFO Panel of the National Enquirer

Between 1972 and 1979, I participated in a panel of educators and scientists, the "Blue Ribbon Panel" of the *National Enquirer.* Some UFO researchers were appalled at what they perceived to be an unholy marriage (or sordid affair) between "pure" UFO investigation and "impure" tabloid journalism. However, panel members had hopes that Bill Dick, editor, and Bob Pratt, reporter, could make good use of the panel. (Some of the newspaper reporters were, in my opinion, boozers, muck-rakers, and womanizers; however, Bill Dick and Bob Pratt were honest and reliable persons.)

The panel was composed, initially, of Jim Harder, Allen Hynek, Frank Salisbury, me, and Robert Creegan, Ph.D., professor of psychology/philosophy, University of New York. We met once each year, usually in Palm Beach, Florida, to review various UFO reports. Our task was to recommend to the publisher one or two cases that we had evaluated as "good reports," i.e., those reports, from multiple witnesses, which might include photographs, radar recording, landing traces, and/or other kinds of physical evidence. The purpose of the panel was to evaluate the evidence; the promise of the newspaper was to award $50,000 (later, $100,000, then one million dollars) to anyone who could "prove" the existence of flying saucers from outer space. The panel, of course, had an (unspoken) agenda: to generate more UFO research; the editors had an (unspoken) agenda: to generate more newspaper sales.

After a few years, the editors expressed disillusionment with the panel, and vice versa. When J. Allen Hynek left the panel, the panel enjoyed neither the leadership nor the status with which it began.

I truly enjoyed my part in the panel. Other panel members emphasized the cases with physical evidence, e.g., the Delphos, Kansas soil samples; the Iran Air Force pilots, who reported radar readings and weaponry malfunctions during a UFO encounter; and police officers and others who presented photographs from triangulated positions of UFO activity.

Lucille McNames. However, I emphasized the trunkful of letters from thousands of persons who responded to the publisher's request to describe

---

3. Extrasensory Perception and Psychokinesis
4. Lorenzen and Lorenzen, 1976.

their own UFO encounters. During one meeting, when each panel member read some of these many letters, Frank Salisbury showed me a letter from Lucille McNames. Not only did she describe her UFO experience, but she also described her psychic impressions of each panel member. "Does Dr. Salisbury walk too fast?" "Does Dr. Harder tap his pencil while he is thinking about a solution to a problem?" "Does Dr. Sprinkle enjoy his work with UFO witnesses?" I was impressed. Of course, she might have guessed, or she might have employed a spy who told her about these personal characteristics. But the probabilities of guessing, or spying, were low; the probability was high that she was apprehending, intuitively, the personal information about our panel members.

I wrote back to Lucille McNames, and to this day I continue to correspond with her. Like many other UFO contactees, she has continued to grow psychologically and spiritually; she has written two books about her "channeling" procedures, and the information which has been given through her about a variety of topics, including "spirit communication." I value the knowledge, charm, and good humor that shines from her. It would require a chapter, perhaps a book, to describe the unusual circumstances of meeting her in person, and the "psychic readings" she provided for those persons who had accompanied me.

Mrs. Ema Franck. Another person with whom I continue to correspond is Ema Franck, of Casper, Wyoming. In the 1960s, after I arrived in Laramie, she had written to me to describe her UFO encounters and psychic experiences. When I visited her and her husband, Mario, Mrs. Franck introduced me to her friend, Mrs. Olson, a large farm woman who charmed us with stories of her UFO encounters. During the discussion, she looked at me quietly and steadily, then in effect she exclaimed, "Now, don't laugh, but I'm getting an impression about you! In my mind, I 'see' you in a high building in about two-and-a-half years, engaged in UFO research, and there's a lot of money involved. Maybe it's a government project or something like that." I thanked her for sharing her impressions with me.

Later, when Mrs. Franck and I walked away from Mrs. Olson's house, Ema turned to me and gave me her opinion. "You remember when Mrs. Olson said that she thinks you'll be involved in a UFO project in two-and-a-half years? "Yes," I nodded. Ema shook her head. "I think she's wrong. I think that it will be more like five years."

In 1968, when I served as a consultant to the Condon Committee, University of Colorado-Boulder, I was reminded of that incident. I met with some members of the Condon Committee on the 2nd floor of Woodbury Hall (near the spot where Joe Waggoner and I had viewed a "flying saucer" almost two decades earlier). I recalled Mrs. Olson talking of a high building, a lot of money, a government UFO project, etc. But I was skeptical about the claim, and I dismissed it from my conscious awareness.

I Saw a Deer! Then, a few years later, when *The National Enquirer* panel met at the home of Dr. Jim Harder, I was reminded once again of Mrs. Olson's comments. Usually, the panel met in Florida; once, we met in New Orleans; and once, we met in Los Angeles when Dr. Hynek was serving as a consultant for Stephen Spielberg, in the movie, *Close Encounters of the Third Kind.*

When the panel gathered for the meeting in Berkeley, we were introduced to the small platform, and outdoor elevator, that Jim Harder had used to transport equipment and materials up the steep hill in order to build his house. The large structure, with long wooden deck, overlooked the San Francisco Bay.

In the gathering darkness, the lights of the area were an impressive display. Then just below the house, in the large bushes, I heard a sound and I saw a small deer, bounding away. I called out to other members of the panel, "I saw a deer!" Dr. Bob Creegan, who had walked out onto the deck at that very moment, said to me, disapprovingly, "You didn't see a deer." I replied, "I saw a deer." Now, Bob's voice sounded louder, with some agitation, "You didn't see a deer!" Just then, Jim came out onto the deck and Bob turned to him, almost in supplication. "Leo says that he saw a deer. He didn't see a deer, did he?" Jim's reply was so typical of his scientific and intellectual style. "I don't know if he saw a deer or not, but, there are deer in the area."

I was so amused, but also humbled by the incident. I wondered, "If I can't convince a colleague that I have seen a deer, what is the likelihood that I can persuade professional persons to believe that I have observed UFOs?"

But that inner question was pushed aside by the magnificent display of lights below us. And suddenly I was struck by the precognitive impressions of Mrs. Franck and Mrs. Olson: seeing Leo, in a high building, engaged in a UFO project that involved a lot of money! I knew that I could not convince a skeptical person, but, my own internal state, excited and joyful, was confirmation for me!

Opportunities and Doubts

During the next few years, there were more and more doubts, expressed to me and to my university colleagues, that I was a "real" scientist because of my insistence that an important task was to investigate the claims of UFO witnesses.

Fortunately, there also were many opportunities, often provided by Jim and Coral Lorenzen of APRO. For example, one journey I took was to Las Vegas, Nevada, to meet John and Robin Romero and to discuss their UFO investigations. Such a delightful couple!

Johnny Sands. A 1975-1976 case was that of a country-western singer, Johnny Sands. He described a strange encounter with an alien entity, while he tried to start his stalled automobile. The encounter seemed to be a "lesson" as well as a "display" to the young man; however, Johnny had as much difficulty in analyzing the meaning of the event as he had in accepting the reality of the experience.

Travis Walton. The journey continued on to Arizona, where I talked to Travis Walton and his family and friends. I was asked to assist other investigators to formulate questions for another polygraph examination. Once again, I was more impressed with the sincerity of the witnesses than I was with the proclamations of scoffers who had not interviewed the witnesses. Travis was upset, at the time, by the adverse publicity, so he and I did not utilize hypnotic suggestions to explore his UFO memories. Instead, we practiced self-hypnosis for relaxation.

Marilyn and I had the opportunity, years later, in Aspen, Colorado, to talk with Travis. We were participating in a UFO conference that was arranged by Larry Koss, UFO investigator and UFO experiencer. I was pleased to note that Travis seemed more at ease with his own experiences, as well as more comfortable in talking about his experiences to other persons. Of course, the movie, *Fire in the Sky*, was not an accurate portrayal of his "on-board" memory, so, Travis and Mike Rogers have traveled around the U.S. to inform the public of their experiences.

Three Kentucky Women. Then, there were more and more opportunities to interview UFO abductees, and to assist them to come to terms with their emotional anxieties, if not with their intellectual doubts. For example, in 1976, Bob Pratt met me at an airport and drove me to interview three Kentucky women: Louise Smith, Mona Stafford, and Elaine Thomas. (Investigation of the case was hampered by internal conflict between APRO and local UFO investigators, who had conducted the preliminary investigations. Finally, Leonard Stringfield—bless his soul—showed his grace and confidence by encouraging cooperation among all of the interested groups.)

The three women had experienced a two-hour loss of time while driving a lonely road, on a return trip from a birthday celebration. The women were members of a local art group, and—after the encounter—each drew her impressions of what she saw: a large object with flashing lights that, initially, they perceived as an airliner about to crash. Suddenly, it stopped, circled, and approached their car from behind them. Later, when they recognized the "loss of time" events, they were puzzled and frightened. A variety of psychic phenomena occurred, along with nightmares and strange "memories." Then, as neighborhood rumors increased, they decided to "go public" about their experiences.

During the weekend hypnosis sessions, each woman described a strange, but somewhat different, experience; their reactions indicated memories of bodily examinations by alien entities. After the difficult and demanding conditions were ended, I recall the haunting question by Mona Stafford, asked in an anguished tone, "Leo, what do they want?"

I was reminded of my ignorance about UFO phenomena, and my wish that I could assist UFO witnesses—and UFO investigators—to deal with their anxieties. (I had been troubled by the insistent, sometimes inconsistent, questions by field investigators as we conducted the hypnosis sessions with each participant. In their zeal, the investigators sometimes whispered, "Ask her about the height of the aliens. Ask her about the number of fingers." etc.) I was trying my best to conduct each session in a psychotherapeutic manner, assisting each participant with her fears and feelings, and allowing the procedures to bring out details rather than adjusting the procedures to the individual concerns of the field investigators. Leonard Stringfield included his comments about the women in his book *UFO Siege*[5]. His steady influence was helpful in dealing with the aftermath of the sessions.

Later, Louise Smith and I appeared on the *Tomorrow Show* with Tom Snyder. He treated her courteously, although I felt the skepticism in his voice. She responded well to his doubts, expressing her own doubts about the meaning of the experiences, but certain that she experienced the events.

I wrote a paper for the IUR (*International UFO Reporter*) about the Kentucky abductions.[6] Then I wrote a paper about hypnotic procedures in UFO investigations for Jim and Coral Lorenzen and their book *Abducted!*[7] I tried to identify with the roles of hypnotist, UFO experiencer, and UFO investigator, with the doubts and frustrations of each of these roles. My intent was to assist hypnotists, UFO witnesses, and UFO investigators to work together, sharing their mutual suspicions, and seeking ways to minimize conflict and to maximize outcome.

Margery and Carl Higdon. One of the most significant UFO experiences (UFOEs), in my opinion, is that of E. Carl Higdon, Jr. Carl, and his wife Margery, have been so gracious to me, and so courageous in dealing with Carl as a UFO experiencer. My one major disappointment, among the many joys in my work with UFOErs, is the loss of Carl's bullet.[8] Now, many years later, I continue to puzzle—and to feel deep disappointment—about my part in the disappearance of that memento from his encounter with a strange entity, Ausso One. While hunting south of Rawlins, Wyoming, Carl aimed his rifle at a bull elk, heard a muffled sound, saw the bullet exit the barrel—then watched it as it stopped and fell to the ground. He went over and picked it up, then experienced his ET encounter.

---

5. Stringfield, 1977.
6. Sprinkle, 1977.
7. Lorenzen and Lorenzen, 1977.
8. Sprinkle, 1979.

It would take a book to describe, and analyze, the various events in Carl's life. For our purposes here, I shall mention two incidents that seem to be related to his initial encounter: an interview with Mr. Wantanabe, and an interview with Carl and Margery Higdon about Carl's reactions to the experience of being—consciously—in three locations simultaneously.

Mr. Wantanabe, a citizen of Japan, had traveled to Laramie, accompanied by his interpreter, to share with me some information about his "onboard" spacecraft experiences, and his message that humankind must prepare for communication with ET (extraterrestrial) entities. (Later, a friend, Ken McLean, told me of his meeting with Mr. Wantanabe: the little man walked into a room full of people, walked over to Ken, looked up at him, and repeated, in a forceful tone, "Wake up! Wake up!" Ken was startled but, somehow, felt that the message had meaning for him as a person, as well as a UFO investigator.)

I enjoyed my conversation with Mr. Wantanabe. His interpreter, a young man who had been born in Japan and raised in the U.S., was pleasant and competent. At one point, Mr. Wantanabe claimed that he continually receives information about the inner character of many UFO researchers. When I asked him if he had received information about me, he smiled and said something to his interpreter. The young man smiled and replied, "Yes! You are a salty apple!" I smiled and asked, "Is that good?" "Yes, that is very good!" No further comment was provided about that information, yet I wondered if there was any connection with the claim of an early UFO contactee (George Hunt Williamson?) that ETs have "seeded" many souls, and now they are returning to Earth for the "harvest."

At the end of the interview, and after the men had departed, the young man suddenly returned to my office with a question. "Mr. Wantanabe wishes to know your answer to this question: Are you ready?" I paused, while feeling an inner "click"; I nodded. "Yes, I think I am ready."

Was there a connection between that interview and the initial interview with Carl Higdon that took place within a few months? Was there a connection between the visit of a little man from Japan and my visit to Rawlins, Wyoming, to investigate the character and experiences of Carl Higdon? I hope that, someday, I might know the answers to these questions. Also, I hope to learn more answers to questions about Carl's encounter with Ausso One. Was it a physical display? A physical/psychical display? Was it programmed mentally? Was it a scenario that was meant primarily for Carl? Was it a scenario for all hunters, and all environmentalists? Was it a warning to humankind about our planet, and how we are polluting Mother Earth? Was Carl selected at random for his "abduction" and "journey" to another civilization? Or was the encounter an opportunity to bring UFO experiencer and UFO researcher together, so that a variety of psychological procedures could be followed in order to investigate the encounter?

Carl was willing to be videotaped by the excellent crew of a capable researcher, Junchi (Jim) Yaoi, Nippon TV Network. Also, he was videotaped by the crew of *In Search Of...*, narrated by Leonard Nimoy. He responded to many letters and telephone calls from interested persons all over the globe. However, he and his family sometimes experienced ridicule by thoughtless and fearful persons. I admired his steadfast conviction that, according to the hypnosis sessions, these events happened, and it didn't amount to a "hill of beans" whether other people believed him or not.

One of the many interesting—and puzzling—events was the late-night call from Margery, when Carl was traumatized by a strange experience. He was sitting in bed, aware of his consciousness in three separate locations: at home, in bed; several miles south of Rawlins, in the woods, and watching a deer; and several miles north of Rawlins, on the prairie, watching a pronghorn antelope. Carl is a strong and capable woodsman, but that event was difficult for him to handle; his sense of reality was sorely tested. Thanks to the support of Margery, and the opportunity to discuss the incident, he seemed to heal, once more, his inner doubts. I admire Carl and Margery, now living in Texas. I wish that, someday, Carl's bullet could be returned to him. Also, I wish that he, and thousands (millions?) of UFOErs, could be recognized by scientists and governmental officials as true heroes, acknowledged for their selfless service and social sacrifice so that the rest of humanity can face the reality of ET presence.

Richard F. Haines, Ph.D. A chapter on Carl's experience appeared in the 1979 book, *UFO Phenomena and the Behavioral Scientist*, by Richard Haines, Ph.D. Dr. Haines has so many credits: experimental psychologist, former NASA scientist, author of several books on UFO investigation, expert on pilot observations of UFOs, organizer of U.S.-Russian research groups, innovator of several technical and hypnotic techniques, etc. In my opinion, he is among the best of true skeptics in ufology. (I believe that scoffers sometimes assume that they are the only skeptics, just as some physicians assume that they are the only "doctors." The word "doctor" refers to a teacher, or learned person, and there are doctors of education, dentistry, medicine, philosophy, science, etc. The word "skeptic" refers to a person who has doubts, especially about fundamental religious beliefs. Thus, it could be said that a UFO skeptic continues to doubt, to question, and to suspend judgement.) Dick Haines truly believes that *conventional science* is the best method to understand UFO phenomena, yet he also is a person of strong religious faith. We care deeply for one another, yet we gently poke at one another for what we see as an inappropriate "mix" of science and religion. Perhaps each of us is correct. Perhaps, someday, we all shall know whether "science" must change in order to study UFO phenomena.

Rev. Mary Teal Coleman. Another good outcome of the Carl Higdon investigation was the opportunity to meet Mary Coleman, R.N., psychic researcher, TV director, and Buddhist priest. (She has developed, with the Dalai Lama, a documentary videotape, *Faces of Sorrow*, about the Tibetan people under Chinese rule.)

Mary tells a story about her introduction to the Carl Higdon story. She was meditating, in her apartment, when some friends yelled to her, "Mary! Come here; we have something to show you!" She resisted, she was in a trance state, and she was obtaining some impressions of a name: "Leo S." She thought to herself, "Who the hell is Leo S.?"

Her friends continued to call to her, until she ended her meditative pose. She went to talk with them and they showed her a copy of a *National Enquirer* article about Carl Higdon and his UFO experience, which was investigated by Rick Kenyon, Bob Nantkes, and Leo Sprinkle.

Later, with her own funds, she traveled to Laramie so that we could drive to Rawlins and visit Carl and Margery and their family. During a later visit, Mary and I were talking at the same moment that I was scheduled to talk with Pat McGuire, a Laramie rancher and UFO contactee. Another "coincidence" in a long series of "coincidences!"

Rev. Coleman has experienced many unusual events, in her personal life and in her professional activities with movie and television personalities. Despite some setbacks, and a few betrayals by some unscrupulous persons, she continued on her spiritual journey and her task of presenting public information about UFO activity, including scientific and spiritual transformation.

Her work with Pat McGuire lead to the ABC's *That's Incredible* episode about his UFO experiences, cattle mutilations, and the amazing water well that he and his (former) wife developed. Now, the ranch is an experimental farm that was given to the University of Wyoming-Laramie.

1975 Arkansas Conference

I enjoyed my participation in a 1975 UFO Conference in Arkansas, partly because it was an opportunity to return to the area where earlier I had spent some time in U.S. Army basic training and leadership school. Also, it was an opportunity for three little "soul samples" about UFO research, through the help of Allen Hynek, Phil Klass, and a friend, who is an engineer and UFO investigator.

During the conference, Allen Hynek and I were discussing an unusual UFO report, and a young man approached us. His badge identified him as a member of a new UFO organization. After introductions, he launched into a monologue about a new era in scientific UFO research. I nodded, smiled, and inwardly reflected on the good work of Dr. Hynek, considered to be the dean of U.S. UFO researchers, who for years had worked diligently to persuade other scientists to become involved in UFO studies. And, somewhat immodestly, I reflected briefly on my own early attempts to use psychological procedures for investigations of UFO reports.

Then, I heard the young man repeat his comments about a new era in UFO research. Suddenly, I "heard" what the young man was saying to us: "Step aside, you Old Guards; we Young Turks are coming through!" I almost laughed out loud; I was so surprised that, without warning, I had been moved from one stereotyped group to the other. In one way, I was pleased, but also I was troubled. Was I out of the scientific circle before I was in?

Philip J. Klass. One of my expectations for the conference was to meet Philip J. Klass, then editor of *Aviation Weekly*, author of several books on UFO reports, and a well-known debunker of those of us who reported our UFO experiences.

It so happened that Mr. Klass and I entered the same limousine, as we left the airport to drive to the conference. I introduced myself. "Mr. Klass, I'm Leo Sprinkle. We've been corresponding." He turned and shook hands. "Ahh, yes, Dr. Sprinkle." Then, he turned to his left and talked with the attractive and vivacious woman to his left, Ms. Sue Wallace. Occasionally, he turned back toward me, rolling his eyes, as if he were asking me mentally, "This woman, who talks of astrology and numerology, is she one of your kooky contactees?"

A young man, seated opposite Phil Klass, spoke to him. "Mr. Klass, what do you think of the Antonio Boaz Villas case?" (The ABV case, investigated by Dr. Olavo Fontes, a Brazilian physician, was an early abduction report—before the experiences of Betty and Barney Hill. I had met Dr. Fontes, now deceased, in a New York City meeting when he renewed his association with Jim and Coral Lorenzen. I was impressed with his competence, as well as his character.)

At the mention of the ABV case, Phil Klass beamed, and he responded with his eloquence and wit. In effect, he asked, "Now, what would people say if I claimed that a flying saucer came down in my back yard; several little entities get out. They grab me and take me into the craft; undress me; and then, with a young woman, I perform sexually, not once, but twice! What would people say?" To his left, Sue Wallace inquired sweetly, "Why, Mr. Klass, are you a stud?"

I have listened to Phil Klass on several platforms, and during several TV programs; this was the only time that he was—temporarily—at a loss for words.

Unidentified UFOs? Another lesson occurred at that Arkansas conference while I was talking to a friend, who was trained as an engineer. He was complaining that he had never experienced a UFO sighting. His complaint, and my rejoinder, went something like this:

"Leo, I've been a UFO investigator for fifteen years, and I've never had a sighting!" I told him about my UFO experiences, but he continued to complain. In an attempt to help, I explained, "Well, there are two ways to experience a UFO sighting. One method is to camp out, night after night, in an area where many sightings are being reported. Keep looking, and you'll have a sighting." He interjected, "I've tried that, and it didn't work!" I continued. "The other method is to sit in your room or your apartment and meditate. Send up a message to the UFO entities that you will do something for them and, in exchange, you wish to have a UFO experience."

He snorted angrily. "I tried that method and it didn't work!" I was puzzled. "You tried that method and it didn't work? I've never heard of that method not working. Are you sure that you haven't had a UFO sighting?" He responded with emphasis. "Yes, I'm sure!" I continued, "Or something that might have been a UFO sighting?"

He paused, looked around, and lowered his voice. "Well, one time I was camping out with these friends. Along about dusk, we saw two lights on the horizon. But as they came overhead (he motioned south to north with his left hand, extending his index finger and middle finger), there was no sound. So we knew that these lights were not airplanes or helicopters. They were just two satellites." Puzzled, I repeated, "Two satellites?" "Yes," he responded once more, as he repeated the movement with his hand and two extended fingers, "Two satellites." I asked, once more, "Two?" "Yes, two!" He growled, as if he were telling me, "Listen, dummy!" I commented, "I've never heard of two satellites traveling together. Have you?" He paused, with a stunned look on his face. He gasped. "That's strange!" "Yes," I agreed. Then, with excitement in his voice, he proclaimed, "Another strange thing! Just after those two satellites (south to north) passed overhead, two more satellites (right hand, west to east) came by!"

We looked at each other. I asked incredulously, "Two? And then two more? Doesn't that sound strange to you?" He sighed deeply, "That's weird!" He paused and then, in a very confidential whisper, "What do you suppose that was?" I smiled. "Perhaps it was a case of misidentified UFOs!"

He was puzzled and I was puzzled. I wondered to myself, how many UFO investigators are not reporting their own UFO experiences?

A Subtle Shift

A subtle shift was taking place in my own awareness. The good news was that many UFO researchers began to confide in me by writing, or calling, with requests that I—confidentially—listen to their own UFO experiences. The bad news was that—in public—I was viewed as biased and lacking in scientific objectivity because I was willing to talk about my UFO sightings.

At one conference in Esalen, California, I was told by a well-known researcher, "Leo, if I had a UFO experience, I wouldn't report it." I asked, "Why not?" He replied, "I don't want to lose my credibility!" I understood; I know that credibility is important to any authoritative person. But I also know that integrity is important to the mental health of every person. Which is more important, credibility or integrity?

I began to recognize the verbal (and/or nonverbal) message of some scientists: UFO reports are anti-science. In other words, the "morality" of these scientists was offended by these "immoral" reports!

I also recognized a related truth. In only two disciplines, or fields of study, is it inappropriate to experience the phenomena: parapsychology and ufology! In brickology, cloudology, or woolology, it is appropriate for the investigator to experience bricks, or clouds, or wool! But, somehow, it has been taboo to experience ESP and UFOs!

I felt as if I were losing ground in my ambition to become a scientist, gathering "sticks" and contributing to the science of human behavior. In consolation, I hoped to become a good psychologist, even if I were not able to be recognized as a scientist. Yet, there were doubts about my credibility as a good psychologist.

Trained Observers

I learned a lesson about credibility, and precognition, one Sunday morning. Sitting at my desk at the campus office, in my jeans, and unshaven, I was busy completing a manuscript for possible publication. Suddenly, the telephone rang, and Dr. Hal Wedel (then director of the local mental health center and program coordinator for the Unitarian Church) asked, "Leo, are you coming to speak to us?" I apologized for my delay; bolted out of the building; drove home; shaved and changed clothes; gathered equipment; drove to the meeting place to show slides and to discuss UFO reports.

I was so embarrassed! In my memory, I had never been late—much less absent!—for a professional presentation.

In attendance at that meeting were members and guests of the church, many of whom were professional men and women including other professors of the University of Wyoming. I tried to ease my guilt about my extreme tardiness, but I remained puzzled about my behavior. Never before had I forgotten a commitment for a presentation!

Later, I wondered if subconsciously, I "knew" that I would be taken to task by some of those in attendance. After the presentation, one professor approached me; his comments and my responses were something like this: "Leo! All of these reports from farmers and ranchers are not worth anything! How about UFO reports from trained observers?"

I knew what he meant, but I asked, "You mean policemen and airplane pilots?" "No," he replied impatiently, "I mean *trained* observers!" "Like who?" I asked. He emphasized, "Astrophysicists!" (Guess what? He was a professor of astrophysics.) I asked him, "Do you know Peter Sturrock?" He answered, "Of course, he is president of the American Astronomical Association." "Are you familiar with his survey?" "No." (Dr. Sturrock had conducted a survey of astronomers and found that a small percentage of respondents had described anomalous aerial phenomena—not UFOs!—which did not conform to known astronomical and meteorological principles.) The professor of astrophysics was intrigued by the brief comments about the survey.[9] Then, I added, "And, you know, many people in Wyoming are more likely to trust a farmer or a rancher than they are likely to trust a professor." He nodded, almost sadly, as he recognized the ways in which people choose to trust or distrust those around them.

---

9. Sturrock, 1994.

Psychologist or UFO Investigator?

*Reason is the horse we ride after we have decided which
direction we wish to go.*

—*Alfred North Whitehead*
U.S. Physicist and Philosopher

Introduction

"Leo, you can't be a 'real' psychologist and also be a UFO investigator."
Those words—or words to that effect—were bothersome to me. The message
came to me from some members of the faculty of the University of Wyoming
Department of Psychology.

I thought to myself, "Damn! I had wished to become a 'true' psychologist."[1] At the University of North Dakota, I had served as an assistant professor of psychology and, briefly, as director of the counseling center. At the
University of Wyoming, I served as associate professor of guidance education;
assistant professor of psychology; then, associate professor of psychology. I
attained the status of a tenured professor, which meant that I could not be
fired except for gross negligence or misconduct.

Professor of Psychology?

But when I sought to become a professor of psychology, my application
was rejected. At that hearing, among other tenured professors, there was general agreement that I presented excellent ratings, from students and clients,
about my teaching and counseling activities; I presented sufficient publica-

---

1. One of my pet peeves is the use of the word "real," when the user actually means "true." In
my opinion, "real" refers to that which is tangible or material; "true," refers to that which is
accurate, or reliable.

tions (journal articles, chapters in books, and entries in encyclopedias, etc.). However, many of my publications were not in "scientific" (prestigious) journals; my writings were viewed as "popular" (non-scientific), which did not meet the criteria for becoming a full professor of psychology.

After the meeting, a few of my colleagues encouraged me to conduct the kind of studies that were publishable in the leading journals of psychology. The head of the department, Dr. Wilson Walthall, asked me if I wished to pursue the application process with the University committee on rank and tenure. I thanked him but I declined; the departmental vote was an answer to the question, did I wish to be a professor of psychology or did I wish to be a UFO investigator? I knew the answer.

Later, I applied for, and received, the title of professor of counseling services. I rationalized to myself that my title was less important than the opportunity to become a full professor and to continue the research that was of interest to me.

Hobby or Obsession? One colleague, while attempting to coax me into more rational behavior, asked me; "Leo, this UFO research...is it a hobby?" I replied, "No, it's more of an obsession." I knew from my inner guidance, my higher self, that I must pursue my internal bliss and my external burden. However, I was disappointed by the decision of the tenured faculty to reject my application.

Director of Counseling and Testing

Beginning in 1970, for thirteen years, I served as director of counseling and testing. We had four full-time staff, an intern, and six half-time counselors (graduate assistants who were Ph.D. candidates from the department of psychology or the department of counselor education.) Occasionally, we also supervised one or two graduate students who were at the Master's degree level; and, occasionally, a member of the faculty of the department of counselor education would serve part-time as a counselor and supervisor of graduate assistants.

I enjoyed the activities of counseling, teaching, supervising, researching, advising, and administering; however, the paperwork and the tasks of hiring and firing were the unpleasant aspects of the position. Most of the staff members viewed me as a "good boss," who was very busy but willing to listen and willing to share in decisions about procedures and services to clients.

Starting in 1980, the demands and difficulties of the position were greatly increased. Many faculty of the University of Wyoming were building excellent reputations for their research, as well as their teaching and service. Several university administrators became more concerned about public relations and the appropriate image of the university. My interests in hypnosis, parapsychology, reincarnation, and UFO research were viewed by some administrative officers as detrimental to my reputation as an excellent psychotherapist, a good teacher, and a fair administrator. Indeed, a few administrators expressed concerns that my research activities and public announcements were detrimental to the counseling center, student affairs, and the university.

Stress Management. I attempted to deal with the mounting pressures by increasing my efforts to serve well in all phases of my work. Every day, including vacation and holidays, I was spending long hours of hectic professional activities.

My only comfort, other than Marilyn's constant support (God bless her soul!), and a few minutes of meditation each day, was my exercise program—noon-hour basketball (Monday, Wednesday, Friday) and a three-mile run on Tuesday, Thursday, and Saturday.

One graduate student asked me, incredulously, "Is it true that you and your wife get up and run at 5:30 A.M.?" When I nodded, he shook his head and gasped, "Just think about it!" I shook my head and replied, "Oh, no! I don't think about it! Otherwise, I might not do it!" Puzzled, he asked, "Then why do you do it?" I replied, "Well, I sleep better, eat better, work better..." His eyes glazed over, as if he were thinking, "Boring!" I continued, "...and I enjoy a good sex life." His eyes lit up, as if he were thinking, "Oh! Maybe there is a good reason!" Yes, all humans can rationalize their behavior.

Playboy Article. One day, while stretching, prior to a noon-hour basketball game, I was approached by another player. He was a professor of mathematics who, for several years, had hooted whenever I came on the basketball court: "Hey, Sprinkle! Have you seen any little green men lately?" On this occasion, he had a comment and question. His jocular comment was about a *Playboy* magazine article on UFO research. He expressed his displeasure at the article, because—as he put it—"Until that issue came out, I didn't know that *Playboy* had any articles! Hah!" His question dealt with the current research activities of those persons who were involved in UFO investigations. After he had discussed current activities, I asked him a question. "Has your position changed in regard to UFO research?" He seemed puzzled as he shook his head and replied, "No, why do you ask?" I stated that for years he had made comments that were critical of UFO research, and now it seemed as if his position had changed. He disagreed—he said he had been critical of the data! Now, the data were better! Once again, I was wrong!

But I was pleased for two reasons. First, because he was showing an interest in UFO research; and second, because I understood more clearly the morality of many professional persons who see themselves as steadfast and unswerving in their dedication to scientific evidence. If the evidence changes, then they are willing to change their evaluation of the evidence.

Mission or Madness?

By 1982, my wife Marilyn began to wonder if I were crazy. I was attempting to serve well as director of counseling and testing, publishing professional articles, and counseling many student clients.

During the 1970s, once or twice a week, there were late-night (or early morning) calls from campus police, or residence hall staff, about disruptive students. My task was to intervene, and to assist the student and staff member to resolve the situation. Sometimes, a student was experiencing a psychotic episode; sometimes, there were relationship difficulties, including suicide attempts; often, there was abuse of drugs, usually alcohol.

In the 1980s, we developed a team for emergency interventions, so that other student affairs staff could be "on call." In that way, the dean of students, Tom Mattheus, and I were not always the persons who were called by campus police and residence hall staff.

However, in addition to the late night calls regarding campus episodes, I often received calls from persons who were frightened by their UFO experiences. In 1982, I worked with more that fifty UFO "abductees" who sought hypnotherapist services with me, so that they could deal with their trauma. I was willing to assist them, without payment, so that I could learn more about their background and characteristics and—in exchange—they could participate in the continuing survey of their ESP and UFO experiences.

To Be or Not Be Director. By 1983, my colleagues in the counseling center were engaged in a variety of reactions to their own personal and professional frustrations. Each of the other three full-time staff members viewed herself or himself as being more capable than I, or the others, in leading the staff and directing the center. (During one staff retreat, when we completed an inventory of professional styles, we were not surprised to learn that Leo scored highest on the "analyst" style, while the others scored highest on the "driver" style!) Also, the vice president of student affairs, a well-known counseling psychologist, was a capable and ambitious person. His style, in my opinion, was to foster competition, and subtle rivalry, among staff members; then, the "winner" was expected to dismiss the "losers." In this way, the "dead wood" could be trimmed, and new (fresher and lower paid?) professional persons could be hired.

Another Brazilian UFO Conference. The subtle pressures from the vice president, and the not-so-subtle conflicts among our full-time staff, became more and more burdensome. Finally, a meeting was called by the vice-president to discuss—and to defuse—the anger and anxiety. However, I also feared that the meeting was designed to force Leo to resign "for the good of the counseling center." I had been criticized openly because my "personal," not "professional," interests were reported in the campus newspaper. I had used vacation days to accept an invitation to speak (again) at an international UFO congress in Brazil. (I always was required to use personal vacation days to attend a UFO conference, including our own annual Rocky Mountain Conference on UFO Investigation that was held on the campus of the University of Wyoming.)

Dr. Bob Fetch. As the meeting convened, I presented copies, to the vice-president and other staff, of a professional article that, minutes before, had arrived in the mail. (Coincidence?) The article, which I had co-authored with Dr. Bob Fetch, a young assistant professor of Colorado State University, Fort Collins, had been published in a mental health journal and was based upon the results of his doctoral dissertation study at the University of Wyoming. (He had asked me, rather than his regular adviser, to serve as his dissertation adviser; his study, comparing supportive self-talk and jogging for treating depression in adults, provided data to support both procedures.) The article apparently minimized the contention that only "personal"—rather than "professional"—research was being conducted and published by Leo! We left the meeting with continuing uncertainty about how to resolve our interpersonal difficulties.

Resignation as Director. I was conflicted: I wished to retain the pay and the prestige of my role as director. (My salary at the University of Wyoming had gone from $10,000 in 1964 to—eventually—$42,000 in 1989.) However, I was willing to resign as director of the counseling center if it meant that our staff could enhance our relationships and our services to students.

I called a meeting to discuss my plans to resign as director and to remain as one of the psychologists. One staff member expressed surprise that I planned to remain, apparently assuming that the pressure on me was intense enough that I would wish to leave the campus.

When the temporary director was selected by the vice-president, she was surprised at the amount of duties, and paperwork. She asked me, "How did you find time to counsel students?" However, in the mode of being the vice-president's "new broom," she placed me on probation; she claimed that my services, as rated by student clients, were "unsatisfactory"; yet she did not allow me to view the rating results, contrary to our long-standing policy.

When I demanded an opportunity to view the rating forms (writing letters not only to the vice-president, but also with copies to the university president and director of personnel services, et al.), I was denied access to the data. However, my service rating was changed from "unsatisfactory" to "satisfactory." (For years, ratings by supervisees and clients of my services were "excellent," or occasionally, "above average.")

Despite the fact that the new director was not a licensed psychologist, she apparently hoped to gain favor with the vice president by pressuring me and another full-time staff member to resign. Eventually, the strife was so bad that the other two staff members (without tenure) resigned from the university for other positions. Soon, the "new" director became another "old" director; then, she finally recognized the nature of the game that we were playing with the vice-president: "Let's you and him fight." (See Eric Berne, *Games People Play*) But the emotional hurt and the professional damage to all of us had been immense.

The next director, trained as a counseling psychologist, was African-American, Jewish, gentle, and very perceptive. He was supportive of me, partly because I endorsed his application for state licensure as a psychologist, and partly because of my cooperative stance with him. His brief stay was a welcome relief for me, because *he* was in the "line of fire"—not I! I was able to "lick my wounds" and to maintain a low profile.

Ruth Montgomery and Scott Jones, Ph.D. In 1984, I had the opportunity, in Washington, D.C., to have lunch with Ruth Montgomery, investigative reporter and author of many books on science and spirituality.

C.B. "Scott" Jones, Ph.D., had shown me his office on Capitol Hill and then had driven us to meet Ruth Montgomery. (Scott is a man of many talents—former U.S. Navy pilot and intelligence officer; former professor of political science, Casper College, Casper, Wyoming; and former special assistant to Senator Pell [D] Rhode Island; now he directs the PEACE Foundation in Kerrville, TX.)

I enjoyed the luncheon and the opportunity to "feel" the probing mind of Ruth Montgomery. Her 1985 book, *Aliens Among Us*[2], contained a chapter about my activities. Her book—once more—demonstrated her ability to comprehend much information about many persons and their experiences, and yet to write in a manner that educates and entertains a wide variety of readers. May her soul be blessed for her contributions as the "Herald of a New Age."

When the book, *Aliens Among Us*, was published, I received (and continue to receive) telephone calls and letters from some of her readers, many of whom ask for more information about ESP, hypnosis, and UFO research. Despite the additional correspondence, I was pleased to learn of the many descriptions of UFO and paranormal experiences from persons around the globe.

One negative consequence was a news item that appeared in *The National Enquirer*, June 23, 1987. The article sensationalized my claim of the 1980 hypnosis session with Dr. Ed Paradis, a professor and a friend, who helped me to explore my memories of a childhood encounter with ETs while "on board" a spacecraft. Apparently, the article was bothersome to some uni-

---

2. Montgomery, 1985.

versity administrators, who wished to maximize good public relations and to minimize any notoriety.

Marilyn also was upset, and bothered by some coarse comments among acquaintances, as well as the rumors in the Laramie community about this "weird" professor.

Childhood Encounters

And what was the ruckus about? It was about my decision to do as I had recommended to hundreds of other UFOErs: if you are willing to tolerate ridicule, then talk to others around you about your UFO experiences.

In 1980, when I was 50, I learned more about my memories of some childhood events. The exploration followed our first Rocky Mountain Conference on UFO Investigation.[3] The "contactee conference" (Chapter 8) provides a forum for interested persons to speak about their UFO encounters.[4]

I had been asking myself the question: "Why am I so concerned about UFO contactees?" I asked Dr. Ed Paradis to provide hypnotic suggestions for me. As I relaxed deeply, and focused on childhood memories, I mentally "regressed" to feelings about 1940, when I was ten years old and in the fifth grade. I sensed that I was in a large room. I was looking through a big window at a black sky that was filled with shining stars. Standing at my left side was a tall man, dressed in strange clothing (not like my dad's overalls or his business suit). The strange man's clothing was tight-fitting, and the pants continued down the legs and ankles like stockings that formed into his shoes or boots. The tall man had his arm around me, and his right hand was on my right shoulder. I heard him talking (or thinking) to me. "Leo, learn to read and write well. When you grow up, you can help other people learn more about their purpose in life." As that ten-year-old fifth-grader, I felt burdened and blessed: blessed by the awesome awareness (subconsciously) of that encounter; and burdened by the awesome awareness (subconsciously) of that task: How can a little ten-year-old boy help other people learn more about their purpose in life?

Reactions and Evaluations. After the 1980 session, I accepted—tentatively—the "reality" of that memory. However, when I spoke to other persons about the session, I recognized the need to tolerate their reactions; they implied (or implored!) that my memories were fantasies, daydreams, or productions of a vivid imagination in a fantasy-prone personality! (Whew! What a relief!)

In 1990, when I was almost 60, I experienced another rush of emotions. I sobbed publicly, during our 11th UFO Conference, in front of more than 150

---

3. Sprinkle, 1981.
4. Gordon, 1991.

persons. I had been listening to Marika Shields, a Denver woman, describe her childhood encounter with an alien being. When she spoke of the stockings/boots, my suppressed feelings of fear emerged with my (claimed/fantasized?) memories of that event. My conscious recollection of the hissy fit, about old stockings over my shoes, now made psychological sense to me. Others could continue to suspend judgment and to doubt, but I no longer had that intellectual luxury. I "knew"—because of my own gut feelings—that those childhood events, at some level, had occurred. (As I sobbed, one woman in the audience said, "Good! Now, Leo is suffering like the rest of us!")

Many persons will not believe the story. Those persons who might be willing to believe the story would assume, probably, that my emotional reaction was an indication of my fear of the man. However, my interpretation is that my fear of the man was not nearly so great as the fear of myself! My greatest concern was about the possibility that his message about my mission was true! The work of UFO investigation is difficult, but the work of soul development is much more difficult!

Another experience, which continues to this day, also was significant to me. During that 1980 hypnosis session, I was reminded of a body sensation that is very important to me. Whenever I perceive "truth" (personal truth, such as beautiful music; an elegant solution to an intellectual puzzle; or some psychic impressions of the inner world of a client; etc.), then I experience a little shiver on my right shoulder. Somehow, that fifth-grade experience in 1940 is associated with a "knowing" that I am moving in the appropriate direction for further "truth." I do not claim that this personal truth is absolute truth or universal truth; however, when I follow this feeling, then usually I am rewarded with opportunities to gain further knowledge that has both personal meaning and professional satisfaction.

The Parnell Study

The year 1986 was very significant for me. During that year, June O. Parnell, Ph.D., completed her dissertation study.[5]

My pleasure was two-fold: I was pleased at her success in completing the program and receiving her degree, Doctor of Philosophy; and I was pleased that the results of her study were consistent with my 1964-1968 study.[6]

Her dissertation was among the (then) half-dozen dissertations on the UFO issue, and the first dissertation that dealt with the personality characteristics of UFOErs. Also, I was glad that I had completed a major professional task. I had the (naive) hope that my UFO research could go forward with fewer frustrations.

---

5. Parnell, 1986.
6. Sprinkle, 1976.

APA Ethics Committee

In 1988, I wrote a paper titled, *The Changing Message of UFO Activity: From Experimental Science to Experiential Science?*[7] This paper was presented at Colorado State University during an international conference on paranormal research, hosted by Maurice L. Albertson, Ph.D. (Maury is a big man, and a bold scientist. He is a co-founder of the Peace Corps; a tireless worker for research and development in Eastern nations; a professor emeritus, CSU, of engineering; and while he served as CSU Director of Research, he helped their faculty to obtain more research funds than any other university in the Western region of the U.S.)

After my presentation, two young reporters (a man from Fort Collins and a woman from Denver) asked me some questions. The questions focused not so much on my paper, but on the policies of the U.S. government about UFO information. Of course, I had no answers for their questions. However, when pressed, I (foolishly?) responded with some speculations about the answers to their questions.

Later, their newspapers ran a short article about this "self-proclaimed" UFO contactee and his speculation that the "Star Wars" project is an attempt by the U.S. to prepare for intergalactic warfare.

Shortly after the news item was printed, I received a notice from the Ethics Committee of the American Psychological Association (APA) that I was being charged with unethical scientific behavior, based upon a complaint from an anonymous source about the newspaper articles.

I knew that the APA Ethics Committee was required to investigate any complaint about an APA member, without revealing the name of the person who submitted the complaint. Marilyn was very upset. She feared that my tenuous tenure at the University would be eroded further; she worried that I might be dismissed from APA membership, which would end my listing as a licensed psychologist.[8]

I tried to calm her, and to point out the need for these procedures. (I had consulted with a few clients, in my career, who had complained about the immoral behaviors of other psychotherapists; these few clients were glad that they could provide information to me and to agencies without the worry of confronting those therapists who had wronged them.)

I told Marilyn that the committee would be objective and would consider all of the evidence—not merely the newspaper articles.

Nevertheless, despite my outer confidence, I was shaken. I had no wish to embarrass the APA, the University of Wyoming, or any other group. Indeed, my wish was to enhance science, psychology, and public trust in psycholo-

---

7. Sprinkle, 1988.
8. #20, 1 Jan 1966, WY.

gists. I had high hopes that the charges would be dismissed, so that I could be viewed as a moral and ethical psychologist not only in the eyes of the APA Ethics Committee, but also in the eyes of colleagues at the Counseling Center, University of Wyoming.

The Newest Director. The issue became more complex when the newest director of the counseling center (yes, the "Interim Director") viewed the situation as a direct threat to my professional career. His position was (in effect), "They are out to get you, Leo. You have to be careful in your response to the Committee."

And so, one Saturday morning, we met in the other department that he was managing. I sat at a table, while he stood at the blackboard and provided me with a systems analysis on what was happening and how I should deal with the system.

I thought to myself, "This is ironic." I was a licensed psychologist, he was not. In fact, he did not hold the Ph.D. degree; his training was in mathematics, and he did not have training as a counselor or psychotherapist. He did have extensive experience as a manager, with computer analysis as a specialty, and he had a reputation for demanding "data-driven" decisions.

My respect for him as a manager, and my anxiety about my professional welfare, influenced my decision to follow his advice. I responded to the APA Ethics Committee with a cautious letter, written from a defensive position. Then, as the committee chairperson asked for more information, I threw caution to the wind. I responded as I had wished to do from the start: I provided the committee with an audiotape and videotape of my presentation, as well as a copy of the prepared paper. Later, as requested, I provided letters from other psychologists who knew of my work as a counseling psychologist as well as a UFO investigator.

The deliberations of the committee were completed within one year. The Ethics Committee unanimously dismissed all charges. I was relieved, and yet I was puzzled. Was there a direct connection between the APA charges of unethical behaviors and the pressures on me to resign from the University of Wyoming? During the year of deliberations by the APA Ethics Committee, I was conducting my own deliberations. I was conducting an "internal audit" of my own resources, body/mind/soul. I knew that I was experiencing a severe case of "burn-out": job-related stress. I tried to joke about it, telling others that I was uncertain if I were burned out, burned up, or burned down. I did not wish to lose the salary or the security of the position; yet I was participating in a situation that I abhorred. Earlier, when my former colleagues and I were struggling about the issue of who should serve as director, I could feel the tension, daily, in my body. I experienced anxiety and stomach cramps; I sometimes awakened at night, unable to go back to sleep. I sought chiropractic treatment and sessions of "body work" to release and relieve the aches and pains in my neck, shoulders, hips, and feet.

However, during the year of the "interim director," I could feel my strength and courage dissipate. My rationalization was that I could tolerate any pressures on me, but I could not tolerate what I perceived to be undue pressures on those staff who were not involved in my struggles.

The interim director had instituted many changes. Now we conducted only two staff meetings each month (rather than the weekly staff meetings, which had been held since the inception of the counseling center in the 1960s). Also, the staff meetings were attended only by the part-time staff (the counselors or graduate assistants) and me, as training coordinator. The other full-time staff members and the interim director did not attend. My task was to inform the counselors of the decisions by the full-time staff. The graduate assistants complained that they had no "input."

During one fall meeting, the issue became more intensified. Some graduate assistants (Ph.D. candidates in clinical psychology) complained that their training and experience were being ignored; they wished to tell the interim director that he was wrong in his decisions about how they should consult with their clients. I cautioned them to be careful, but they insisted upon their right to talk with the director and to express their views.

Ka-Boom! They came back with the good news: they were told to accept the situation or to get out! Further, they were given the bad news: they were told that they would not receive a favorable recommendation for next year's employment.

One capable doctoral student, who later received an internship at a prestigious psychoneurological clinic, was talking to me about the way he had been treated. He looked at me evenly and said, "Leo, I think that I felt a little bit of what you have been feeling for a long time."

Deep within me, I knew that I must resign from the university—not only for the sake of the graduate students—but also for the sake of my own health.

Resignation or Re-creation?

In November of 1988, I submitted my resignation, effective September 1, 1989. Immediately, in my opinion, the pressures for this or that project, as well as pressures on the graduate assistants, ceased. Later, I became aware of rumors about the game between the interim director and the vice-president; each—according to the rumors—was attempting to oust the other and to obtain the dominant position in the new organizational chart for student affairs.

In that scenario, the rest of us were pawns, not major players. I do not know if the rumors were true or not; however, I noted (with little satisfaction, but a sense of ironic justice) that both men were involved, the following year, in a dispute over misused funds. I could imagine their stress about newspaper articles which carried complaints from staff and students about the alleged misconduct of these two administrative officers.

By that time, I was involved in my own private practice. One dear friend, a woman in Jackson, Wyoming, had written to me about her reactions to the announcement of my resignation. First, she wrote that she was shocked. "How can they do this to such a fine professor?" Next, she was angry, "How dare they treat Leo in this manner!" Then, finally, she accepted the news as appropriate. "Oh! Leo is being prepared for something better!"

I wrote back, thanking her for her perspective. I tried to rationalize that I was getting my wish: an unofficial "chair," so that I could be free of regular university duties, and I could conduct my professional activities as I saw fit to do so.

New Science and New Cents

When I resigned from the University of Wyoming (Professor Emeritus, Counseling Services), I was 59. Marilyn and I were fortunate to share office facilities with two friends: Drs. Lynne and Darrell Pendley. (Both received their Ph.D. degrees from the U of WY, and they serve in Special Services of the local school district as diagnostician and school psychologist, respectively. Both are knowledgeable and skillful, not only in conventional psychological services, but also in transpersonal psychology.)

Although my private practice is not lucrative (approximately $25,000 each year), it provides enough income to pay for expenses and continue my research. I am so grateful to Ida Kannenberg —author[9] and long-time contactee extraordinaire—for her gift that gave me enough courage to separate from the campus and begin a new stage of life. (At age 59, I was not yet eligible for retirement payments or Social Security benefits. Thus, our personal income was limited; I did not have funds to attend professional meetings or UFO conferences.) I did have enough money to attend the IANS (International Association for New Science) conferences in Fort Collins. However, I drove my car back to Laramie each night to ease food and lodging expenses.

IANS was developed by Maury Albertson, Ph.D., and Brian O'Leary, Ph.D., with the able assistance of Robert Siblerud, D.O., and his volunteer staff. Dr. Brian O'Leary is another one of my many heroes. I told him, when we shared campus campaign stories, that I was pleased to know that a "real" scientist from a prestigious university could suffer slings and arrows like a mediocre psychologist from a medium-sized university.

Also, I was able to attend three of the TREAT conferences.[10] These conferences were convened in various states in order to bring together UFO researchers and mental health practitioners and explore various anomalies.

---

9. Kannenberg, 1992, 1993, 1995.
10. TREAT: Treatment and Research of Experienced Anomalous Trauma, initiated by Rima Laibow, M.D., New York psychiatrist.

I am pleased at the increasing numbers of good scientists and professional practitioners who are joining various organizations, such as International Society for the Study of Subtle Energies and Energy (ISSSEEM); and Society for Scientific Exploration. Although a lack of funds prevented me from attending most of these conferences, I was able to attend TREAT II.

Treat II. The second annual TREAT conference was held at Virginia Polytechnic Institute (VPI), Blacksburg, Virginia.[11] During the conference, I experienced several "treats." First, I was able to talk briefly with Dr. Helen Crawford, Professor of Psychology, who had transferred from the University of Wyoming to VPI. Her experimental studies in hypnosis were well done and well known. (She had served as a former colleague of Drs. Ernest and Josephine Hilgard, as well as a student of Dr. Charles Tart.) Helen had come to the TREAT conference to listen to Ken Ring, Ph.D., a professor of psychology from the University of Connecticut. I sat next to Helen as she listened to Ken's presentation on his comparison of NDErs (near-death experiencers) and UFOErs. I was pleased that Ken's careful study showed similar results to those of my simple surveys: a connection of UFOEs and ESP experiences.

I assumed that Helen was willing to tolerate my whispered "Yes!" whenever Ken's slides revealed more significant correlations between NDErs and UFOErs. I perceived Helen as a "closet" transpersonal psychologist, yet her public presentations maintained the conventional explanations for psychic phenomena: dissociation and/or fantasy. I mentally prayed that, someday, Dr. Crawford and other good psychologists would demonstrate a public interest in paranormal research.

Second, I enjoyed my reacquaintance with the now deceased David Cheek, M.D., a world-renowned obstetrician and gynecologist. I had met Dr. Cheek briefly, in the 1960s, when I attended a meeting and workshop presented by the American Society of Clinical Hypnosis. His workshop presentation, in my opinion, was brilliant; he presented himself as a true *doctor*—a teacher and learned person.

Then, in the 1970s, I had the opportunity to meet Dr. Cheek again. He had traveled across the U.S., visiting laboratories where sleep and dream research was being conducted. Dr. Dave Foulkes, then professor of psychology at the University of Wyoming, called me one afternoon to tell me that David Cheek was on campus; Dave invited me to his office for a chat with the two of them.

When I arrived, they were involved in a discussion of birth memories. I volunteered to demonstrate my "reliving" of my birth memory, based upon my reactions to a self-hypnosis trance state. They watched as I relaxed deeply, closed my eyes, and focused on "returning" to earlier memories. Then I sug-

---

11. See Sprinkle, 1995.

gested to my subconscious mind that I relive the birth experience. My neck and head began to twist. My shoulders turned; I groaned and moaned, tears rolled down my cheeks onto my shirt, as I recalled the dual feelings of anger and guilt: anger at my mother because of the pain that she was causing for me, and guilt because of the pain that I was causing for her.

As I completed the "emergence," I ceased my groaning. David Cheek skillfully eased my anguish by suggesting verbally that I could return to the normal state without pain and with a deeper appreciation of the birth memory. Also, he prepared me for my tearful condition by stating (in effect), "When you open your eyes, you'll notice some moisture on your face and your shirt." I responded, with a smile, "That's OK. A little Sprinkle never hurt anyone." It was a therapeutic moment for me as I accepted the double meaning of the pun. As I opened my eyes, Dave Foulkes had a better pun: "That's quite a condensation!" I appreciated his comments, and the comments by David Cheek that my head and shoulder movements were consistent with his observations of babies during the birthing process. I began to trust more fully the possibility that my "memory" actually represented the movements and emotions of my own birth experience.

Then, in 1989, at TREAT II, I looked forward to seeing Dr. David Cheek again. I wondered if he would remember me and our discussion of birth memories. When I arrived at the conference, I saw him across the room, surrounded by other conferees. I went to the men's room. Then, while standing at a urinal, I heard a booming voice: "A little sprinkle never hurt anyone!" Instantly, I laughed. "David Cheek!"

A third treat was the opportunity to meet a colleague of Dr. Cheek: James S. Gordon, M.D., professor of psychiatry, Georgetown University, Washington, D.C. Dr. Gordon was a writer for *The Atlantic* magazine and other publications, as well as author of *The Golden Guru*. Although Jim was very skeptical about UFO reports, he was willing to attend the TREAT conference because of his friendship with David Cheek. When he learned about the annual Rocky Mountain Conference on UFO Investigation, he made arrangements to attend. He wished to watch Dr. June Parnell and me while we conducted hypnosis sessions with individual UFOErs. Later, he wrote an article about his reactions and observations.[12]

Some of my friends viewed the favorable article as "vindication"; they reminded me that a professor of psychiatry at Georgetown University has credentials that are as good, if not better, than professors of psychology at the University of Wyoming. I was pleased with the article because many professional people, as well as UFOErs, called or corresponded for more information about the conference and about UFO research.

---

12. Gordon, 1991.

One woman, a university staff member, told me that she had attended a committee meeting during which a question was raised (by the vice-president of student affairs?) about the UFO conference. Should the university discontinue permission for the UFO conference to be held on campus? The woman stated that several committee members pointed out that other organizations, e.g., Girl Scouts and religious societies, were using the facilities of the U of WY Conferences and Institutes. Further, some university staff and faculty viewed *The Atlantic* article as favorable to the university and the community, rather than as unfavorable or detrimental.

Psychical Analysis of UFOEs

The article in *The Atlantic* also provided an opportunity for rethinking my view about the significance of UFO activity. For a decade, I had been nurturing my views about the taboo topic of reincarnation (See "Past Life Exploration" on page 79.) and the connection with UFO activity. However, I had been struggling with the task of bringing that connection into focus for my work with others.

Then, a client, who herself is a hypnotherapist and a UFO contactee, suggested that we conduct a workshop for hypnotherapists, so that they could come to terms with their UFOEs. The workshop never was scheduled, but the challenge provided me with a method to apply the PACTS Model (Sprinkle, 1987).

I began to write an article for the 1992 Denver UFO Symposium, sponsored by the International Association for New Science. The Symposium speakers were selected by Dr. Albertson and Dr. Siblerud, based on a list of researchers that was developed by the steering committee: Steven Greer, M.D., Brian O'Leary, Ph.D., and me.

Linda Moulton Howe. I was pleased that many members of the audience expressed their appreciation of the concepts and demonstration of psychical analysis.

My one disappointment was my failure, somehow, to include references to the work of Linda Howe, TV director/producer, investigative reporter, and author of *Alien Harvest*, and *Glimpses of Other Realities*. Linda and I had worked together on several UFO cases, including the Judy Doraty UFO experience. She is a delightful person, as well as a dedicated professional researcher.

Steven M. Greer, M.D. Of course, the star of that conference, as well as the keynote speaker at our 1992 Laramie UFO Conference, was the director of CSETI (Center for the Study of Extraterrestrial Intelligence), Dr. Steven Greer, emergency physician, now of Virginia. His proactive approach, rather than waiting passively for UFOs to appear, is the next level of UFO experience: CE-V (close encounter of the fifth kind).

In my opinion, the protocol for CSETI field of experiences is not for the benefit of ETs; however, it may be that the sounds (chanting), lights (directing high intensity flashlights), and meditation (sending mental messages for landing instructions), are beneficial for the teams of human participants.

During our field experience, north of Laramie, in June of 1992, several participants described their impressions that our rituals may have been helpful—not only to ease our human anxiety, but also to allow ET observations of our attitudes, motives, and efforts to establish mutual communication.

Perhaps, someday, we may learn if these field experiences can lead to onboard experiences for mutual benefit of humans and ET entities. Greer's new book, *Extraterrestrial Contact: Evidence and Implications*, compiles his research to date.[13]

PART ONE: Summary and Conclusions

In these first three chapters, I have described the personal experiences that encouraged me to become a UFO investigator and UFO researcher. I gradually learned about my repressed memories of childhood ET encounters that caused me to view myself not only as a UFO observer and UFO witness, but also as a UFO abductee and UFO contactee.

In the 1950s, I had begun my investigations from the conventional viewpoint: *sensing* and gathering physical evidence about UFO activity.

However, I found myself unable to make further progress until I became aware—and accepted—the psychical aspects of UFO phenomena. My *intuiting* of UFO phenomena, and my *feeling* about the significance of UFO evidence, provided me with doubts about the methods of the conventional model of science.

I found myself becoming more and more skeptical—not of the reality of "flying saucers"—but of the concept of "reality" as defined and developed by the current leaders of the scientific community.

I found myself increasingly attracted to the perspective that the model of conventional empirical science must be modified in order to incorporate experiential methods and techniques. I wished to understand ESP and paranormal phenomena in hopes that I could understand and evaluate the range of evidence for UFO activity.

---

13. Greer, 1999.

PART TWO

Personal Analysis of POLS

*It is absolutely necessary that the soul should be healed and purified,
and if this does not take place during its life on Earth,
it must be accomplished in future lives.*

—St. Gregory (237-332 AD)

Part Two is written in order to describe my "intuiting" of hypnosis, ESP (extrasensory perception), and reincarnation. In my opinion, explorations of these topics are necessary for a fuller understanding of the significance of UFO activity.

I can understand why some researchers (e.g., Jerome Clark, editor of *International UFO Reporter*; former editor of *FATE* magazine; and author of *UFO Encyclopedia I, II, III*) choose to differentiate between ESP experiences and UFO experiences. Some UFO researchers avoid the topic of ESP because they wish to maintain their sense of scientific respectability; some parapsychologists use the same argument in their refusal to study UFO phenomena. However, I appreciate the efforts of those many researchers (e.g., David Cassirer and Rhea White, et al.) who are showing the connections between parapsychology and ufology.

These next three chapters describe my personal explorations of hypnosis, ESP, and reincarnation, and the many "soul samples" that I gathered in my work with clients and colleagues.

Legitimate Suffering

Neurosis is always a substitute for legitimate suffering.

—Carl Gustave Jung
Swiss Psychoanalyst

Introduction

I feel it is important to describe some of the events that helped me to become more aware of the moral/ethical dilemma of hypnosis and subconscious processes. In my opinion, the "key" to the UFO puzzle is not what we shall discover about ETs, but what we are discovering about humanity—how can we suffer without being "neurotic" about it!

Hypnosis Doesn't Smoke

The young man sat in my office, counseling center, University of Wyoming. Leaning forward in his chair, he stared intently at me. Then he challenged me: "I bet you can't hypnotize me!" I leaned forward in my chair, looked intently into his eyes, and replied, "I bet you that I can't hypnotize you, either!" Puzzled, he leaned back and complained, "But you're supposed to be an expert on hypnosis." I retorted, "I am, but I can only hypnotize one person." He grinned. "Who's that?" (As if he were asking, "Who's the dummy?") I responded, "I can only hypnotize myself." (He slumped, as if my words had taken the starch out of him.) Then his face brightened as I continued, "But I can teach you how to hypnotize yourself."

He responded well to hypnotic suggestions, and we both felt that our session was helpful to him. Yet, I knew that his initial concern was less an issue of *hypnosis* and more an issue of *power*. Essentially, his verbal, and non-verbal, communications were asking, "Who is in charge here? Are you more dominant than I? Or am I more dominant than you?" When I showed him, verbally and non-verbally, that I regarded us as co-operators, then he responded with his commitment and courage as I responded with my commitment and experience.

There are so many mistaken notions about hypnosis that I often hear myself as a teacher, as well as a hypnotist, in my dialogues with clients.

For example, the following discussion occurred spontaneously with a U of WY student who demonstrated his wit and curiosity. He opened our initial interview with this question: "Does hypnosis stop smoking?" I answered, "Hypnosis doesn't smoke." He did a double-take, and he sputtered, "You don't understand the question!" I responded, "What is the question?" He mumbled, "Oh! I know. Can you stop smoking with hypnosis?" I replied, "I don't smoke." He gasped, "You don't understand the question!" I smiled. "What is the question?" He grinned and giggled, "Yeah! What is the question?" He paused. "Hmmm!" He looked at me in amusement and then, "Oh! I know! The question is: If I learn hypnosis, can I use hypnosis to stop smoking?" I nodded my head and responded, "That's a good question, but there is a better question." Impatiently, he asked, "What's that?" I replied, "The better question is: When I decide to stop smoking, can I use self-hypnosis procedures to ease my anxiety?" He glared. "Why is that a better question?" I stated, "Because you can stop smoking anytime you wish to do so." He looked incredulous. "I can?" (As if he were asking or begging, "Mother, may I?") "Yes," I said. He asked, "How?" I retorted, "Just don't put cigarettes in your mouth." He sputtered, "Oh, yeah? Well, how about the anxiety?" I smiled. "Ahhh! Now, we are asking good questions!" He smiled, as if to tell me that he recognized the gist of our discussion: Hypnotic procedures are not "weapons" to cut out bad habits, but more like "tools" to enhance good habits.[1]

Convergence of Client and Counselor

As a graduate student at the University of Colorado-Boulder, I was impressed with the writings of various psychoanalysts and psychologists, e.g., Alfred Adler, Sigmund Freud, Carl Jung, Carl Rogers, Harry Stack Sullivan, et al. I learned much from the supervision of Dr. Dottie Sherman; she had the ability to assess—intuitively—the motives of others, to *hear* both the verbal and nonverbal messages of clients. Both she and Dr. Victor Raimy had been students and colleagues of Dr. Carl Rogers, and they continued the tradition of "client-centered therapy."

As a graduate student at the University of Missouri (UMO), I learned more about their Communications Model (from Ohio State University) and

---

1. Prochaska, Norcross, and DiClemente, 1994.

the Empirical Model (University of Minnesota). The UMO professors spent much time with doctoral students in designing the methodology and assessment procedures for dissertation studies. We learned that the scientific approach was based upon the art of asking good questions in order to arrive at better answers. For example, an early dissertation study showed that student clients responded well to either a "cognitive" (thinking) approach or an "affective" (feeling) approach by their therapist. Yet, for years, at various counseling centers, the debate raged over which approach was better: cognitive or affective?

I recognized the significance of asking good questions, not only in group studies, but in individual sessions as well. The psychological grammar of client and therapist might be very different, initially, but a successful therapeutic relationship will show a *convergence*, or an integration, of commentary as the sessions continue. Thus, I learned that a good therapist can be both scientist and practitioner in listening and interacting with each client.

That integration took place for me, both intellectually and emotionally, when I sought personal counseling with John McGowan, Ed.D. Dr. McGowan was helpful to me in recognizing that I was trying to be two kinds of therapists: "cognitive" (like my advisor, Dr. Robert Callis) and "affective" (like Dr. Carl Rogers). However, I was neglecting the important rules of life: know thyself, like thyself, and be thyself.

On the one hand, I was attempting to be thoughtful, logical, and rational; on the other hand, I was seeking to become intuitive, emotive, and caring with each client. Thus, my pace was sometimes slow and patient, sometimes fast and hectic. For a few clients, that was difficult, even bothersome. By learning more about my relations with other persons, and childhood feelings, I came to a greater self-awareness and self-acceptance. It was OK to be myself; I could integrate my experiences as a client with my experiences as a therapist.

Quartet Harmony. I enjoyed writing papers in various graduate courses, particularly in Bob Callis' class on advanced theories in counseling practice. He had the capacity to state his position and to defend that position with both empirical evidence and professional philosophy.

However, one of the most satisfying projects was an assignment by Robin Clyde, Ph.D., clinical psychologist. Dr. Clyde had acquired the skill of looking at an inventory profile (e.g. MMPI: *Minnesota Multiphasic Personality Inventory*) and accurately hypothesizing the behaviors of the examinee. On several occasions, when I consulted with him about the MMPI profiles of my clients, he not only showed an awareness of the personal dynamics of each client, but he also suggested ways of dealing with each client. His views were excellent. (On one occasion, I listened as he observed the behaviors of a visiting speaker and he hypothesized the likely MMPI profile. I could not discount the likelihood that he could "reverse" the process of diagnosing.)

During a course on abnormal psychology, Dr. Clyde gave us an opportunity to write a brief but creative paper; I chose to write about the "music" of a "male quartet": Freud, Jung, Rogers, and Alfred Korzbyski, author of *General Semantics.*[2]

The concept of four voices in the mind of the psychotherapist was appealing to me: Alfred Korzbyski, the bass (sensing), who provided the scientific basis of general semantics; Carl Rogers, the mellow baritone (feeling), who allowed the client to explore self; Sigmund Freud, top tenor (thinking), who penetrated the neurotic nexus; and Carl Jung, lead tenor (intuiting), whose voice spanned all of the levels of physical and psychical phenomena. I wished that I could incorporate and blend each approach in my own professional procedures.

3 + 1. The model of 3+1 had been growing within for many years. I could see the model everywhere! For example, I could recognize the religious views of some of my friends as a foursome, rather than their professed belief in a Trinity: God, the Father; God, the Son; God, the Holy Spirit; and (ta da!) God, the Devil. A few of my friends seemed to be much more excited about God the Devil than the other Gods. (For other models of human behavior see Chapter 10.)

Another example: I was raised in a family of three sons and one daughter, as was one of our cousins. Many years later, Marilyn and I raised three sons and a daughter. In my work as a member of many doctoral committees, I served as major advisor for four doctoral students: three men and one woman.

Another example: in the early years of post-doctoral experience, I found myself collecting articles and newspaper clippings about 3+1 topics: physical sciences, biological sciences, social sciences, and a category that I initially called religious or mystical events. Not until later was I able to recognize the need within me to seek—and find—a model to integrate each of these four levels of science. Meanwhile, hypnosis became the "clutch" between the "gears" of my mechanical model of science.

Hypnosis or Self-Hypnosis?

Everything I heard about hypnosis indicated that it was a process which was conducted by the "hypnotist," and the result was a response by the "subject." Yet my own personal experience was different; I learned that all hypnosis was "self-hypnosis," which might be facilitated by the so-called hypnotist.

---

2. As a high school student, I enjoyed my participation as a member of the male quartet. The blending of our voices in four-part harmony was most gratifying. One of our songs was "Ezekiel saw a wheel, way up in the middle of the air. The big wheel run by faith, and the little wheel run by the grace of God; wheel in a wheel, a-turning, way up in the middle of the air." I did not recognize—until many years later—that the African-American gospel song was a UFO story!

I learned about the 1964 book *Self Hypnotism*, by Leslie Le Cron, from a client at the U of W counseling center. The student/client was a bright, well-read, and thoughtful person, who wondered if he might become the ruler of the planet! He did not wish for me to dissuade him for his grand plan, indeed! He wished for me to enhance his potential for the project!

Despite my personal objection to his fascist philosophy, I attempted to assist him. Our efforts, however, were not successful; he continued to view himself as failing to make progress. We tried every approach with which I was familiar: analysis of dreams, client-centered explorations, behavior modification, existential discussions, personality and vocational inventories, etc. Alas! He continued to feel frustrated and unhappy, but he would not accept my viewpoint that his project was the source of his unhappiness.

Finally, in desperation, he asked me about the use of hypnosis. My initial inner thought: "Oh, sure! You wish me to give you hypnotic suggestions so that you can follow the suggestions and get better!" Then, I thought to myself, "Well, if it works, what's wrong with that?" So, I listened to him as he showed me a copy of Le Cron's book and described the procedures for self-hypnotism.

I bought a copy of the book, practiced the procedures, and joined the American Society of Clinical Hypnosis. I traveled to the University of Chicago for professional training. When I returned, the young man discontinued counseling sessions. My first failure with hypnotic procedures! Nevertheless, I recognized the value—for myself as well as for my clients—of following procedures for deep relaxation and exploration of the inner self. I collected many soul samples and learned many lessons.

Training in Hypnosis. One lesson I learned was that most professional practitioners of hypnosis are more open and more productive than their peers. In 1965, when I attended a University of Chicago workshop, I was curious about other participants. I walked along the hallway toward the conference room. I tried to be inconspicuous while eavesdropping on a conversation of a group of men and women. I overheard a riddle: "If one continues to wear riding clothes, does it become a habit?" I laughed out loud, then I apologized for my intrusion. They were cordial, and I was pleased to be associated with these dynamic and compassionate persons.

But the most important lesson I learned was not that of professional uses of hypnosis; rather, it was a lesson about the reach of the subconscious mind. I learned that lesson on the railroad train between Laramie and Chicago.

A Train of Thought. I sat in the evening shadows. I was bored, but it was too early for sleeping and the light was too dim for reading. So, I decided to play a mental game: I would pretend to place myself in the mind of other railroad passengers around me, and I would pretend to become aware of their thoughts and emotions. I relaxed deeply; I focused my awareness on a man walking by, and I imagined that my thoughts were his thoughts. Suddenly, I experienced a strange feeling: "Damn! I need a drink!" (Although I do not enjoy drinking alcohol, except for a glass of wine at a special dinner, I truly felt—at that moment—a strong desire to go to the bar and buy a drink.) Interesting!

Next, I focused my awareness on a young woman who walked by me. I felt a rising anger, almost a rage, within me; then, I heard an inner voice saying, "Those damned men! I wish I could cut off their balls!" The feeling was strong, but the attitude was not one that pleased me! I discontinued playing the game. Of course, my usual skepticism returned after the experiment. I tried not to think about the implications of the game.

Age 35 or Age 5? One night, while the children were asleep, and Marilyn was at a meeting, I continued the self-exploration that I had conducted during that noon hour. I had relaxed deeply, and suggested that I go back in memory to an important childhood memory. My conscious thought was that I would remember more about my fifth birthday anniversary. But what happened was not pleasant; in fact, it was frightening!

My jaws sprung open; I gasped and shuddered; I groaned loudly; I wept bitter tears, as I felt an almost uncontrollable rage. Then, my jaw snapped shut, as if I had bitten something or someone. Gradually, the tension eased, and I returned to my normal state of awareness, but, I was puzzled and confused.

I tried to learn more about the significance of those emotional reactions by asking myself questions, and allowing ideomotor responses (finger and thumb movements) to provide answers to these questions.[3]

Q. Am I five years old?
A. Yes.
Q. Did something happen to my jaw when I was five years old?
A. Yes.
Q. Was I alone?
A. No.
Q. Was my father with me?
A. No.
Q. Was my mother with me?
A. No.
Q. Older brother?
A. Yes.
Q. Can I remember, consciously, what happened?
A. Yes.

---

3. Cheek & LeCron, 1968, p. 85.

Then, I had a faint visual image, but a powerful emotional feeling, that I was sucking on a blanket (showing my infantile level of development?). My brother, Bob, in an effort to teach me not to be a "baby," pulled on the blanket. It hurt my jaw, and I was angry!

That night, sitting in my chair and reviewing the information that came out of the noon-hour session, I decided to explore further. I relaxed deeply and focused on the question: Is there anything else that is important about that memory?

My jaw sprang open, almost cramped; I groaned; tears spilled down my cheeks. I thought to myself, "Am I five years old?" My right index finger signaled yes. My jaw and my head nodded yes.

I recognized that, now, I had dual controls or dual communications. Not only could I use my fingers and thumbs to signal yes and no, I don't know, or I don't wish to say, but I could also use my head and jaw to signal yes (head up and down), no (head back and forth), don't know (lips lightly touching), and don't wish to say (jaw firmly clenched).

I continued my self-exploration.

Q. Is there something else that is important to remember about that five-year-old experience?

A. *Don't wish to say.* (Jaw firmly clenched!)

I asked again and received the same answer. I cajoled and pleaded with my subconscious mind, to no avail.

I was stumped—and upset! How can this be? Here I am, I thought, a 35-year-old adult, with a Ph.D. in counseling psychology, serving as a university professor and counselor, and skilled in working with many clients who have experienced all kinds of traumatic events. How can I refuse to answer my own questions?

Finally, I thought to myself: What is the morality involved? Which is more moral, to respond or not to respond. To answer the question or to refuse to answer the question? To be or not to be? as Shakespeare's Hamlet had pondered.

So, I thought, OK, subconscious mind, listen up!

Q. Does the "don't wish to say" refer to my concern that the answer might be bothersome or hurtful?

A. Yes.

Q. To others?

A. No.

Q. Only hurtful to Leo?

A. Yes.

Hell! I thought if I'm only protecting myself, then I can handle the information! What is it that I have been hiding from myself? Immediately, the five-year-old thought was clear in my conscious awareness: I am so angry that I could kill my brother!

The Murderous Impulse. That recognition was like a lightning bolt: not only was I aware of that powerful feeling, but also I was aware of the implications of that murderous impulse. Two memories stood out clearly in the relationship with my brother, plus the memory of bruxism (grinding my teeth) during the hectic nights as a residence hall director at the University of Colorado-Boulder. Now, I had a better understanding of my rivalry with my brother, and my male colleagues.

The two memories were these: an episode while Bob and I were hunting jackrabbits (hares) with .22 caliber rifles, and an episode when I loaned Bob's rifle to a friend of mine.

The hunting episode, in retrospect, showed my ambivalence about my guilty feelings, on one hand, and my (repressed) murderous feelings on the other hand. Both Bob and I were standing next to a car that had been driven by an older boy. We were getting ready to climb into the car and drive to another section of the prairie. I was holding our father's rifle, and Bob asked me if I had cleared the bullet in the chamber; I said that I had done so. He expressed his doubt, and I reacted impatiently. (Younger brothers, in case you weren't aware, don't like to be bossed by older brothers!)

Inside the car, with my rifle pointed safely upward, I reacted angrily when Bob again asked me if I had cleared the chamber. "Yes! If you don't believe me, watch this!" I pulled the trigger; the rifle fired; the bullet went through the roof of the old car. I was aghast! I had been taught, through family and Boy Scout training, to be careful with tools and weapons. No one was hurt, but I was puzzled and felt guilty.

The second memory was of an incident that occurred during our high school years. I had loaned Bob's rifle to a friend, but the friend had not returned it. Bob complained to me, but I was unable to retrieve it. I rationalized to myself that our friend was responsible for the return, or repayment, of the rifle. Then, at age 35, with that five-year-old memory of my murderous impulse, I recognized my own pattern of guilt, anger, fear, and love. I recognized the ambivalence of holding—or releasing—that murderous impulse.

I wrote to my mother and brother, asking if either could remember a childhood incident in which I "popped" my jaw with a pillow or blanket. Neither could recall such an event. (In my mind's eye, I could see my brother shaking his head and saying, "There goes that psychologist brother again!") I also wrote a check to Bob, in order to pay for the loss of that rifle, years ago. I eased my old guilt with new self-esteem.

The Morality Impulse. My self-hypnosis session was helpful to me in two ways: to establish a new level of love for me and my older brother, and to establish a better understanding of the power—and potential pain—of the morality impulse. I came to a greater appreciation for that Biblical phrase, "'Vengeance is mine,' saith the Lord."

I recognized more fully what some of my clients were showing me: An overemphasis on morality (being "good") can be as destructive to the inner self as an overemphasis on immorality (being "bad").

Neurosis and Legitimate Suffering

Carl Jung, M.D., said it best: "Neurosis is merely a substitute for legitimate suffering." When I first read that statement, I was puzzled. I did not understand the meaning of *legitimate suffering*. Later, I recognized at least four levels of suffering: physical or environmental stresses; bodily stresses; mental stresses; and spiritual or psychical stresses.

I noted that some theorists have written about three levels of suffering: normal, neurotic, and creative suffering. Normal suffering refers to everyday concerns about job, family, health, etc. Neurotic suffering refers to existential issues, such as death and dying, meaning of life, the suffering of others, etc. Creative suffering refers to concerns about fulfilling one's mission in life, serving God and community, etc. (The ancient Greek proverb, with sexist terms, said it well: man helping man is God.)

I became aware of the meaning of the term "Shrink." Some clients are asking, "Hey, Doc! Can you shrink my head/mind so that instead of neurotic suffering I can go back to normal suffering?"

I began to view myself as a mind expander rather than a brain shrinker. I wished to assist other persons to move from "normal" to "neurotic" to "creative" suffering. No wonder that some clients were afraid of me—or were they afraid that I would expose their inner selves as strong and purposeful?

Hot Rocks and Hay Fever

I learned another valuable lesson from my own inner self (body/mind/soul) as I continued to practice procedures for self-hypnosis. One day, during the noon hour, I relaxed deeply; then, I suggested that I could recognize the conditions that were significant in causing my "hay fever" symptoms.

I had experienced allergic reactions, each spring for thirteen years. The sneezing, runny nose, and itchy eyes were very noticeable—whether we were living in Missouri, Germany, Colorado, North Dakota, or Wyoming. As a graduate student at the University of Missouri, I had consulted with a physician who conducted a series of skin tests; the results showed my allergic reactions to various tree pollen.

When I learned self-hypnosis procedures, I was eager to try some techniques in order to end or ease my allergic reactions. At the moment that I suggested to myself that I could learn the cause of my symptoms, I had two related reactions: a hazy mental image of myself as I stood at the base of a large tree, and a strong feeling of anxiety about my inner self.

The image of standing at a tree was connected with a conscious memory of events in the spring of 1952, when Marilyn and I were engaged to be married. One night, I had bid her good-bye, right after a period of heavy petting. As I walked away, I remember the pain of what my friends called "hot rocks": sexual tension that burned throughout my groin. There, under the moonlight, standing at the base of a large tree, pounding the trunk with my fist, I gasped, "I can't stand this!"

Immediately, in my relaxed trance state, I recognized what had happened in the spring of 1952: my conscious mind, unable or unwilling to tolerate the "suffering" of sexual denial, merely asked my subconscious mind to handle the suffering. Then, every spring, the subconscious mind repeated the message: "Warning! Warning! Tree pollen! Tree pollen!" My body "suffered" various symptoms so that, mentally, I need not suffer; emotionally, I could handle the stress by dumping the suffering out of *mind* but into the *body*.

The difficulty was that message, and reaction, was developed while I was engaged to be married. (In those days, according to a popular song: love and marriage...go together like a horse and carriage...you can't have one without the other. In other words, we "learned" that we first are married—then we can engage in sex!)

In 1965, after thirteen years of marriage, it was no longer necessary to maintain the symptoms. So, mentally, I thanked my body, and then recoded the message: now, it is OK to engage in sex; I am married! If there is pollen in the air, I can breathe normally and I can tolerate any anxiety at the psychological level.

Then, my symptoms eased in a dramatic manner (despite the fact that *The Denver Post* newspaper had carried an article, by a specialist in allergic conditions, which stated that "only medication" can be helpful in easing allergic reactions.)

I learned what many physicians and healers have learned throughout human history: We have the capacity to harm—and to heal—ourselves. The task, I believe, is to balance *ethics* and *morality* of body/mind/soul.

Personal Ethics and Social Morality

E. Erickson was quoted as saying: "Morality is expendable where ethics prevail." I do not know if my interpretation is an accurate representation of his viewpoint; however, I view "ethics" as personal choice: doing what *I* believe to be best. I view "morality" as social choice: doing what *others* believe to be best.

Thus, if I choose what seems to be best for me and for others, then I am acting both in an ethical and moral manner. The difficulty, of course, is "knowing" what is best for me and what is best for my community.

I came to recognize the fact that many of my clients were trapped within two sets of belief: I wish to view myself as a "good and moral" person, yet I cannot accept my "bad and immoral" feelings and emotions. Thus, these persons continued to badger themselves, or punish themselves, in many ways self-defeating behaviors (SDBs).

My task was to assist them to recognize, and modify, their personal philosophy and interpersonal behaviors, so that they could view themselves, if possible, as "moral" (in the eyes of others) and "ethical" (in their own eyes).

Fingernails and Sister's Eyes. A student client, a young attractive woman, displayed her hands; the fingernails were chewed down to the bloody quick. She asked in a plaintive voice, "Can you help me find out why I chew my fingernails?" "Yes, we can find out quickly why you chew your fingernails." She almost gasped. "We can?" (Her voice sounded somewhat incredulous, but with a hint of optimism.) "Oh, yes," I replied, but then I cautioned her: "Finding out is easy; the difficulty may be in learning what to do about it." She smiled, knowingly.

She was willing to practice hypnotic procedures, so I began to teach her how to follow procedures for self-hypnosis. She was a "quick study," and soon she was in a deep state of body relaxation and mental concentration. Then, I encouraged her to picture herself in a special room, a place of security and comfort, where she could call upon the knowledge and wisdom of her inner self, with courage and confidence.

When she indicated that she was ready, I suggested that she mentally picture her fingernails becoming long and beautiful. She smiled as she apparently admired the image of the long and beautiful fingernails. Then, I suggested that she gather her courage and confidence, that she allow her fingernails to do anything that they wished to do. "Oh! Do you know what they want to do?" "No," I replied, "what do they want to do?" She almost yelled: "They want to scratch my sister's eyes out!" "They want to scratch your sister's eyes out?" (I was tempted to ask her if it were she—not her fingernails—who wished to scratch out her sister's eyes. I knew, however, that the therapeutic task was more important than the comic comment.)

I asked her to describe the feelings of the fingernails. Then, as she explored her feelings of hate and rage, she came to the awareness, and acceptance, and acknowledgment (the AAA of self-healing), that she could learn to suffer in a legitimate fashion, rather than in a neurotic manner. She could give herself a message like this: "I truly suffer; and I shall continue to suffer! However, I choose to suffer by not scratching out my sister's eyes. Maybe she deserves it, but I can refrain from doing it. If I decided to scratch out her eyes, I could do it with a knife or scissors, but, then, there would be social shame, and personal guilt, as well as a host of legal problems. Thus, I can find other ways to explore and experience my anger. And I can allow my fingernails to grow, without biting them, so that they are long and beautiful. My long and beautiful fingernails can be lovely reminders of my choice to suffer and to tolerate my sister."

When she returned to the normal state, we evaluated the exercise. She expressed pleasure at her new awareness, and she was satisfied that her new suffering was more mature than her old suffering. We agreed that there is something noble about suffering for a good cause: Our spirits are lifted and our self-esteem is enhanced!

Self-Improvement Program

In 1969, I began a group-counseling program called the Self Improvement Program. My individual counseling sessions were scheduled with students who sought assistance, including self-hypnosis training. Usually, I was busy from 8:00 AM to 5:00 PM; sometimes, I scheduled additional sessions at 7:00 AM, noon, or 5 PM. Then, during those weeks when most students were on vacation, I dealt with the "waiting list": students, faculty, and staff who wished to meet with me.

I decided that a group program in self-hypnosis would be helpful in two ways: to ease the heavy load of clients, and to prepare interested clients with those procedures that we would be following in individual sessions.

Some of my colleagues expressed concern about the use of hypnotic procedures. One colleague stated his view of my proposal: Leo should conduct an "experiment" in order to determine if hypnosis exists or not. I wrote to the director: I am conducting an experiment; the experiment is to determine if my colleagues will, or will not, support me in this project. The project was approved by W. Harry Sharp, Ph.D., Director.

The Self Improvement Program (SIP) consisted of seven weekly meetings, each for one hour. Interested students, staff, and faculty were invited to participate. Participants were encouraged to practice procedures for relaxation and concentration, including ideomotor responses, pendulum technique, clenched fist technique, study habits, ego strengthening, self-reinforcement, (Premack Principle), directed daydream technique, bracketing technique, and various approaches to meditation. Later, a booklet, the *Self Improvement Program Handbook*[4] was written and duplicated so that participants could be informed about procedures and topics. SIP (one professor apparently told a student: "SIP? Yes, a 'sip' of Sprinkle is quite enough.") became so popular that we had two groups each week, repeated twice each semester, fall, spring, and summer session. There were approximately two hundred participants each year.

In the 1980s, when I was speaking about UFO research on the campus of a Nebraska college, I was approached by an instructor who identified himself and stated, "You probably don't remember me. But I participated in SIP when I was a student at the University of Wyoming in 1970. I want you to know

---

4. Sprinkle, 1976.

that I continue to practice self-hypnosis. That self-hypnosis class was one of the most helpful classes that I ever took." He grinned: "Almost as helpful as my typing course!" I laughed: "Wow! Right up there, next to typing!"

Cancellation of Self-Improvement Program. The satisfaction that I received from the continuing success of the Self-Improvement Program was offset by the disappointment that I experienced when the SIP was cancelled.

I knew the true reason for the cancellation of the program: in 1983, when I resigned as director of counseling and testing, the SIP was viewed by some administrative officers as Leo's "pet project," along with his inappropriate activities in ESP, past-life therapy, and UFO research. Thus, the decision to cancel SIP—and to cease past-life therapy and UFO investigation during office hours—was the method by which I could be pressured to resign, or at least to *clip my wings*.

That year, 1984, was very difficult for me. I had never experienced any period in my life, or any activity (athletic, academic, manual labor, military, etc.) where I was expected to fail, or expected to admit that my life-style and work ethic was *wrong*. I had always been challenged and encouraged to be successful. But, in 1984, I was hurt, angry, and fearful.

Sometimes, during early morning jogging, I found myself swinging my fists at unseen enemies. If I put faces on those invisible enemies, I gained temporary vengeance and temporary satisfaction; yet, my deeper wish was to reform my colleagues, just as they probably wished to reform me.

Marilyn (may God bless her soul!) finally put the situation in proper perspective. She said, "Leo! Do as you tell your clients: If you are handed a lemon, make lemonade!" I understood the philosophy, but I didn't know how to apply the wisdom. She continued, "Let's make a videotape on self-hypnosis and market it."

Well, it wasn't my idea, so I didn't think that it was such a good idea. (Smile.) Later, as I reconsidered, I recognized: "Yes! That's a great idea!" Marilyn and I established a company, Trance Formations Unlimited.

Trance Forming Yourself

We talked with our grown children, and they agreed to participate in the project. Nelson and Eric and their friend, Eric Bittner, collaborated on the opening scene: a cowboy showdown (with gold watches). Matthew played his guitar in one scene; Kristen played her flute. Dudley, our little white dog, provided a sterling performance as he "played" the piano. A professor of music, and author, Ron McClure, provided background music on his guitar. (He had enjoyed his participation in SIP and encouraged many others to learn to use self-hypnosis procedures.) Mike Lewis and Coney Pownall (formerly co-owners of High Country Images, a photographic and videographic company) videotaped the proceedings at our cabin in Red Feather Lakes, Colorado.

On the morning of the videotaping, a deep fog rolled onto the lake; later, the sun shone brightly on the calm surface of Lake Hiawatha. All in all, it was a lovely and magical day in a delightful setting.

After editing by Mike and Coney, the videotape was ready for market. In 1985, we introduced our project, titled "Trance Forming Yourself: Self Hypnosis for Stress Management and Self Improvement."[5] The videotape provides group instruction in self-hypnosis procedures, with our family members as participants in various "daydream" scenarios.

We sold our first cassette to the staff of a local hospital for their program in community mental health. The videotape has not (yet?) been a commercial success. However, the project has provided me with a deep sense of satisfaction, both personally and professionally. Professionally, I was pleased to introduce the videotape at a 1987 APA symposium in Washington, D.C. Personally, I was pleased to reintroduce myself to my family! Those long hours together, for planning and reviewing the project, were jolly and joyful. Marilyn and I are so pleased that these creative and competent souls decided to join us in this lifetime.

I recognized, once more, that the test of a developing soul is not what happens to the body/mind/soul, but how that person responds to what happens. Once again, I was reminded that my work is important; further, I recognized, once again, the significance of altered states as the pathway—as well as the map—for the journey of the soul.

Whose Altered State?

"Boy! There certainly are a lot of drugs going around these days!" Those words were spoken to me by an acquaintance, a Laramie physician. I laughed, and replied, "You're right!"

I thought that he was joking, and I laughed to show my appreciation for his joke. However, later into our conversation, I recognized my error: he was not joking. He stood there, soft and obese, with a drink of alcohol in one hand, and a burning cigarette in the other hand. The year was 1976, and we both were guests at a Christmas party at the home of a mutual friend. I wished to remind him that alcohol and tobacco represented the most difficult drug addictions in the U.S.; and also the misuse of these products leads to many deaths annually, as well as a major cost of our public health bill. However, I didn't have enough courage (or compassion?) to remind him.

The physician turned the conversation to another topic. "Your daughter did very well before the operation; she seemed calm while she waited for surgery." I agreed with his viewpoint about our daughter Kristen, who was nine years old at the time. She had been hit by a car, when she was attempting to

---

5. Sprinkle, 1985.

cross a street near our home. I told the physician that one of the reasons Kristen did so well was due to the assistance of her mother: Marilyn had lain down on the street, next to Kristen, and talked to her in a calm voice about relaxing her body, mentally going to another place that was comfortable, etc. The hypnotic suggestions had been helpful to Kristen, so that she could deal with the pain of a broken leg, a broken collarbone, and a serious cut on her broken leg.

The physician was almost incredulous: "Your wife?" He asked the question as if he were asking several questions: "Your wife? A woman? A layperson? Using hypnosis?"

I didn't have the courage to ask him: "Isn't it much better to use meditation or hypnotic procedures to produce altered states of consciousness than to use tobacco and alcohol?" Thank goodness, the physician was not Kristen's surgeon, who was (and is) very mindful of *health* as well as *medicine*. And thank goodness, more and more health practitioners as well as physicians are aware of the harm from alcohol abuse and public smoking.

Premonition or Planning?

After talking with the physician, I recalled an incident when Kristen was five or six years old. I had been reading her a story, as she was tucked in bed and preparing for sleep. She looked up at me and asked, "Dad, what's it like to be in a hospital?" I offered a few comments about hospitals, medical treatment, and good health. When I asked why she had raised the question, she replied, "Oh, I just wondered. Maybe someday I'll have to go to the hospital." I suggested that we could visit, so that she could be well-informed about the hospital—without becoming seriously ill. She seemed so positive in her comments that I was puzzled.

Was she experiencing a premonition of events to come? I did not know. If she were experiencing a premonition, was it best to be prepared with a courageous and optimistic attitude about any future stay in a hospital? Apparently, at some level, she was aware of that possibility.

Bugged by a Moth

I was reminded, during the late 1960s, that "coincidence" and "premonition" are deeply entwined in everyday life. The reminder came from a client who set an appointment at the University of Wyoming Counseling Center. When she sat down, and I asked her how I could be helpful, she stated that she wished to deal with her phobia; she claimed that she was *deathly afraid* of moths.

As she spoke of her fear of moths, she shuddered and gasped. I encouraged her to continue talking, but I also encouraged her to relax her shoulders and to deepen her breathing. The sun was shining outdoors, and the warm summer air was blowing gently through the open window behind her.

As she increased the relaxation process, she seemed to ease her emotional distress as well as her bodily tension. She continued to associate more and more memories with her fear of moths.

At one point in our session, I felt impelled to tell her a story about Dr. Carl Jung, Swiss psychoanalyst. I told my client that Jung had written about a woman who came to him because of her fear of beetles. He reported that, while he was talking with the woman, a strange coincidence or "synchronicity" had occurred: He heard a scratching sound at his window; he turned and saw a strange beetle, like a scarab (an African beetle). He wondered not only at the timing, but also at the event: how did a scarab-like beetle, with such ancient Egyptian symbolism, appear at his window on a wintry day in Switzerland?

I am not certain of this part of my memory, but it seems that one of us— or both of us—joked about the possibility of a moth visiting us, just as a beetle had visited Carl Jung and the woman.

I do, however, recall vividly the next event: A big, beautiful, brown moth floated inside the window, around the room, and landed gently at her feet. The moth was oriented toward her, a few inches in front of her shoes; the wings hovered, with a slight pulsing movement, as if waiting on behalf of the client.

The woman was so frightened that she seemed to be paralyzed, unable to move, and almost unable to speak. She whispered, "Dr. Sprinkle! What— what—what shall I do?" I tried to assure here that everything was OK; however, I admit that not only was I shocked, but I also wasn't certain about any recommendation for her! (This situation was not covered in any of my graduate courses!)

Finally, I said something like this: "Well, why don't you talk to the moth?" In an incredulous voice, with a hint of anger, she exclaimed, "Talk to the moth?" Then, when she noticed that I was serious, she sputtered, "Oh!" and she whispered, "What shall I say?" I swallowed a couple of times, trying to sound calm as well as logical and reasonable—and feeling that I was not being very successful. (Jung wrote that the best style in psychotherapy is to be intuitive or "artistic" during the therapeutic session, then, rational or "analytical" after the session.) I replied, in effect, "Why don't you thank the moth for coming to visit? Tell the moth that you are afraid, but that you are here to learn more about your fear of moths. Then, ask the moth to help you as you learn more about your fear." When she protested that it was silly, or crazy, to talk to a moth, I suggested that she communicate, mentally, those thoughts to the moth.

If anyone else had seen us, he or she might have been puzzled by the proceedings. We, all three, were transfixed: I was watching the woman; the woman was watching the moth; and the moth seemed to be resting, with a rhythmic flutter of its big brown wings.

After a long silence, the woman told me that she had been communicating those thoughts, silently, to the moth; next, the moth flew up and away, out of the window, and out of our session. But that moth remains in my memory and—I suspect—in the memory of that woman. She said, in a quiet and thoughtful tone, that she continued to experience her fear of moths, but she also felt a "shift" in her attitude about herself and moths.

Guru or Chela?

When are we guru, or teacher, and when are we chela, or pupil? Perhaps we are both teacher and pupil in every important lesson. Certainly, I feel as if I have learned from my clients about "suffering." Over and over, they have taught me that everybody suffers. To be human, and in the body, is to suffer. The important task is to learn how to suffer creatively, and legitimately, rather than to suffer neurotically, without awareness of our purpose in suffering. How can we suffer so that we do not harm ourselves and others? How can we suffer so that we help ourselves and others to heal?

Past Life Exploration

*Every soul...comes into this world strengthened by the victories
or weakened by the defeats of its previous life. Its place in this world as a
vessel, appointed to honor or dishonor, is determined by its
previous merits or demerits. Its work in this world determines its
place in the world which is to follow this.*

—Origen, from DePrincipitis
(Early Christian theologian, 185-254 AD)

Introduction

This chapter provides a brief review of some events, and little lessons, which influenced my views about ESP (extra-sensory perception) and reincarnation. Despite my initial intellectual skepticism, and emotional resistance, I came to accept the reality, and personal significance, of paranormal phenomena and memories of possible other lives.

Thesis Advisor?

"Doctor, are you willing to serve as my thesis advisor?" The slender young man who stood before me was distressed, but he controlled his anxiety with his very deferent and professional demeanor. (I had suggested to him that he call me "Leo," but he continued to address me, and other faculty, by the title "doctor." I was reminded of the conversations between some physicians where the title almost becomes a first name.)

The graduate student was very bright; I knew that his academic test scores were much higher than mine. I also suspected that he was as bright as his committee members, yet they had rejected his thesis proposal. They apparently had told him to develop another proposal, or else to arrange for another advisor to supervise his experimental study.

I was an assistant professor of psychology, University of North Dakota. I had overcome, almost, my fear of ESP; several of my clients had demonstrated to me their psychic abilities, e.g., "knowing" that I was in my office, when I had told them of my plans to be out of town and had to change my plans, etc. At first, I had hypothesized "luck," "coincidence," etc., whenever these strange events occurred. However, after several episodes, with one particular client, I had become so unnerved that I had sought relief by reading the literature on experimental studies by parapsychologists. (Professors sometimes accept the written word more often than the spoken word, especially if the word is written by another professor!) I came to the tentative conclusion, despite my doubts and fears, that clairvoyance, telepathy, precognition, and psychokinesis were demonstrable, by some individuals, under controlled laboratory conditions. Later, I joined the American Society of Psychical Research and the Parapsychological Association.

Yet, at the moment that I was asked to serve as the young man's thesis advisor, I hesitated. My uncertainty was due less to my anxiety about ESP, and more to my anxiety about being accepted as a peer by other faculty members.

However, because of his fervent plea, and his interesting proposal, I agreed to serve as his thesis advisor. The proposal involved a study of thirty graduate students who were Master's degree level counselors; they and their clients would be monitored through a one-way viewing window. The purpose of the study was to compare the behaviors of the counselors on the basis of two conditions. The "good news" were the rigorous conditions; the "bad news" were the topics: rapport and telepathy (mind-to-mind communication).

After the study was completed, the young man was relieved, partly because the results were not significant, and partly because his committee members accepted his completed thesis. He told me, "Leo" (yes, he finally agreed to call me "Leo," rather than the other first name), "I'm not going to conduct a doctoral dissertation in the study of ESP. It's too lonely." I nodded, and told him that I understood that feeling, and that decision.

Gardner Murphy, Ph.D. Although I felt, somehow, that I had not been fully supportive of the wishes of my colleagues, I also felt that they had not been supportive of the graduate student. He was an excellent researcher; he had worked as an assistant to Robert Rosenthal, Ph.D., who had moved from UND to Harvard University.[1] The topic of his thesis may have been unusual, but his methodology was appropriate for the study.

When I applied to become an associate member of the Parapsychological Association, I supplied a copy of the study. I was pleased that my application was supported by Gardner Murphy, Ph.D. Dr. Murphy, a former president of the American Psychological Association, was well known for his work, including a 1961 book, *Challenge of Psychical Research* (Harper). (In a book edited by Farberow on the difficulties of "taboo topics," Murphy had pointed

---

1. Rosenthal, 1966.

out the burdens of researchers who study topics such as handwriting, death and dying, homosexuality, etc. However, he noted, wryly, that the other researchers were investigating recognizable phenomena; he was studying something that did not exist!) I renewed my uncertain belief that it was OK to be a psychologist and parapsychologist.

Paranoid or Psychic?

My interest in psychical research received another boost when I recognized the connections between ESP and abnormal psychology. I was serving as an instructor for 85 students in the U of WY. Usually, the course in abnormal psychology was taught by Richard Pasewark, Ph.D.; however, Dr. Pasewark was on sabbatical leave, and he asked me to teach the class that semester. I was pleased to do so because of my admiration for his work. Also, the textbook was one that I had read, a decade earlier, when I was a doctoral student at the University of Missouri. Despite my ignorance in neurological and physiological psychology, I assumed that I could assist these students to learn more about psychopathology and unusual human behaviors.

One day, while I was preparing my class notes, I re-read a section of the textbook that caused me both anxiety and exhilaration. The section was a case study of a man who had been hospitalized because of his rageful behaviors and his "delusional system" of perceiving his world. The man had been accused of attacking his wife. He claimed that he had a "screen" in his head; he claimed to "see" his wife and another man engaged in sexual activity. The man had been diagnosed as exhibiting the pattern of a "paranoid schizophrenic" personality. What caused my anxiety, and exhilaration, was my new perspective. On the one hand, I viewed the case study from my conventional, pre-ESP position; on the other hand, I viewed the case study from the position of "possible psychical phenomena." Although I did not know the answers, I was able to ask new questions: What if the man were telling the truth? What if he did have the ability to perceive a mental image of his wife? (According to the case study, the wife had denied engaging in sexual intercourse with another man; however, she had admitted that she had engaged in social dancing with that man.) What if the husband "tuned in" to his wife's behaviors and mentally pictured what was happening, physically and/or psychically? What if his paranoid behaviors also were psychic behaviors?

Psychopathology of Everyday Life

One day, while talking with a colleague who was sympathetic to topics about anomalous behaviors, I remarked—jokingly—that I should write an article about "psychic pathology" of everyday life. He appreciated the pun; as a clinical psychologist, he was familiar with Sigmund Freud's book on the psychopathology of everyday life. (Freud had described three "slips" of pen/ tongue: those that we recognize and understand; those that we recognize and do not understand; and those of which we are not aware.) My colleague, Dr. Don Fish, was genial in his awareness and in his acceptance of the behaviors all around him that indicated the neurotic attitudes of other persons.

He had watched me, one day, when I came out of my office with a young African-American student. The student was an attractive woman, with a high "Afro" hairdo that was popular in the 1970s. She wore a sweater and jeans—and an angry expression! Later, when she returned for a second interview, she was in a much better mood; I had referred her to a department where she could enroll in a program that fit her interests and abilities. However, the first interview was a recital of all of her troubles at the university: the racist attitudes of some students, and the "fouled-up" (close!) enrollment procedures, etc.

When she walked away from my office after that first interview, my colleague was able to see the cloth patch that had been sewed on the crotch of her jeans: a roaring lion with fearsome teeth! As she walked on down the hall, he was able to observe the cloth patch that had been sewed on the rear of her jeans: a locked padlock!

I watched him, in amusement, as he watched her, in amazement. I asked him after she departed, "Well, what do you think?" He smiled. "There goes a tight ass!"

Psychic Pathology of Everyday Life

My colleague and I were reminding each other of various unusual events (counseling center "war stories"), including his first week on the job. Don had dealt with a homicidal student, who had threatened to kill some other students who had taunted him. And the tauntee had a rifle, pistol, and hand grenades to support his threat! Thanks to the psychologist's quick and skillful intervention, he was able to ease the student's rage, and to diffuse the situation, with the able assistance of the Campus Police.

When I joked about "psychic pathology," he responded in good humor. Shortly thereafter, the postal carrier delivered an excellent book by Jule Eisenbud, M.D.[2] There, in Chapter 14, was that title: "Psychic Pathology in Everyday Life." Once again, I was enthralled with his writing. I commended Jule, when I wrote to him, not only for his new book, but also for his many erudite articles, and his 1967 book, *The World of Ted Serios: "Thoughtographic" Studies of an Extraordinary Mind.*[3] He and his wife, Maggie, invited me to visit them when Ted Serios was in Denver.

When I arrived at their home, Ted and Jule were at work planning another session for exploring Ted's ability to produce mental images on photographic film. I watched in fascination, as well as the usual skepticism, while

---

2. Eisenbud, 1970.
3. Eisenbud. 1967.

Ted and Jule engaged in their serious/silly activities: bantering with each other and raising the energy level of all of us in the room. The Polaroid camera was kept busy!

Ted was not successful in his attempts to provide me with a gift: a photograph of his mental image of a "flying saucer." However, I was impressed with what he did: he obtained several Polaroid photos of his face and the room; the photos displayed increasing distortions of angle and distance. I came away from that session with more questions than answers. But my admiration for Ted's courage, and Jule's compassion, was matched only by my wonderment at their enormous efforts in time and money. I felt that my own efforts were rather puny, yet I also was pleased to be associated with such fascinating characters.

I recognized the contributions by Jule, not only in his experimental procedures for assessing Ted's abilities, but also his clinical skills in helping Ted to display his abilities. I came to appreciate, more and more, the morality/immorality issues of developing and using one's paranormal powers.

Jule had pointed out (Chapter XIV, again a Chapter 14!) in his book about Ted Serios that we humans exhibit emotional resistance to ESP. In his articulate and penetrating style, he described what he called the anatomy of resistance: the emotional denial that we humans experience whenever we come closer to being aware and accepting our psychic abilities. And the conflict? Well, if we accept our potential ability to help or heal, then we also have to accept our potential ability to hurt or harm ourselves and others. Most of us have no wish to confess our murderous impulses, so we deny them. Thus, we deny our psychic impulses as well. And the result? We claim that our individual minds are not connected; we claim that anger, anxiety, and depression "belong" to the individual—not to the family, the neighborhood, and the community. Thus, we are able to ease our fears of ourselves, but we also lose our connections and our sense of community.

Fear of Dogs? In the late 1960s, I stumbled into past-life therapy. At that time, I was interested in all kinds of psychic phenomena, but the one topic that troubled me was that of reincarnation. I resisted any impulse that suggested there could be some truth in stories of possible past lives. (Old proverb: we become what we resist!) One day, a young man came to the University of Wyoming Counseling Center for an appointment with me. His opening question: "Can you help me overcome my fear of dogs?" I responded warmly and affirmatively. (I was in the "power" mode of my development as a professional practitioner of hypnosis.) We discussed our treatment plan: I would teach him self-hypnosis procedures; I would guide him back to memories of earlier stages of development, i.e., ages 10, 8, 6, 4, etc.; when we arrived at the crucial memory, e.g., being bitten by a dog, we would help him become "desensitized" to that emotional image and those bodily reactions; after easing the traumatic symptoms, we would enhance his self-esteem and his control over the phobic reactions to dogs! He agreed to the plan, and we began our work together.

As he relaxed deeply in his chair, he responded well to the hypnotic suggestions. But when I suggested that he recall any buried memory of a bothersome episode with dogs, he was unable to identify any image or feeling. We went back to the memories of age 6, 5, 4.... Being impatient, and eager to assist him, I suggested, "Go back to the earliest experience that is connected with your fear of dogs." Immediately, he began to groan and writhe in his chair. He talked about himself as if he were a woodsman, in Medieval Europe, being chased through the forest by wolves.

As a "good" psychologist, I had no wish to harm the student/client, so I asked him if he wished to return to the normal state. He asked me to leave him alone; he said (in effect) "I'm OK. This is interesting!" He continued to groan, describing himself—as the woodsman—being pulled down and his body eaten by the wolves.

Later, when he returned to the normal state, he stood up, shook my hand, and said, "Thanks a lot! Now, I know why I was so afraid of dogs!" He left my office, while I stood there with my mouth open. I thought to myself, "This is nonsense. But apparently this is helpful nonsense."

Fear of Drowning. Within a few days, (Inner Guides often speed up one's lessons!) a 30-year-old woman came to my office. Her opening question was, "Can you help me overcome my fear of drowning?" I responded warmly and affirmatively. We agreed upon our therapeutic alliance, and we began our work together. When I suggested that she recall memories of age 6, 5, 4, etc., she could recall no unusual memory about the fear of water. Being impatient, and eager to assist her, I suggested, "Go back to the earliest experience that is connected to your fear of drowning." Immediately, she began to cough, groan, and writhe in her chair. She described herself as a pirate, who was so obnoxious that his buddies decided to "keelhaul" him (tie him to the ship and shove him overboard, so that he almost drowned, over and over). I was bothered by the student's discomfort, and I asked her if she wished to return to the normal state. Impatiently, she replied, "Leave me alone! I'm learning something!" She continued to moan, cough, and sputter, but, gradually, her emotional reactions subsided, and she returned to the normal state. After evaluating the session, she stood; she shook my hand, and she stated, "Thank you! Now, I know why I was afraid of drowning." She left my office; I stood there with my mouth open. I heard my inner voice, "This is nonsense, but it is helpful nonsense."

Later, in that fall semester, the young woman returned for a follow-up interview. She smiled with pleasure as she told me of her success: she had gone to the university pool, taken swimming lessons, and now she no longer experienced a fear of drowning. I was pleased for her, but I was puzzled for me. How could these strange reactions be explained?

Ian Stevenson, M.D. When I learned of Ian Stevenson, M.D., a professor of psychiatry, University of Virginia, I bought a copy of his 1966 book, *Twenty Cases Suggestive of Reincarnation.*[4] When I began to read the book, I slapped my forehead with my hand: "Wow! What if this stuff is true?"

Leo's POLs

Noon-hour activities (basketball, Monday, Wednesday, and Friday, and self-hypnosis procedures, Tuesday and Thursday,) now took on a new flavor: POLs (Possible Other Lives). I continued to practice the procedures for deep relaxation, but now my time-regression procedures included the suggestions to go back to memories of adolescence, childhood, infancy, birth experience…and beyond!

I obtained a variety of scenarios: Roman soldier, champion soldier (I was surprised at the intensity of satisfaction when I recalled—or fantasized—my killing another champion soldier); shepherd boy; a woman who was raped brutally; an African slave who was killed by his master after being accused, falsely, by his master's wife of being her lover; a young woman in Peru who wished to learn to read, but only the priests were allowed to read and write; et al.

Most of the scenarios were interesting, and some were exciting, e.g., the scene of the champion soldier: I exalted as I felt my sword plunge into the body of the opposing champion! The victory was ours! (That exaltation was not what was expected of a pacifistic, bleeding-heart liberal!)

However, I continued to experience skepticism. I continued to meditate and pray for information that could be viewed as reliable information. Then, one day, that wish was realized.

My pony. One day I sat at my desk; I relaxed deeply. I drifted, in memory, back through adolescence, childhood, infancy, and the birth experience. Then, there was the familiar "gray" period: in-between lives? Or merely the opportunity for my subconscious mind to create an interesting fantasy?

Mentally, I saw sagebrush, as if I were moving quickly, peering down at the prairie. After a while, I became impatient and bored. (After all, sagebrush in Wyoming is not unusual!) I began to doubt whether any other scene would appear. I felt as if I were "stuck." I debated within myself whether I should continue or discontinue the session. However, I also knew the inner feeling: anxiety about morality!

I thought to myself, "OK! I'm ready! With courage, let's go on to the significant experience!" Immediately, I felt a shift: I felt myself to be a brown-skinned lad, holding onto the mane of a pony with my left hand, and holding onto a wooden spear with my right hand. Lo! We were chasing a buffalo, an American Bison. The shaggy beast rumbled up a ravine, staggered, and rolled

---

4. Stevenson, 1966.

back down upon my pony and me. Tears rolled down my cheeks. I thought to myself (as Leo), "Oh! I must have died." I began to shift from an experiential mode to an observational mode: I wondered about the possible purpose or meaning of this fantasy or POL?

But no! I (as the skinny boy) was not dead! I felt myself arising and listening to the most awful screams. I turned and saw some fierce-looking Amerinds (native Americans) with painted faces, waving spears and yelling, "The kid got a buffalo!"

Sure enough! As I turned back, I saw the body of the dead buffalo! But also I saw the body of my beloved pony! Instantly I knew what had happened: I had been so afraid of being perceived as lacking in courage that I had pushed my pony into a dangerous situation. As a result, my pony died; I had been successful, but only at a high price. My tears were not only a remembrance of my grief, but also a reminder of my guilt.

From an evidential point of view, the scenario produced very little that could be used by me to show skeptical persons the meaning of that memory. The only connection that might have been useful was a Boy Scout Camp event, one summer in New Mexico. One morning, some other boys and I managed to corner a horse in a large field, and—one by one—we grabbed his mane, swung up on his back, and rode around the field. When my turn arrived, I experienced a great deal of anxiety, especially when he balked suddenly at a small stream: I slid along his neck, almost falling, as I swung down to the ground. I stood there, looking under his neck, watching my laughing buddies, and experiencing dejà vu. Later, I puzzled about my anxiety: not only had I feared for my safety, but also I was worried about the safety of the horse.

Despite the lack of empirical evidence, I "knew" that the hunting scenario was "real." Deep within, I knew that the experience had occurred. I was reminded of my sad feelings whenever I saw horses being abused. (Now, whenever I write or speak about the memory, my voice feels choked, and tears well up in my eyes.)

Bridey Murphy/Virginia Tighe

I noted, rather humbly, that my views about reincarnation were becoming less dogmatic. (My karma ran over my dogma!) I recalled my student days in Boulder, Colorado, when we learned of Bridey Murphy. We joked about that silly woman, who was hypnotized by Morey Bernstein, and who described a former life as an Irish lass. Our jokes included a crude notion that it was appropriate for the woman to be living in Pueblo, Colorado, where the state hospital for the insane was located!

I recalled a former friend, and co-worker in a residence hall kitchen, who was very bright and studious. Not only was she awarded a Phi Beta Kappa key for her high grades, but also she was a Buddhist by choice. I was puzzled at her professed beliefs, especially the concept of reincarnation. I had thought to myself, how can such a bright person believe in such a weird concept?

Yet, I decided then that I had little religious knowledge, other than my training as a Methodist youth, so I enrolled in a course titled, "Psychology of Religion." The experience was as enlightening (and bothersome) as another course: "The Bible as Literature." As a result of increased historical knowledge, and, later, enhanced experiences in my inner world, I changed my views about Bridey Murphy.

The important influence, however, was the opportunity, many years later, to meet Virginia Tighe, the true Bridey Murphy. I had learned about Virginia from a friend and former high-school classmate, Marianne (Clute) Pearce, who had known Virginia as a neighbor in Denver.

When I met Virginia, at a New Age conference at Sheridan College, Sheridan, Wyoming, I was impressed with her intelligence and her humility. I apologized to her for those crude adolescent jokes that emerged from me and other college students, many years earlier. She smiled, and dismissed my concerns, saying in effect, "That's all right; sometimes I'm not certain that those are past-life memories. I try not to force my views upon others. I encourage them to keep an open mind and explore their own past-life memories."

Exploring POLs

I continued to search for other methods to explore possible other lives (POLs). Marilyn and I belonged to a "gourmet group," four couples who met monthly to enjoy good food and a bottle of wine. Sometimes, after dinner, we would stretch out on the floor and relax deeply; then, we followed the voice of the temporary group leader to recall a previous lifetime; after a few minutes, we returned to the normal state and we shared the images and feelings of various scenarios. We enjoyed these impressions, partly because of the friendly atmosphere, and partly because we did not worry about the obvious question: Are these fantasies or are these memories? However, I was fascinated with the eventual outcome: Several of us seem to resonate to the imagery of a group of primitive people, pinned down by enemy arrows behind some rocks, without food and water, in a sun-blistered climate, slowly dying. After that, for whatever reason, the gourmet group seemed to lose its cohesiveness, and the dinners were discontinued.

Fear of Snakes? I learned a painful but valuable lesson from another student at the University of Wyoming. She was a participant in the self-hypnosis group, Self Improvement Program (SIP).

One day she asked me if I could help her to overcome her fear of snakes. I referred her to a doctoral candidate in clinical psychology; he was conducting a desensitization program for persons with snake phobia. (The program included incremental conditioning techniques, such as looking at snakes; watching someone handle a snake; and, eventually, handling a snake.) However, her fearful reactions were so strong that she discontinued the experimental program. Once again, she asked me if I would help her. I agreed to do so.

I suggested that she relax deeply, focus on the feeling that she could be in a safe place, then return to the memory of that experience which was connected with her fear of snakes. She groaned, and twisted in her chair; I asked her if she wished to return to the normal state; however, she acted as if she did not hear me. Suddenly, she screamed, and continued to scream. She sobbed; she described what seemed to be a scenario of a jungle, and watching her boyfriend who was struggling with a huge boa constrictor that was coiling around him. She sobbed hysterically, but finally she was able to ease her discomfort and return to the normal state. Then, she glared at me, and she accused me of putting those terrible thoughts and painful pictures in her mind. She demanded to know the name and telephone number of my boss. I gave her the name and telephone number of my supervisor. She stomped out of the room, while telling me that I could expect a visit from her boyfriend.

The next day, her boyfriend asked to talk with me. When we talked, he criticized my methods, but he recognized my sincerity in wishing to help his girlfriend. Later, her residence hall director, who also was a participant in SIP, arranged a meeting with the young couple. When the four of us met, I showed the young woman a copy of the letter that I had written to her (which she had viewed as an example of my evil motives). We managed to ease her anger, and her fear that I could place those terrible images into her mind. I never did learn whether she was able to ease her fear of snakes, but I learned an important lesson: These scenarios may be nonsense, but some people react to them as if they are true!

Helen Wambach, Ph.D. When I learned of Dr. Helen Wambach, I wrote to her and arranged a meeting during the 1976 APA conference in San Francisco. (Later, when her work was publicized, a well-known psychiatrist was quoted in a women's magazine; he stated, in effect, "If I thought that a California psychologist had regressed thousands of persons to memories of previous lifetimes, I would be the first person to get on a plane and visit her." I thought to myself, "Why didn't you visit her?")

For over two hours, Helen and I sat at a restaurant table, while we discussed her research methods and results. At one point, she said, "Leo, I like a past-life story as well as anyone else does, but I want data! When I talk on a TV program, I want the director to show my data. If necessary, I'll pin the data on my boobs"!

And Helen had a lot of data! Helen also had a lot of intelligence, common sense, and courage. Her wit and wisdom were warm and wonderful, but she had little patience with arrogance and ignorance. During a June 1978 workshop that she arranged in Walnut Creek, California, she taught two dozen participants her group method of exploring memories of possible past lives. During a break in the workshop (Father's Day), I was contemplating the impressions of a POL with the soul of my father in this lifetime. I stood outside the ranch style bungalow; then, as Helen walked outside, I seemed to be in a daze, as if I had entered another time zone. I pictured the house as a huge tent; Helen seemed to be a man, a commanding officer; the rest of us seemed to be field officers; we were preparing for battle. Then, as the scene shifted back to Father's Day, 1978, I felt as if this same group of participants had gathered. Now the purpose was not to battle other soldiers, but to struggle against apathy and ignorance.

Roman General. I was hesitant to share with other workshop participants my memory, or fantasy, so I remained quiet about it. A few years later, when Helen came to our UFO Conference in Laramie, Wyoming, I mentioned to her that scenario. She nodded and said, "Oh, yes. I was a Roman general. I was a slob, but I was bright, and they needed me." When she said the word "Roman," I felt as if the word were a fist, and the fist had hit me in the abdomen. I felt a shift, internally, and I "knew" that years of service at the University of Wyoming had an important purpose; I felt as if I were a solitary guard at a lonely post; yet, I also felt that there were many other servants, around the planet, who were serving well and who were aware of their social/spiritual tasks. Then, I heard Helen telling her story about her reason for coming to Laramie.

Future Dreams or Another Cigarette? Helen described her NDE (near-death experience) during triple by-pass heart surgery: a classic event of perceiving herself in a tunnel, moving toward a bright light, with a father figure who told her that her work (reincarnation research) was not finished. She stated that, when she returned to the conscious state, her first comment was, "I must talk to Leo about those future impressions of UFO contactees!" Her companion shook her head and said, "No, Helen's first words were, 'I want another cigarette!'" For years, Helen and I enjoyed teasing each other about healthy life styles. Helen liked to eat, drink, and smoke! I liked MEDS: meditation, exercise, diet, and sociability/sexuality/spirituality/smiles! She joked, "Leo, the body is a vehicle. When you are finished with the body, you get out and go on." However, at the following UFO Conference, Helen extended her foot, with amputated toes, and lamented, "I have one foot in Heaven; and I'm experiencing trouble in dropping the rest of the body."

When her body died in 1985, her friends saluted her soul! I am sure that she continues her work at many other levels.

Edith Fiore, Ph.D. There were many special souls at that 1978 Wambach Workshop. One important person was Dr. Edith Fiore, a clinical psychologist from Saratoga, California. Edie is well-known as a master hypnotherapist and as a master teacher of other therapists. Marilyn and I went to San Francisco so that I could attend an advanced workshop in past-life therapy, hosted by Edith Fiore, Ph.D., and Lee Pulos, Ph.D. The workshop was valuable to me, both personally and professionally. My partner, during practice sessions, was a California physician, who is courageous, competent, and compassionate.

It Ain't Nice to Push Other People Off a Cliff. As I guided my partner to a significant POL, he described himself as a well-dressed gentleman, standing at the top of a white cliff (Dover?), standing next to a young woman who was pregnant. Somehow, he knew that he was the father of the child-to-be, but, for some reason, he did not wish for the fetus to be born. So, he pushed the young woman from the cliff to the rocks below, which caused the death of the young woman—and her unborn child.

Then, in another POL scenario, he saw himself falling from a cliff to the rocks below; he agonized as he experienced his body, broken and bleeding, lying in it own waste, slowly and painfully dying.

When he returned to the normal state, he was very thoughtful; he stated that he now was aware of the reason for an event, in this lifetime, which he had experienced as an infant: lying on a table, knowing that he was about to fall to the floor, and wondering why adults could be so neglectful of the health of a little baby. He said that he had another insight: He now knew why he was so neat, almost fastidious, about cleanliness, as he reviewed his POL, and death, while lying in his own waste.

Then, with a twinkle in his eye, he said, "I learned a valuable lesson today." I asked, "What's that?" He smiled, "It ain't nice to push other people off of a cliff."

Head Hunter or Soul Rescuer? As we switched roles of patient and practitioner, the physician guided me to an important POL. I viewed myself as a primitive hunter, with dark skin, quietly walking through a heavy forest. The tension, almost terror, seemed to increase.

Suddenly, I was attacked and captured by others. They cheered wildly as they tied me to a wooden pole and carried me into a clearing. The tribal members were ecstatic. Their enemy was captured!

As tribal members taunted and poked at me, I gradually recognized what was happening. I was a headhunter! And I was such a skillful and successful headhunter that a "roast" was being held in my honor!

Gradually, the pole was lowered; my feet were exposed to the flames of a huge fire; slowly, I was tortured and, finally, the body died. As I rose out of that body, I could feel the fear and rage of tribal members. I knew that, someday, I would return and ask these people to forgive me for what I had done to their families and to their tribe.

Also, I was experiencing a childhood memory, but from a different perspective. For many years, I had been puzzled by my reaction to a photograph in an old encyclopedia.

The Chicken or the Egg? As a young boy, I was a voracious reader; I especially liked to read biographical comments about great leaders, as well as women and men of achievement. One day, I sat on our couch, turning the pages of a big book. Suddenly, I was horrified as my eyes focused on a photograph of a dark man with a headband and bushy hair. The caption: head hunter in Borneo, New Guinea.

I could not understand the intense fear, until many years later, when I experienced myself as a head hunter. Of course, the conventional psychological explanation would be simple: little Leo is afraid of a photograph of a fierce headhunter; years later he fantasizes a POL memory of being a headhunter.

However, the psychical explanation also could be simple: the soul of Leo has a life as a headhunter; in a later life, he remembers that lifetime, and he experiences the guilt of his former violence and destructiveness.

Which comes first? The chicken or the egg? Which explanation is better? The causal conventional hypothesis, or the causal karmic hypothesis? (Karma: action or cause.)

I didn't know the answer to the question, but I knew my inner feeling. Yes, this memory is not only an emotional experience, but also an intellectual insight. I knew why I had been such an assertive therapist, seeking a variety of helping techniques for a variety of clients. Yes, I had been a headhunter in a past life; now, in this life, I am helping clients to "get their heads on straight!" (I know! I know! Punsters deserve punishment!)

Tardy or Terrorized? The question of neurotic morality versus legitimate suffering was raised, once more, when I worked with a young man, a U of WY student. He stated that he had worked with various psychiatrists and psychologists in an attempt to ease his symptom: arriving about a half-hour after any scheduled activity. He hated his tardiness, but he claimed that he could not change his behavior.

Of course, he was late for our first appointment! When he arrived, he stated that he had tried "everything," including medications, behavioral conditioning, dream analysis, hypnotic suggestions, etc. Wearily, he asked for my opinion. I asked him if he had sought past-life therapy; he had not. He was skeptical, but willing to try the procedures. He was a good participant in the hypnotic process, and soon he was deeply relaxed.

When he felt ready for a "special journey," I suggested that he go to the time and place that was connected to his tardy behavior. His voice sounded as if he were puzzled, but he described a scene—ancient Greece?—of small hills and trees; he was on a path, walking toward his village. He felt happy, even joyful, because he anticipated a holiday celebration. He also was eager to arrive, somehow knowing that he was late for the joyful celebration. Then, with horror in his voice, he "arrived": With anguish, he described the bloody bodies of his family and friends; all around him, he saw the bodies of villagers who were dead or dying. Apparently, he was the only survivor of a raid by some "barbarians."

He was horrified, on the one hand, by the ghastly scene, but on the other hand, he was glad to be alive—all because he was a few minutes late! When he returned to the normal state, he clearly was shaken emotionally by this unexpected scene. He did not set another appointment, so I was unable to help him in any formal evaluation of the session. However, my feeling was that he knew, inwardly, that the scenario was meaningful and insightful to him.

Despite the feeling, I sought better experiential evidence that these sessions were helpful to clients. That goal was realized with my assistance to a young man, by the name of John G. Williams.

Allergies and Neuroses. John and I shared information (and photographs) in *The National Enquirer*, along with Dr. Edith Fiore, who was recognized for her work with clients for past-life therapy, and her book, *You Have Been Here Before*. (Later, she wrote a book, *The Unquiet Dead*, on spirit releasement, then, another book, *Encounters*, on UFO abductions.)

With permission from John, who was a U of WY student at the time, we shared information about his experiences. He had sought counseling services with me because of his desire to learn self-hypnosis procedures. He had hoped that he could learn to ease his discomfort from allergic reactions. He often sneezed and coughed as he described his reactions to dust, dog fur, etc. He also experienced very strong reactions to eating various grains. (See page 130 for information about John's UFO experience.)

As John developed skills in self-hypnosis, he eased his discomfort and increased his optimism that he could end his symptoms. He was willing to engage in past-life therapy as a means to that end. After several POLs as "victim," I suggested that he go to the significant POL: the lifetime in which he "caused" the conditions that resulted in his allergic reactions.

He described himself as a Mongolian soldier, who was the leader of a fierce group of soldiers. His orders from superior officers were to burn a village and kill the women and children. When he refused to follow those orders, he was punished in a most painful manner: He was forced to eat a quantity of grains, then forced to swallow much water; as the grains expanded, his body experienced a protracted and painful death.

As John accepted the significance of the POL emotions, he forgave himself for refusing to obey those orders; he freed his "inner self" from the past guilt/fear/anger.

It seemed almost miraculous! John had eased his former symptoms: He was able to rub his face in his dog's fur and was able to eat those grains that previously were so bothersome to him.

However, when he tried to discuss his insights and changes with his family, he experienced their deep denial. (The situation was rather ironic, because he said that both his father and brother were MD specialists in treating allergies, and his mother, for years, had experienced many allergic reactions. Coincidence or connection?)

When the article on reincarnation and past-life therapy appeared in *The National Enquirer*, I received letters and telephone calls from interested persons. However, some of my U of WY colleagues were dismayed by what they perceived to be some unwelcome notoriety. I attempted to offset their criticisms by a demonstration: I videotaped a session of past-life therapy with a client, who had given her permission to show the videotape during a counseling center staff meeting.

The videotape session followed five sessions of conventional psychotherapeutic procedures, with little change in the client's behaviors and verbal insights. During the POL session, she seemed to gain greater self-awareness and self-acceptance; she seemed ready to engage in some behavioral changes. But, my colleagues were not ready! They rejected my claim that hypnotherapy and past-life therapy were more efficient and effective than traditional psychotherapy. When I suggested that they read the literature, and seek training in these procedures, they looked at me as if I were asking them to engage in immoral actions. (And from their perspective, I suppose that I was!) An article in the campus newspaper about the principles and applications of reincarnation research was welcomed by some of my friends; however, some readers complained to the vice-president of student affairs. Eventually, I was told to discontinue my activities, during office hours, in reincarnation and UFO research.

As a "life member" of APRTs (Association for Past Life Research and Therapies), I continue to associate with these courageous and compassionate persons. I am pleased to know that there are so many good psychiatrists, psychologists, counselors, and hypnotherapists who are exploring these procedures.

Self-Mutilation or Murder? I relearned an important lesson with a young man who was referred to me by a U of WY residence hall advisor. The young man was feared by others because he had many cuts on his chest and arms. Apparently, he was engaging in self-mutilation by slicing his skin with a knife.

When the young man and I met, he told me about his background. He was completing an undergraduate program in 2-3 years, so that he could enter law school; his goal was to combine law and economics. His academic test scores were much higher than those of most students, and I knew that our strategy must appeal to his intellect, as well as his expressed wish to change his obsessive/compulsive behaviors.

Obviously, he was bored with the approach of several psychiatrists, who apparently had prescribed medications and presented moral persuasion for procedures. I suggested self-hypnosis procedures, so that he could concentrate more fully and really "enjoy" the slicing of his skin! That suggestion appealed to his sense of humor!

Later, as he recognized the direction in which we were going, he expressed an interest in past-life therapy. We met outside office hours, so that I would violate neither my morality (the external policy of no past-life therapy during office hours) nor my ethics (my internal policy to assist my clients as well as I could).

The scenarios that emerged were painful to both of us. He experienced several POLs in which he was stabbed, or he stabbed others in revenge. Eventually, we recognized the "neurotic nexus": He was reluctant to give up his inner need for self-mutilation; his fear was that, in rage, he would murder his tormentors. Yet, he also came to recognize his pattern of "setting up" others around him so that they would ridicule or torment him. He was so bright (and so psychic) that he could intuit their attitudes and observe their patterns of behaviors. He seemed to influence others, almost without trying, to mistreat him or to discount his importance. Thus, he constantly hovered between feeling threatened, on the one hand, and demeaned, on the other hand; the urge was to harm others in retaliation for the fear and anger; but the guilt prevented his harming others and, thus, he merely harmed himself. We sometimes joked among ourselves, "Which is more moral, murder or self-mutilation?"

Once again, I relearned the lesson: neurosis is merely a substitute for legitimate suffering.

The young man and I explored the important question: how can he suffer nobly? Could he learn to suffer the ignorance, and stupidity, and the hatefulness of others? Could he suffer his own ignorance, and stupidity, and hatefulness? Was it necessary for him to suffer neurotically, by cutting himself? Or could he learn to suffer more creatively, by finding another way to "cut" himself and others?

We learned that he could use his intelligence and wit to "cut," with words, the behaviors of others that he deemed to be inappropriate. Thus, as a budding attorney, he could use this cutting edge of his mind to separate good and evil, right and wrong, legal and illegal. Now, he could begin to address the suffering of others and use his sharp mind to help them rather than to harm himself.

Professor or Practitioner?

It should be the chief aim of the University Professor to exhibit himself in his own true character—that is, an ignorant man thinking, actively utilizing this small share of knowledge.

—Alfred North Whitehead
U.S. Physicist & Philosopher

Introduction

This chapter is a description of events that resulted in some procedures for helping clients to explore their inner world. These procedures have been helpful, apparently, to many persons, especially in the search for self-awareness and self-direction. I pray each day that these procedures be continued for the benefit of those with whom I work. However, in some ways, these procedures also contributed to my resignation as a professor at the University of Wyoming.

How Did You Know About My Pet Rat?

As Joan sat down in the recliner chair, she introduced herself as someone who is very anxious, but she didn't know the source of her anxiety. Thus, she didn't wish to be a client for counseling services. However, her persistent anxiety was affecting her studies, as well as her sense of well-being. She asked me if I could help her to find some way that she could ease her anxiety.

I commended her for her courage and honesty, and I provided her with information about the effects of meditation and self-hypnosis procedures. Then, she expressed an interest in practicing these procedures in order to relax more deeply and—possibly—to learn more about the source of her anxiety.

As she leaned back in the chair, I leaned back in my chair and relaxed my arms and shoulders. She looked surprised. "Are you going to do this, too?" I joked, "Of course! You're not the only person who should benefit from these procedures."

I suggested that she mentally repeat some phrases for deep breathing, muscular relaxation, and a directed daydream. Some suggestions that, in her imagination, she place herself where she feels comfortable, pleasant, and secure. I mentally pictured myself as merging with Joan, so that I could focus on those concerns and reactions that might be helpful to her in reducing stress and enhancing her self-esteem.

After fifteen or twenty minutes of deep relaxation, we returned to the normal state of awareness. When she opened her eyes, she expressed enthusiasm about the "pleasant glow" that she was experiencing, rather than the usual body tension.

Then, I told her that I was puzzled about a mental image that came into my awareness during the session: the head of a small animal (dog or cat?) with short white fur and pointed ears. She immediately burst into tears and, sobbing, she covered her face with her hands. After a minute, she regained her composure; in a quavering voice she asked, "How did you know about my pet rat?"

She described a childhood incident. She was in the backyard, playing with her pet rat. Her parents called to her, saying that they were driving to town; if she wished to go with them, she must leave immediately. So, leaving her pet in the cage, she went with her parents. While she was gone, a sudden rainstorm soaked her pet; her pet became ill and eventually died.

Joan said that she had been so stricken with guilt, and grief, that she told no one about that incident until our counseling session. Later, she experienced more release from these negative feelings about herself. She learned that she could decrease her anxiety, enhance her self-esteem, and increase her concentration on her studies.

Psychological Resonance

I learned a valuable lesson from Joan and her pet rat. I learned that it was OK to talk to clients about my "fantasies" or psychic impressions that occurred to me while I focused on their concerns and feelings. Indeed, I recognized that some clients seek counselors who are empathic and/or telepathic in order to release themselves from their guilt/anger/fear. Previously, I had been reluctant to share my psychic impressions for two reasons: the moral, or external, concern that I might not be "scientific" in the eyes of others, and the ethical, or internal, concern that I might be foisting my fantasies on my clients.

Yet I recognized that I had been interested in "psychological resonance" for several years. In the early 1970s, I had attended a conference on hypnosis at Stanford University. I participated in a workshop by John Watkins, Ph.D., of the University of Montana. I recognized an important principle: The shared experience of client and therapist could go beyond an introspective level, and become a more active process.

I had not recognized that principle when it could have been apparent to me. Earlier, I had watched a man on the television program, *The Tonight Show*, who was able to resonate with another person and repeat—word for word, with proper inflection—what the other person was saying. The process seemed to be magical, as if he were a telepathic person who was "receiving" and then "sending" the verbal messages of the other person. Indeed, he was so successful that he could repeat, almost simultaneously, the comments of "Professor Corey," who tried to confound the man by using his skill in "double talk."

Resonance and Healing

As I contemplated the principle of psychological resonance, I recalled an incident, in Denver, Colorado. I was seated in a large auditorium with 500 other persons (Global Sciences, Phyllis and Dean Stonier). We were listening to Andrija Puharich, M.D., as he described his experiences in psychic-healing procedures. I listened, almost in awe, as he described the work of Aldous and Laura Huxley. He reported his observation of Laura Huxley, while she placed her hand above the chest of a man with a weakened heart condition; both "healer" and "healee" were connected to biofeedback devices and two screens that displayed their brain waves. Then, as healer focused awareness on healee, the waves of each participant became synchronized; they were experiencing—and displaying—psychological resonance.

My fist slammed down on the wooden arm desk on my chair. Without thinking, I yelled aloud, "I knew it! I knew it!" Suddenly, I was aware of a thousand eyes, and 500 puzzled faces, turning to look at me. Embarrassed, I mumbled an apology for my outburst, but I was exhilarated at the notion that my own modest mind could grasp such an important principle, which was being described by the mind of a genius.

Of course, if my colleagues were to attend such a conference and listen to my outburst, they probably would shake their heads and assume that I was engaged in more dissociated mentation. From my perspective, however, the event was not one of divergence but one of convergence.

PRIME: Psychological Resonance In Mutual Experience

I continued to contemplate what others had observed and what I had experienced in psychological resonance. I selected the term "priming" for the process of resonating and verbally sharing inner impressions. (The term appealed to me because, as a child, I had to prime the hand pump in our kitchen by adding some water before pumping more water. Similarly, I had to express my own impressions in order to access the internal impressions of other participants.) I wished to credit Dr. Watkins for his original work.[1] However, I did not wish to burden him with any extension of his procedures that might reflect adversely on his work.

Based upon my own experience, I have grouped procedures into four stages:

1. **Preliminary Procedures.** After discussion of plans with the client, I relax deeply, close my eyes, imagine a "flame" cleansing each corner of the room, and "white light" surrounding both participants. I silently pray for helpful impressions, and mentally view the client and myself as one personality.

2. **Verbalized Impressions.** In a few seconds, I begin to speak subvocally and to move my hands as if these movements were associated with the verbalized impressions. I become aware of the next word to be spoken as if I were reading from an imaginary script. Sometimes, I am describing in these impressions possible childhood feelings, possible past life impressions, and possible life goals or future experiences as if these impressions are an outline of vocational and personality development. Sometimes, there is a release of emotional reactions (smiling or weeping) as if these feelings are related to the inner world of the client (or mutual personality). Then I summarize the impressions and return to normal awareness.

3. **Reactions to Impressions.** The client is encouraged to comment on the possible meaning and significance of the impressions.

4. **Evaluation of Impressions.** Finally, the client and I discuss both short-term and long-term ways in which the impressions can be evaluated, including further meditation and interactions with significant other persons. The session is audiotaped, and the cassette tape is given to the client.

Jackson, Wyoming. By 1981, I was writing articles and giving lectures on the possible connection of reincarnation and UFO activity. Several persons in Jackson Hole also shared these interests. I provided priming sessions (or "life readings") to these good people and their families and friends.

Among these many good persons were Todd Berkenfield, Melinda Cullinan and Fred Hernandez, Jean Jorgensen, Ann Kreilkamp, Ph.D., and Dodie Stearns. Marilyn and I provided weekend reincarnation workshops and individual sessions for life readings.

On one occasion, Todd Berkenfield telephoned and asked me to conduct a "long-distance" session. I protested, "I can't do that!" She responded, "Sure, you can. You and I know that psychic impressions are not limited in terms of space and time." Of course, she was correct about ESP. However, I was not so

---

1. Watkins, 1978.

sure about my own ability to respond to the demands of the situation. I finally agreed, because she was willing to try the procedure. The session seemed to go very well.

I developed a brief evaluation form that could be completed by participants. I wished to learn if they rated the verbalized impressions as meaningful to them. Also, I wished to compare the "sitting session" ratings with the ratings of "long-distance" sessions.

A Study of Priming Procedures

My confidence in using these procedures was given a boost by two excellent psychologists: John Thorn, Ph.D., and Elizabeth "Liz" Hickman, Ph.D. Both John and Liz are well trained. His doctorate is from the University of Minnesota, hers is from Colorado State University. They are associates in a private counseling center in Jackson, Wyoming.

Both John and Liz were willing to explore the possible significance of these procedures for themselves, as well as for several of their clients. At one point, John invited me to stay at his home, while a workshop was conducted for colleagues from the University of Utah, Salt Lake City. The purpose of the workshop was to develop a methodology for evaluating the procedures.

In some ways, the study was a failure. Personality inventory scores did not seem to correlate with the verbalized impressions that we obtained when I resonated with several of these psychologists.

However, in some ways, the study was a success. Many participants expressed satisfaction, even surprise, at the meaningful relationship of the verbalized impressions and their self-perceptions. Also, friends and co-workers often were able to relate examples of how the priming impressions were similar to the attitudes and actions of the participants.

As Soon As I Get My Voice Back!

John Thorn, Ph.D., is not only a big bear of a man (former heavyweight wrestler and former U.S. Navy officer), but he is also a tireless worker for high professional standards for psychologists in their work with clients.

One year, while he was serving as president of the Wyoming Psychological Association, I submitted a brief paper on procedures for psychological resonance. A few of my colleagues from the University of Wyoming were critical of my activities; there was a serious question about the "professionalism" of my paper. Sensing my apprehension about my presentation, John courageously volunteered to participate in the demonstration.

As we both closed our eyes and relaxed in front of the other conferees, I pictured myself as asking for helpful information and mentally merging with John. I do not recall now the words that came to me then, but I do recall the powerful feelings of anguish. Tears rolled down my cheeks as my hands moved in response to the inner messages.

As I returned to the normal state, I looked over at John. With tears in his eyes, he nodded, quietly acknowledging the significance of the verbalized scenarios. When I asked him if the impressions were significant, he wiped his eyes; then, mocking his own reactions, he growled, "Naaaa!" Then when I asked him if he would be willing to discuss his reactions, he laughed, "As soon as I get my voice back!"

As we discussed his reactions, I was pleased to note that other conferees were listening respectfully to his evaluations of the procedures.

I admire John for his tough-minded insistence on data, and for his tender-minded compassion with others—including me and my situation!

Multiplication of Labor

During the 1980s, I felt increasing "pulls" from several directions: my colleagues in the U of WY counseling center wanted more from me; UFOErs wanted more from me; and, lastly but most importantly, Marilyn wanted more from me. She pointed out that our four children were becoming adults, and my time at home was important to her and to them.

Two good decisions came out of one discussion: first, Marilyn and I agreed to work together in presenting reincarnation workshops; second, we decided to meet regularly for further discussion!

Every Friday, whenever it was feasible, Marilyn and I went together for lunch at a local restaurant. She would order a cup of soup, and I would bore the waitperson, who would turn to me and ask, "The usual?" (Black cherry spritzer, a fruit punch, and veggie stir fry with no sauce!) The getaways were such a relief from office pressures. My zest for life was enhanced by my feeling that I was involved, in an ongoing affair, with a beautiful and intelligent woman.

The other getaways were on the road. Every month or so, we would load the car with overnight bags and workshop materials, travel to some town in Wyoming (or Colorado, Nebraska, etc.) for a reincarnation workshop a la Wambach. Marilyn would conduct the workshop in her soft and soothing voice, and I would conduct individual sessions of "life readings." These trips were marvelous opportunities to earn some needed money and to gain some valued friends.

Batter or Batty?

Strike One. One evening, as Marilyn and I were driving back to Laramie after a tiring weekend journey, I lamented the conditions that existed among our full-time staff members. I expressed the wish that I could help our staff to become less competitive and more cooperative. I referred to one staff member who was being very disruptive, and I said, "I hope that she settles down. Maybe she will; maybe there will be no more trouble." Just at that very moment, a passing vehicle kicked up a large pebble that struck our windshield, head level, exactly between Marilyn and me. As the loud sound ended and the dent in the glass remained, I experienced a sinking feeling in my solar plexus: "No, Leo, the trouble is not over." I felt a little crazy, but I knew that the feeling in my belly was significant—whether it was or was not related to the dent in the windshield.

Strike Two. A young woman came to the counseling center. She was agitated, almost hysterical; she expressed suicidal thoughts; etc. The receptionist hurriedly asked if I could talk with the student and I agreed to do so.

As we sat in my office, I recognized the extent of the student's psychopathology, but I also perceived her strength and intelligence. Her difficulties were many, including no money, no friends, pressures in her studies, and no emotional support from her family. But her main complaint was her anxiety about the soul of the fetus that she had conceived and later aborted. She returned, again and again, to the theme of her guilt about the soul of the unborn child.

I was perplexed. On the one hand, I was reluctant to introduce the topic of reincarnation and "life readings." On the other hand, I was reluctant to avoid these topics if they might be of interest and assistance to her. As she leaned back in the chair and became more calm and coherent, I decided to trust my inner self and introduce these topics.

As I questioned her personal values and philosophy, she expressed her interest in reincarnation. In fact, she said that she had hoped that I might be willing to share any information I had. I showed her books by Netherton and Shiffin, *Past Life Therapy*; Fiore, *You Have Been Here Before*; and Wambach, *Reliving Past Lives* and *Life Before Life*. I told her that more and more research was being conducted by various psychologists and psychiatrists.

I described my own investigations, and the possibility that psychic impressions could be verbalized, if she and I decided to merge mentally. She agreed to the approach, and she understood that the comments might not be *true* or *false*—merely impressions of our inner feelings.

The comments that came out of our session were very meaningful to her about her own personal and interpersonal characteristics. Then, she asked me if I could "tune in" to the personality or soul of her unborn child. We both agreed that any verbalized impression might not be a "true" expression of that personality. However, the comments that emerged were, in my view, a compassionate and caring dialogue of the mother-child relationship. Further, the comments created a mood of forgiveness, and optimism, about the future relationship between the two souls.

At the end of the long session, I felt good about our work together. I believed that we had avoided the need to arrange hospitalization for her. Further, I believed that she and I could continue our work together in clarifying, and perhaps resolving, some of her problems.

Wrong! The events that followed reminded me of an episode when I was a college student, visiting relatives, and sitting on a porch swing with my cousin's five-year-old son. The boy had pushed the swing, then jumped onto it for a ride. But when he jumped, his momentum flipped the swing. We both tumbled out of the swing, hit the floor and bumped our shoulders and heads. As we sat up, rubbing our shoulders and heads, blinking away the stars, we looked at each other. I could see that he was in a mild state of shock, and was halfway between laughing and crying. I groaned; then smiled. "Wow! That really hurts!" He nodded and checked out my attitude again. I smiled and asked, "Are you OK?" He nodded, rubbed his head again, and looked as if he were ready to laugh. At that moment, out of the doorway, his grandmother rushed to him, with anguish in her voice and concern all over her face. She yelled, "Oh, my poor baby!" The floodgates opened; he cried as she clung to him for comfort. I often wondered (but didn't ask!) if she were in more need of comfort than he.

Similarly, I often wonder if a certain professor of psychology was more upset than the college student. I learned later that the professor and the student talked about the session. Apparently, the professor viewed me as unethical and unprofessional in my work with the student. However, I was not approached directly by that professor.

Instead, two other professors came to my office: Richard Pasewark, Ph.D. and Rod Carman, Ph.D. Both expressed concern about the situation and my methods of assisting that student. I appreciated their concerns and I tried to answer their questions. However, I was puzzled because the questions seemed to focus less upon the welfare of the client, and more upon the procedures and theory I had followed in dealing with the student.

I volunteered to conduct a demonstration of the procedures with one or both, but they declined. They did provide me with an opportunity to discuss these procedures with other members of the department of psychology. I appreciated their frankness, as well as their willingness to discuss these issues.

Later, Richard was willing to explore these procedures with an individual session. He did not perceive the scenarios as "possible past lives," but he perceived the verbal impressions as an expression of a "sensitive clinician." Rod has invited me, in recent years, to speak about parapsychology and ufology in his course on history and systems of psychology. Their professional and personal support has been very meaningful to me.

Ball One. I felt some relief after the departmental meeting. Although there were some members who voiced their disagreements with my views about science and psychotherapy, they also seem to recognize my concerns for students and cooperation with clients.

I was reminded of the lesson I learned with three previous clients. Each had entered counseling with symptoms that puzzled us, as well as frustrated us in reaching some kind of resolution. Then, one day, as I read John White's book on *Frontiers of Consciousness*, I turned to the chapter by a psychologist, Wilson Van Dusen, Ph.D.

As I read Van Dusen's approach, I knew immediately what I must do. (Van Dusen, a clinical psychologist, had moved from Canada to California. In applying the knowledge of Swedenborg, a Swedish scientist and mystic, Van Dusen decided to interview one hundred participants in the back wards of a hospital for the mentally insane. During those interviews, he talked to the possessing spirits of the patients as he investigated the hypothesis that these individual spirits could account for the hallucinations of the patients.) I decided to meet, individually, with the three frustrated, and frustrating, clients, and to ask each person the same question.

Using White's book as a prop, and Van Dusen's chapter as support, I asked each student, "What kind of spirit guide or guides do you have? Are they positive or negative?" (I did not provide the option of no spirit guide.)

Each student reacted somewhat differently, but the theme was similar. "How did you know?" Each client reacted favorably to the discussion and eventually each improved in self-confidence and self-esteem.

One student, who had been hospitalized for severe depression after a car wreck in which her three best friends were killed while she survived, was able to talk openly about the souls or spirits of her deceased friends. She said, "They told me at the state hospital that I shouldn't talk about this; if I do, then people will think I'm crazy. But if I don't talk about it, I'll go crazy!" She was very relieved to learn that it was OK, in my office, to talk about the souls of her friends and their occasional visits with her. She quickly regained her emotional stability and improved her academic standing.

The second student recognized his capacity to ease his anxiety by allowing his "inner guides" to argue, almost quarrel, over his values and decisions; then, he could arrive at a compromise that was satisfactory for "everyone." He preferred to think of these entities as aspects of his basic personality, rather than as possessive earth-bound spirits. In that way, he could conduct his inner dialogue as a "directed day dream," rather than as conversations with other entities. The important outcome was his improved confidence and productivity.

The third student was difficult to assist; she did not like me or my style or my philosophy. However, she preferred to work with me, because she was afraid to talk with her family priest. Her family, apparently, were staunch in their Roman Catholic traditions, and she feared their reactions if they were to learn that her possessing spirit was a male, with black beard and horns!

Sometimes, as she whispered to me the information about the latest threats from the "Devil," she would ask me to push my chair to the other side of the room. I would comply; then I would peer around the corner of the wall and ask her, "What is he telling you now?" Gradually, as she eased her fear that the entity might kill her, she began to recognize that her fear was the entity's strength. She began to appreciate the viewpoint that she could react to his threats in four ways: anger, fear, guilt, (i.e., confusion), or courage. She had tried guilt, anger, and fear; finally, she decided that she was ready to try the courageous approach.

However, she rejected my suggestion that she rid herself of the demon by calling upon the powers of God and the Heavenly Host of Angels. When she balked, I reminded her of the story of Pinnochio: he possessed no "good" friends, so he preferred "bad" friends rather than no friends at all. I asked her if she preferred the companionship of a bully demon or a guardian angel. At last, she came to recognize her fear and anger and guilt was directed toward an unforgiving God—who was personified as a Devil!

She provided me with a valuable lesson, which I am learning over and over: The spiritual crisis, for most humans, is more difficult to resolve than the personality crisis, or the bodily health crisis, or the environmental crisis. However, once we resolve our spiritual task (to go out away from God and then return to God, over and over) then the other tasks are less painful and more challenging.

Ball Two. I learned another lesson from a female student, who sought counseling services to deal with her sleeplessness. She presented herself as a tall, quiet, but determined young woman. She had sought meaning in her life by joining a religious organization and living with others in a commune society.

As she related her story, she began to recognize that she had attributed to Father God, and the male church leader, her own personal need for a nurturing father. She gradually experienced the insight that "God" can be both Mother/Father, and that she herself could embody both Yin and Yang, or both feminine and masculine energies.

We conducted a "clearing" of two entities, whom she recognized as a childhood friend and as an entity from a past lifetime. Later, she told me excitedly, "After that session, I slept all night—the first time in two years!" Selfishly, I secretly wished that I could confide these results with my colleagues. However, I knew that the information would not be received and, even if it were heard, the information would not change the status quo.

Ball Three. Despite my fears and doubts about my position as a professor, I regained some enthusiasm when I was invited to participate in a 1985 special issue of the *Journal of Counseling and Development*. Fred B. Newton, Ph.D., and Richard B. Caple, Ph.D., were guest editors for articles on the topic of Paradigm Shifts: Considerations for Practice.

Fred (Kansas State University) and Richard (University of Missouri) are well known in Division 17, Counseling Psychology, of the American Psychological Association. I wondered what might happen when James C. Hurst,

Ph.D. (U of WY vice-president, student affairs) discussed with Fred the brief article that I submitted: "Psychological Resonance: A Holographic Model of Counseling." Apparently, the discussion included a question of whether Leo should be listed as a psychologist and professor of counseling services at the University of Wyoming, or whether Leo should be identified as a psychologist in private practice. (Remember! The topics of ESP and reincarnation were taboo during office hours!)

Apparently, it was decided that Leo would be identified by university rank and title. When the journal issue was published, my immediate colleagues had no comments. However, I was pleased at the number of letters and requests for copies from other professional persons, including psychologists from other nations.

Strike Three: I'm Outta Here! In my fearsome fantasies, I sometimes imagined what might happen to cause me to resign from the University of Wyoming. One pleasant fantasy was to be selected as a "chaired" professor, but that fantasy was laughable! Even if a "chair" were available for a professor to study her/his special topic, I certainly would not be chosen to fill that chair. Another pleasant fantasy was that of becoming independently wealthy, so that I could donate money to the University of Wyoming and establish a chair for the study of parapsychology and ufology. Of course, there were no prospects for realizing that fantasy. Indeed, I was spending several thousand dollars each year from my own salary to fund my *personal*—not *professional*—research endeavors.

An unpleasant fantasy was one of being pushed out of my position because of alleged misconduct, in terms of my work with clients in past life therapy, spirit release, or UFO investigation. Yet, in my obsessive/compulsive style, I rationalized to myself: "If these topics are now taboo, and I do not engage in them during office hours, then am I less likely to be accused of misconduct?"

I tried to reassure myself that all was well: I could conduct myself appropriately, continue my work at the office, and continue my research activity at night and on weekends. I did not seek publicity, although I did respond to requests for interviews by reporters for newspapers, radio, and TV shows. I told interviewers, as I had been instructed, that I was reporting my findings as a licensed psychologist in the state of Wyoming, not as a U of WY professor.

Then, in November of 1988, I recognized the fact that the "game" was over, or at least my participation in the game; I could not continue as a professor on campus. I did not know it at the time, but my life-style was very reliable. The choice, once again, was between a *little brother* and a *big brother*. (See "Psychologist or UFO Investigator?" on page 43.)

Sprinkle in the Showers

When I recognized the game had shifted, from pressure on me to pressure on graduate students, I felt a sudden loss of professional power as well as a loss of personal will.

I felt as if I were standing at the plate in a baseball game, and I heard: "Strike three!" Yet, I didn't know if I had been struck out by a fast ball, a curve ball, or a slider. (My critics would probably say that it was straight over the plate and I didn't swing!) I looked at the calendar (November, 1988). I hoped that my 25 years of service could result in the title, Professor Emeritus of Counseling Services. I submitted my resignation effective September 1, 1989.

Failure or Success? When I left the University of Wyoming, I had just passed my 59th birthday. I felt old, tired, with little reason to celebrate. I was too young for social security benefits, and too young for retirement benefits. I was known as a good psychotherapist, despite my unusual interests, so I hoped that I could earn a living as a psychologist in private practice. My decision to resign was a difficult choice; Marilyn worried that our income would be low.

Ida M. Kannenberg. The generosity of Ida Kannenberg, in a gift to me, was the factor that permitted me to take a *leap of faith*. She was the first client for services in our new office, shared by two true friends, Darrell Pendley, Ph.D. and Lynne Pendley, Ph.D.

Drs. Darrell and Lynne Pendley. I had assumed that I could learn to heal myself body/mind/soul in one year. Actually, it took three years to regain a sense of confidence, as well as regain the former level of strength (and another three years to write this book).

Part of the healing is due to the supervisory sessions with Darrell and Lynne, as well as family dinners where love and good humor chased away the shadows of yesteryears.

Part of the healing occurred in my body/mind work with a variety of health practitioners: Kent Edlund, D.C.; Pat Righter, a body work therapist; Judy Ginnity, R.N., a therapist for neuromuscular massage and her husband, John, a reflexologist; Christie Anderson, who works with the chakras or auric energies; and Kent Nelson, D.C., who helped me to learn many lessons including the fact that my big feet should not be stuffed into shoes sized 12, but should be honored in size 15AA shoes!

Part of the healing process was the inner capacity for challenge—and for rationalization! For example, I jogged three miles on the day of my 60th birthday. I reminded myself that when I was 40 years old, I ran three miles in 21 minutes; when I was 50 years old, I jogged three miles in 24 minutes. So, at 60, I assumed that I could jog the distance in 27 minutes. But no! It took me slightly longer. I stood there, looking at my watch, sweating and frustrated. Then, I rationalized to myself, "That's OK, Leo. Some guys who are 60 years old are not even able to jog three miles." Then I smiled and thought to myself, "Hell! Some guys who are 60 are dead!"

Good News/Bad News

Relaxing after a shower, I tallied the bad news/good news of three decades of professional activities.

In some ways, my efforts could be viewed as a failure. I had been unable to complete my tenure at the University of Wyoming; I had only fifty-some articles and chapters of published writings; I had failed in my efforts to become a fellow in various organizations; I was not able to achieve the rank of Psychologist III after failing to become a professor of psychology; in 30 years of investigations, I had received only two small grants of approximately $500 for research studies; and I had failed in my attempts to persuade most of my immediate colleagues to collaborate, or even support, my research activities.

In other ways, however, my achievements had gone beyond what I had hoped to accomplish when I was an aspiring graduate student. I had experienced many opportunities to be helpful to thousands of clients. I learned so much from my clients. (Every good idea: self-hypnosis, psychic awareness, reincarnation, spirit releasement, and UFO abductions, etc., was refined by my work with professional colleagues, but initiated and illumined by my work with clients.) I had the opportunity to write papers and to share knowledge with many bold professional persons. I had the opportunity to correspond with tens of thousands of persons who shared their psychic and UFO experiences. I had appeared on national TV and radio shows. I had met many fascinating and courageous persons at international and national conferences. And, most of all, I had many friends, rich and poor, old and young, highly educated and poorly educated. In terms of love, I am a wealthy person!

I decided at that moment to renew my view that my professional glass was not half empty, but half full, and my personal cup was overflowing!

PART TWO: Summary and Conclusions

My "intuiting" about the inner lives of clients led me to explore hypnosis, ESP, and reincarnation.

Despite my internal resistance to paranormal phenomena, and my external doubts about any approach that was not approved by conventional science and mainstream professional training, I found myself drawn to those approaches that were helpful to my clients.

As I learned more about the inner world of clients, I began to systematize a method of hypnotherapy and past life therapy that resulted in the technique of "psychological resonance" or "life readings" for interested clients.

PART THREE

Some Studies of UFOEs and POLs

*Get your facts first, and then you can
distort them as you please.*

—Mark Twain

As a youth, I enjoyed reading biographies and autobiographies of famous women and men. I wished to learn how these well-known personalities conducted themselves. I desired to know what they did in order to reach their goals.

I can recall, when I was a skinny kid of fourteen years of age, how difficult it was for me to work nine hours a day in agricultural field work. When I read that Catherine the Great worked from fifteen to eighteen hours a day, I was very impressed. However, I was also very disappointed in myself! Of course, as I grew older, I recognized the possibility that I could maintain a heavy schedule of activities. Like most of my professional colleagues, I worked long hours each day and also on weekends and holidays. I noted one survey of university counseling center directors that showed the average workload to be approximately fifty clock hours per week. I noted that I was providing about fifty hours per week on counseling center activities, plus twenty to twenty-five additional hours on UFO research and correspondence, including vacations and holidays.

Yet, I also knew that hard work was not the only factor in professional achievement. I knew that intelligence and creativity were important factors in success. However, that awareness was bothersome to me because, as a graduate student, I had learned that my academic ability was in the average range for doctoral level psychologists.

So, I continued to obsess about the question of whether I had sufficient creativity to be a successful professional person. I recalled the story about Isaac Newton, the English physicist. He described himself as a curious youth, who used his own body in an experiment on a sandy beach. He ran and jumped as far as he could against the wind; then, using the same mark, he ran and jumped as far as he could with the wind. Then he compared the lengths of the two jumps in order to learn from the difference that was caused by the force of the wind.

I also recalled a story told by the physicist, Albert Einstein, about himself as a young boy. He was watching a man who was standing outside on the last car of a moving railroad train. The young Einstein saw the man drop something, and instantly, the boy had two images of what was happening. He had the image of the man standing on the train and watching as the dropped object fell straight to the ground. He also had his own viewpoint of the situation: He saw the falling object as it moved, at an angle, from the hand of the man to the ground in the direction of the moving train! The young Einstein was experiencing a "fact" and also a "theory": He recognized the significance of his observation about the relative difficulties in perspective between two participants in a field of physical activity.

Whenever I tell these stories to friends of mine, some of them respond—as do I—with enthusiasm about the genius of these young scientists. But, I also feel frustrated in my attempts to discuss the significance of the differences between the two scenarios: Newton was a solitary figure, assessing his own impact upon the system of forces in which he found himself. However, Einstein was a co-participant within the system of forces; his (unwitting?) colleague was a necessary component of that event, which eventually developed into the general and special theories of relativity.

I am not trained as a physicist; yet, in my opinion, many physical scientists have yet to comprehend the significance of Einstein's childhood observation. If I correctly understand what young Einstein discovered, then we are moving into the dawn of a new science. Apparently, he recognized that both truth and science can be multifaceted experiences. Both he and the man on the train, if they had discussed their viewpoints, could have accurately and truthfully disagreed on the motion of the falling object. Yet, they both could have accurately and truthfully agreed on the "fact" that both perspectives were accurate and true.

However, in my opinion, that agreement could only be reached if each participant were willing to accept and acknowledge his own psychic awareness, or compassion, or rapport, or resonance, with the other participant.

The principle is the blessing and burden of new science. No longer is most "science" a solitary activity. New science involves—indeed, it requires—the acceptance and application of mutual psychic experiences, the awareness of common consciousness from individual perspectives.

I wonder how long it will be before this important principle is accepted among the majority of the academic and scientific community. The cultural lag between scientific knowledge and social application is a factor in many areas of human activities. This lag time can occur, also, in the acceptance of scientific knowledge.

For example, according to some historians of science, it was two hundred years before one benefit of Vitamin C was accepted into the mainstream of scientific thought: the prevention of scurvy. For many years, the British sailors ("Limeys") had demonstrated that daily ingestion of a cup of lime juice could prevent the symptoms of scurvy. The British sailors were more healthy than their counterparts from other nations; thus, British shipping was more successful than that of other shippers. Now, conventional scientists "know" about the benefits of Vitamin C: the prevention of scurvy! However, some conventional scientists have not investigated the question of whether additional benefits can be obtained from additional levels of daily ingestion of Vitamin-C supplements.

The interested reader can learn about these benefits, including prevention of the common cold, through the work of physicians like Drs. Irwin Stone[1] and Edmé Régnier,[2] and the biochemist, Dr. Linus Pauling. Apparently, increased levels of ascorbic acid are beneficial for the immune system. Some proponents argue for 2-4 grams daily of Vitamin C, some for 12-18 grams daily. (Because I am a "moderate" in these matters, I take 8 grams of Vitamin C a day. Some of my friends say that 8 grams is excessive, but they are unable to provide evidence of their claim. I can claim that I don't have colds, and until the age of sixty, I was playing organized basketball with fewer aches and pains than I experienced without the additional intake of ascorbic acid.)

When, oh when, will we learn to listen to our bodies, as well as to the experts? Listen to ourselves! And who are the experts? Some philosophers of science said it well: Science advances one funeral at a time, i.e., there is always a better scientist who comes along. Santayana was quoted as saying something like the following: Every science goes through three stages; first, it is ignored; second, it is ridiculed; and third, it is accepted. When friends ask me if I'm bothered by public ridicule of past life therapy and UFO research, I smile and reply, "Hey! We're making progress!"

The purpose of Part Three is to present, as clearly and meaningfully as I can, the findings of some earlier studies that I have conducted. Chapter 7 describes early studies; Chapter 8, our initial UFO Conference; and Chapter 9, more recent studies.

---

1. Stone, 1972.
2. Regnier, 1971.

Caution. If the general reader chooses to read Chapters 7, 8, and 9, then he or she should be aware that some professional readers have found fault with the various surveys and studies that I have conducted. Criticism of these studies have been directed at the methodologies; number and kind of participants; analyses of data; interpretations of findings; and—indeed—the research hypotheses themselves. Many of these criticisms have come from psychologists and scientists who are brighter and better-trained than I am. Therefore, I caution the reader to be careful in accepting any comment from me as "truth," because of the results of these studies.

However, I hope that each reader will accept my statement that I am doing as well as I can. I am interested in phenomena that are difficult to observe, to document, and to interpret. Thus, I have conducted studies that appeal to me, rather than the kinds of studies that might appeal to other investigators.

For example, I conducted a small study of an interesting question: How often can I win when I play Solitaire? Solitaire is a game of cards that is played (surprise!) by oneself.[3]

The variation called Klondike, or Canfield, is played with seven piles of cards, each pile with an increasing number of cards; stock cards are manipulated in order to uncover four Kings and four Aces; in descending order, alternating red and black, the cards are placed on the Kings; then, in ascending order, the cards are placed in proper suite, upon the Aces. If all cards are uncovered, the player "wins."

On Friday, August 14, 1987, Marilyn and I drove to our cabin on Lake Hiawatha, Red Feather Lakes, Colorado (fifty miles west of Fort Collins). We planned to celebrate the weekend of the "Harmonic Convergence," August 16-17, 1987, with a few days of vacation. For diversion, I decided to record my efforts in playing Solitaire.

Each game was preceded by five or six riffs, or shuffles, plus cutting the deck. Then, using every third card, I checked to see if a play was possible.

I recorded these items: minutes of playing time per game; number of cards placed on the row of Aces; number of estimated "dollars" spent and won per game. (I had heard from friends, years ago, that $52.00 per game, or $1.00 per card, was the charge for playing Solitaire in a public gambling house; then, the gambler was awarded $5.00 in return for each card on the row of Aces, or $260.00 for a perfect game.)

Between noon and 10 p.m., I played 100 games. The findings were as follows: average time per game, 4 minutes; the average return per game, $42.80, or the average loss per game, $9.20. I won four games (#11, 27, 56, and 94). Tentative conclusion: I decided not to test my Solitaire ability in a public gambling

---

3.   Morehead & Mott-Smith,1966.

establishment! I did not mind if I could only win four times in one hundred games; however, I did not wish to spend approximately $10.00 a game (plus the initial $52.00) when I could stay home and lose the game for nothing!

Scientific Attitude. The example shows several aspects of my scientific attitude: I am willing to conduct studies that are interesting to me; I am willing to test a hypothesis about the phenomena that I am investigating; and I am willing to make personal decisions on the basis of my interpretation of the findings.

Initial Studies

The mystery of life is not a problem to be solved,
but a reality to be experienced.

—Van DerLeeuw
Philosopher

This chapter briefly describes my early attempts to analyze and to inter-pret my growing awareness of unusual phenomena in my life.

As a boy, I had a burning curiosity about the world around me. My father joked that Bob, my oldest brother, would search and find the cookie jar, while I—with my hands behind my back—would amble along and ask, "How many miles is it from the Earth to the Sun?"

My memories of early childhood Christmas gifts are vague, except for two holidays, one during which our father (as Santa Claus) bought a football, bas-ketball, baseball, bat, and two gloves for us. Wow! The other holiday I received a small microscope set with slides for viewing organisms in a drop of water. I was torn between the wish to become a famous athlete and a famous scientist. (As my friends said later, about either wish, "Not to worry!")

An Early Experiment

My first "experiment" combined my 1939 or '40 interests in athletics and science. One day, when I was nine or ten years old, I was shooting the basket-ball on the dirt courtyard, next to the garage. When my mother backed the car from the garage, I stepped aside, waiting for the car to move forward and out of the driveway.

Then, looking at the tire of the car as it slowly rolled by me, I thought to myself, "I wonder what it would feel like to have the car drive over my toes?" I decided to find out the answer to my question.

I was aware that the car was probably very heavy, so I knew that I should be careful. I kept my toes straight and I placed my J.C. Penny Co. "tennis shoes" just inside of the path of the left rear tire. Then, as the tire rolled over the toes of my left foot, I gasped in pain! I couldn't yell! I almost was in shock! I could feel the blood drain from my face! I stood there as my mother drove away in the car—she did not know what I had done, and I wanted to keep it that way!

I knew later that I had been rather foolish, so I kept quiet about the "experiment." However, I now had the answer to my question, and the results of the analysis were highly significant. Furthermore, there was no need to replicate the experiment!

Another Experiment

My next experiment was somewhat more formal: I conducted a 4-H project. (4-H refers to an educational and social program for rural youth, with an emphasis on activities that foster Head, Hands, Heart, and Health.)

I decided to conduct a study of one of our young pigs. I kept a record of his daily feed and his increase in body weight. Along with the "formal" study, I also conducted an informal study. I tested my own strength against the weight of the pig. (Nowadays, I might call the activity a bit of "shoat boating." But, in those days, I wanted to follow the method of a Greek god who, according to the story, gained great strength by daily lifting and then carrying a young bull.)

All went well at first, until I recognized that my daily increase in body strength was not accelerating at the same rate as the body weight of the pig. Within a few weeks, I was no longer able to pick up the pig. Another scientific study and another experimenter failure!

In high school and college, most of my activities that were called "experiments" were really repetitive rituals that had been developed by others. Even my first important psychological observation was based on Freud's principles about the psychopathology of everyday life.

Freudian Slips. I was twenty-three years old; it was 1953; I was sitting on an army cot in Germany, surrounded by other young U.S. Army draftees. I raised my eyes from a copy of Freud's *Introduction to Psychoanalysis*. (He described three kinds of written or spoken "slips" of the pen or tongue: those that I recognize and understand; those that I recognize and do not understand; and those that are not recognized by me—unless someone else points out the slip!) I decided to test his hypothesis that any interested observer could "listen" and "hear" slips of the tongue in everyday conversations.

I was aghast!

As I relaxed and listened, I became aware of several slips of the tongue from those young men around me. I was pleased at my success, but I was puzzled about my own academic training. Why did some professors of psychology claim that there was no basis for Freud's view of subconscious motives?

Marriage Counseling Services

My first formal academic study, in 1956, was a survey of students at the University of Colorado-Boulder. I asked selected students to provide written opinions about their level of awareness—and interest—in marriage counseling services on campus.

Probably, in retrospect, the study could be interpreted as a better indicator of my internal concerns than my need for external assessment of student opinions. However, the thesis showed my willingness to look beyond some of the conventional studies that were being conducted by candidates for a Master's degree in personnel services.

Permanence of Vocational Interests

In 1961, at the University of Missouri-Columbia, I completed a doctoral dissertation study in counseling psychology, titled "Permanence of Measured Vocational Interests and Socio-Economic Background."[1] The research hypothesis was reasonable: Men from lower socio-economic backgrounds are more likely than men from higher socio-economic backgrounds to experience a shift in their occupational interests. For example, a young man from a poor family, with interests in law, may choose to become a high school teacher of history, then, later, he might enter law school. On the other hand, a young man from a wealthy family, with interests in law, may choose to enter law school immediately after graduating from college.

I heard about the hypothesis in a class taught by John McGowan, Ed.D. The idea intrigued me, partly because of my own changing interests, and partly because the hypothesis was developed by my own advisor, Robert Callis, Ph.D. I expressed my willingness to conduct the study. ('Tis a wise graduate student who conducts a study that is of interest to his or her advisor. Caution: Be careful that the proposed study is not a "pet" theory, in case the results are inconsistent with the research hypothesis!)

I reviewed thousands of folders of former clients of the University testing and counseling center. (The review was rather laborious, and I recalled William James' exposé of the "Ph.D. Octopus." I recorded the number of hours I spent—in case I decided later to expose the ugly truth of poor, unpaid, and overworked graduate students!) I selected the approximately 500 folders of young men who had been former clients, had completed the *Strong Vocational Interest Blank* (SVIB), and had graduated from the University of Missouri-Columbia.

---

1. Sprinkle, 1961.

I obtained current addresses of potential participants. I wrote to them, with a conjoint letter from Dr. Callis and me, asking them to complete and return another copy of the SVIB along with information about their educational, economic, and social backgrounds. Vocational interest profiles were grouped according to their "upper" or "lower" background levels, and SVIB scores—before and after graduation—were compared on three measures, including judge's ratings of profiles.

The results showed no differences in the permanence of measured vocational interests between men of "high" and men of "low" socio-economic backgrounds. The SVIB profiles, as Strong had concluded, were viable indicators of vocational interests. The results of the study did not support my advisor's hypothesis, and, like a good research scientist, he relinquished his belief in that hypothesis.

In some ways, I was disappointed that I had not been able to demonstrate that Professor E.K. Strong's work could be modified. In other ways, I was impressed that his monumental work was reliable. With thousands of men and women, he had shown that various occupational groups can be differentiated on the basis of inventoried vocational interests. Further, he had demonstrated that most U.S. adults, after 25 years of age, continue with their adult pattern of vocational interests.

Although I did not know it at the time, the results of the study were instructive to me in regard to my philosophy of human nature. I eased my somewhat cynical view of others, and I returned to my childhood view that humans are more similar than different in their spiritual aspirations, even if they are different in their levels of spiritual development.

In my current philosophy of science, I am interested in "psychology": the study of the soul. I wish that I possessed the genius to assess the soul level of any person and to estimate the number of incarnations that the persons had experienced (and the number of incarnations needed to complete the spiritual journey?). Perhaps, in the next lifetime, I shall have an opportunity to work on that task![2]

NICAP Study

In 1961-62, as a young professor of psychology at the University of North Dakota (UND), I conducted a survey of 344 participants, including a sample of members of NICAP (National Investigations Committee on Aerial Phenomena). With the kind cooperation of Richard Hall, I asked NICAP members to provide information about their socio-economic background, and to complete the *Rokeach Dogmatism Scale*. Then I compared their results with

---

2. Hawkins, 1995.

the profiles of UND graduate students and professors of psychology. (See Appendix A.)

There are two significant aspects about that 1961-1962 study (along with the difficulty that I experienced in finding a professional journal in which the article could be published): One, the survey was an early attempt to explore the psychological characteristics of persons interested in UFO reports; two, the results were puzzling. How could a group of professors of psychology be more "open-minded" and yet less "scientific" than the sample of members of the National Investigations Committee on Aerial Phenomena?

I knew that my attempt to develop a scientific attitude survey was amateurish, at best; yet, I expected fewer differences between the groups in terms of their attitudes about "science." The SAS (*Scientific Attitude Survey*) was an expression of my belief (bias?) that "science" often was viewed as "SCIENCE," with an emphasis upon that which is "real" rather than "true," an emphasis upon a mechanical and materialistic model of human nature.

A Failed Study of Scientists

In 1963, I attempted a study of my colleagues in the UND Department of Psychology. The study was a failure. I was unable to complete the study, because it was poorly constructed (according to some of my colleagues) and because it featured taboo topics (according to me).

Robert Rosenthal, Ph.D., (now at Harvard University) had conducted a departmental survey on the levels of statistical inference, and size of samples, that provided confidence to any experimenter. He found that those of us who participated in the study were not consistent in the way that we rated our levels of confidence in statistical results. Apparently, as a group, we "swung" from one probability level to another probability level, e.g., .05, .01, .001, etc. Similarly, we were not consistent in our ratings of participant samples, e.g., 10, 200, 500, etc. Rather than moving smoothly toward higher sample size and greater probability levels that the results are not due to "chance," we responded as if the conventional levels were more important than in-between levels of probability and in-between levels of sample size.

Thus, according to my understanding of his findings, he demonstrated that we jumped from benchmark to benchmark. We were using a dogmatic or ritualistic method of inference, rather than using our own scientific knowledge that each sample size and each probability level gradually approaches the total population of participants, and, thus, gradually approaches the highest level of confidence that the results are valid observations of nature and not a result of chance.

According to my viewpoint, I wished to study a similar question: To what extent do we rely on various levels and kinds of scientific evidence? I labeled the levels as follows: anecdotal information, testimony from experts, empirical evidence, and experimental laboratory evidence. I asked my colleagues to rate these levels of information for various topics, e.g., study of dreams, ESP, extraterrestrial intelligence, etc. One professor of psychology refused to complete the survey because he viewed the study as nonsense. (I privately wondered about his attitude toward his rats and whether they were allowed to discontinue their participation in his studies?) My speculation about his refusal was that he recognized the likelihood that his favorite method of scientific evidence (experimental laboratory evidence) would be difficult or impossible to use in the investigation of some of the listed topics, e.g., "life on other planets."

Psychic Impressions of UFO Phenomena

When I discontinued that study, I decided to investigate the personality characteristics of persons who claim UFO sightings.[3] I developed a questionnaire for obtaining background information from participants, as well as a description of their ESP and UFO experiences. (See Appendix A for the UFO Report Form.)

I assumed that—within one year—I could obtain the cooperation of one hundred persons who would describe their background, share their ESP and UFO experiences, and complete some personality inventories. Instead, it took four years to obtain the participation of sixty-three participants in the initial study and nineteen participants in the second study, for a total of 82 participants. (See Appendix C)[4]

Results of Survey. If an investigator accepted the questionnaire and inventory results as reliable, he or she could conclude (tentatively) that the scores were obtained from a sample of persons of average or above average education, with professional and academic interests, with an interest in human behavior, and with no obvious psychoneurotic or psychotic reactions. The results are similar to those of the "upper-middle class" who are viewed as intellectual, creative, and productive; sometimes, these people are viewed as "pace setters" and leaders. Yet, the statements of the participants suggest that they have been observers of strange phenomena which defy explanation through any single body of knowledge.

The results of this survey indicate that most of the participants believe that they have experienced UFO phenomena. The statements of many participants suggest that they experienced direct or indirect communication with UFO occupants. Some participants claim to have experienced "mental communication" with UFO entities.

---

3. Generous cooperation in publicizing the survey was extended by Jim and Coral Lorenzen, APRO; Charles Bowen, *Flying Saucer Review*; Laura Mundo, The Interplanetary Center; and J. B. Rhine, Ph. D., Foundation on the Nature of Man. (NICAP staff declined the request to announce the study.)
4. Sprinkle, 1976a.

Tentative Conclusions in 1968

After conducting the 1964-68 study with eighty-two participants, I concluded tentatively that the survey form was appropriate, there seemed to be a connection between the claims of ESP and UFO experiences, and most participants were normal in their responses to psychological inventories. I decided to conduct a long-range study, in order to learn if more persons would be willing to participate in the survey, and to determine if the initial findings would be replicated. Also, I wished to learn if my more subjective view of individual participants would be confirmed by a more objective measures of their personality profiles. Despite the rejection of my manuscripts by journal editors, I continued to believe that eventually an increase in data would be rewarded by an acceptance of these studies by other psychologists.

Graduate Faculty Committee. In 1973, I was awarded $275.00 from the Graduate Faculty Committee of the University of Wyoming. The small grant was an incentive to continue the survey of UFO reports. Of course, each year, I was spending a few thousand dollars from personal funds for my UFO investigations, including travel, telephone calls, testing materials, and postage expenses. However, the small grant was pleasing, because it demonstrated a recognition of my work by a few faculty members—especially Dr. Michael Massarotti, a professor of educational measurement.

Department of Psychology, University of Wyoming. At one point in time, a female graduate student in the department of psychology expressed an interest in analyzing the data that I was collecting. However, after she consulted with her faculty advisor, she apologized to me for her decision to choose another dissertation topic. She had learned, all too well, the academic and professional risks in conducting a UFO study.

Department of Counselor Education, University of Wyoming. Then, Mrs. June Parnell expressed an interest in analyzing the hundreds of folders that had been collected over the years. She had become a member of our Laramie UFO support group, after attending the second Rocky Mountain Conference on UFO Investigations, 1981. June was well-known for her research skills, as well as her teaching abilities. She had completed a Master's degree in psychology, including laboratory research studies with Dr. Helen Crawford (now at VPI), who was well-recognized for her psycho-physiological studies of hypnotic processes.

When June became a doctoral candidate in the Department of Counselor Education, she expressed an interest in a dissertation study of the personality characteristics of UFO observers. Her advisor was reluctant to approve the study; however, he agreed on the condition that I serve as dissertation advisor. I was glad to serve in that capacity, but I could only guess at the struggles just before us.

June Parnell, Ph.D. Candidate

June demonstrated many qualities of the ideal scientist-practitioner: she was compassionate and courageous in dealing with a variety of clients in the counseling center, and she was analytical and rigorous in her scholarship. She had taught Spanish and German in a New York City public school. When she and her husband, Tom, came to Laramie, she served as a German instructor in the Department of Modern Languages, while he served as a professor of political science, U of W.

The parents of Mrs. Parnell had come from Germany; living well into their 90s, they demonstrated the pattern of many couples from the "old country." Mr. Reis was the patriarch, who knew truth and reality for himself and others! Mrs. Reis allowed him to steer their ship of matrimony, but she prepared the map while trimming the sails. Thus, June was well-trained to be deferent to her committee members—but determined to complete her study.

Advanced Statistics. At one stage of her program, June had doubted whether she could continue. Her graduate committee had been composed of five professors: Dr. Don Forrest, Dr. Arden White, Dr. Wayne Lanning, Dr. Richard Pasewark, and myself.

The other committee members did not agree with my wish to encourage June to conduct a "qualitative" study of Ps, including their ESP and UFO claims. The other members of the Committee expected a "quantitative" study of personality inventory scores. In fact, some members expressed concern about the methods that were used to obtain participation in the survey.

Finally, the Committee recognized that the "sample of Ps" could be construed as a "population," because any interested person had been invited to participate as long as he or she had been willing to complete and return the survey materials.

After Committee approval of the dissertation proposal, there was a delay of another year so that Mrs. Parnell could complete another course in advanced statistics. Apparently, the Committee could not guarantee that the data were gathered in a rigorous manner, but the Committee could guarantee that the data would be analyzed in a rigorous manner!

When June consulted with me and a young professor of educational measurement about the statistical analyses to be conducted, I mentioned the difference between electronic computers and the hand-cranked Munroe calculators that were available when I conducted a dissertation study in 1960-1961. The young professor looked at me; her eyes were opened wide, with arched eyebrows; she gasped, "I've seen one of those!" I was glad that she only commented on the age of the calculator, not on the antiquity of the old geezer in front of her!

June Parnell, Doctor of Philosophy

In 1986, the University of Wyoming awarded June Parnell the degree, Doctor of Philosophy. As her dissertation advisor, I was pleased to walk across the stage with her, during the graduation ceremony, when she received her academic hood and diploma.

Although there have been several dissertation studies on the historical, journalistic, and political aspects of UFO research, her study was the first one that focused on the personality characteristics of UFO Experiencers. I believe that Dr. Parnell is to be commended for her courage and persistence, in the face of considerable adversity. (See Appendix D for a summary of the Parnell Study.)

Conference Profiles

*There are three steps in the revelation of any truth: in the
first, it is ridiculed; in the second, resisted; in the third,
it is considered self-evident.*

—Arthur Schopenhauer
(1788-1860)

Introduction

My "thinking" about UFO activity and reincarnation—including my
own ET connection—took a sharp turn in 1980. Not only did I learn more
about my own childhood memories of ET encounters, but I also learned more
about the personal characteristics of UFO experiencers.

For many years, I had been corresponding with many UFO contactees
and abductees. Some of these good people became impatient with me; they
continued to write often, but they asked questions like these: "Leo, can you
introduce me to other UFO contactees, so that I can correspond with someone who will write more often?" "Leo, when can you arrange a meeting so
that we can come together and talk about our UFO experiences and alien
encounters?"

My usual reply was a good, professorial "explanation": There is no money
for a conference.

I had applied for grant money to conduct a meeting; I had written to
Richard Hall, who was with the Fund for UFO Research. I had known Richard, by correspondence, from the days when he was with the National Investigations Committee on Aerial Phenomena. He had assisted me, in 1961-
1962, to conduct a survey of NICAP members.

When I inquired about funds for conducting a conference for UFO contactees, Richard had responded by asking, "What about real scientists?" I

thought that he was joking. (After all, I was a life member of AAAS and I had received training in scientific methodology during my academic programs.) So, I wrote back with my own little bit of humor, "Oh, yes, scientists are welcome, as long as they are UFO contactees." Apparently, that comment was received as impertinent, as well as unfunny. There was no money for funding a meeting for UFO contactees!

But, my correspondents did not accept my good explanation (which they viewed as a poor excuse); they insisted: "Leo, call a meeting. We'll pay for our own expenses."

Rocky Mountain Conference on UFO Investigation

In May, 1980, our first "contactee conference" was convened at the School of Extended Studies, University of Wyoming, Laramie. Approximately twenty persons participated in the meeting, either by submitting a statement, or appearing in person, or both. In addition to those who presented written statements, there were also five other persons: Carl and Margery Higdon, Pat and Wanda McGuire, and Mike Lewis, photographer.

Of course, some persons expressed initial doubts about the other participants. Bud Hooper, Denver newspaper reporter, was skeptical of any UFO story that came out during hypnosis sessions, because he could remember his UFO sighting and on-board experience without the use of hypnosis or without consulting with anyone else. But, after talking with Ann Canary, and others, he began to consider the possibility that they were honest persons, who were telling the truth as they knew it.

Pat McGuire and Carl Higdon (see Chapter 2) briefly argued about the features of alien beings, until they accepted the possibility of more than one group of ETs who were contacting humans.

Soon, there was an atmosphere of compassion and appreciation for the courage and integrity of all the participants.

Participants. *Gayle P. Bever* could not attend, but she submitted a statement about the changes in her scientific and spiritual philosophy as a result of the UFO encounter (experienced by her and her daughter) and, later, her abduction by an alien entity.

Dorothy E. Burrow expressed her skepticism about whether she was a UFO contactee. However, Dottie described her studies of earthquake and volcanic activity, and her visions of possible Earth changes.

Barbara J. Freund, a university student who later became a science teacher, described her 1977 encounter with little gray entities who examined her body and conducted a healing process on her metal and plastic (Geometic) artificial knee. Before her encounter, she had felt a compulsion to learn meditative procedures; afterward, she changed from a "religious" person (church oriented) to a (cosmic oriented) "spiritual" person.

R. B. (Bud) Hooper described his experience of walking on board a space craft, and communicating through telepathic messages with armored entities who showed him their propulsion system.

Catherine L. Fisher of New Mexico was unable to be present, but she described her years of meditation and communication with extraterrestrial entities. She had channeled much information about the ET plan for Earth and humankind.

Kimberle J. Lenz submitted a statement about the 1974 time loss that she and her brother had experienced. During a hypnosis session in 1979, she was able to recall more about her "on-board" experience, including bodily examination and questions about human sexuality.

Millie Lindsey, Women's Softball Coach, University of Wyoming, Laramie, described five UFO close encounters in California in 1968, and another UFO sighting in Wyoming in 1979.

Lucille McNames submitted a channeled message, *UFO Transmission*, May 19, 1980. (In 1995, Lucille was 87 years old and living in western Colorado. When she was 17 years old, she was a dancer in a chorus line for Hollywood movies.) In 1966, on a bright moonlit night, Lucille saw a "flying saucer." As it floated approximately 500 feet above her house, another UFO began to merge with the first UFO. Lucille tried to project a mental message to anyone in the craft. In her mind, she stated, "If you came to help earthman out of his dilemma, and if you are co-workers for Christ, and if I am not too presumptuous, and if you can use my clairvoyant ability, even in a minute way, I am willing to serve." The UFO then seemed to dissolve instantly.

In 1967, Lucille began to type messages from invisible entities. Her mentors have channeled many messages through her (as Sari), including two books: *Startling Revelations* and *The Crystal Tower*.[1] One message, for scientists who study electronic communication with spirit personalities, contained this statement: "We have methods by which to nudge the patterns awake after having lain dormant, often for eons. Memory patterns are part of the soul's Akasha that are reflections of one's deeds and actions throughout all of his/her lifestreams."

Mary K. Sewall, a public health official (and now an ordained minister in Maine), described her 1956 UFO experience in Fresno, California. While aboard a strange craft, with others, she was given a "black box" to hold. She was told by a "woman" that they would meet a U.S. Navy ship where they would wait for a ship to come in from outer space. The entities seemed to be oriental in facial features, and they seemed to possess great technical skills and to exhibit high ethical concerns.

---

1. McNames, 1980.

On April 12, 1976, Mary awoke and felt a hand on her back. She turned to see two "persons" leaning over her, and one inserted a syringe needle into her rib cage at the lower section. The two entities were of short stature, and as they left the room, Mary could see a soft glow around their space suits that looked like a series of inflated rings connected together.

John G. Williams, Laramie musician, described his June, 1979, camping trip in some mountains of northern Wyoming. He and his dog were on the edge of a double cliff overlooking a waterfall. While he was meditating, some heavy clouds rolled in, but there was a "hole" above him where the sun continued to shine down on them.

Then, a "network" or center of a large room appeared next to the cliff. John was invited by an entity to walk into the "network." While he was standing, a helmet was placed on his head, and he experienced expanded awareness (See page 92 for information about John's exploration of another possible lifetime that was connected to his allergic reactions.) John described the effects of the UFO experience in terms of his personal growth, as well as his interpersonal and spiritual development.

Mr. and Mrs. Anonymous and Son described their experiences in February, 1974, while camping in the Sonora Desert of Mexico. That night, they heard a strange electronic beeping sound. The next morning, they investigated but could not locate a source of the sound. Then, during breakfast, they began to recall more about the "visitation" by little gray entities.

Later, in the U.S., they sought hypnosis sessions in order to recall more about their experiences.

Mr. Anonymous described his memory of standing over a "screen" with a "man" who urged him to consult with governmental officials about a possible nuclear war in 1980.

Mrs. Anonymous said that her first thought that morning had been: "We were visited by a UFO." Then, when her menstrual period began unexpectedly, she thought, "We *were* visited by a UFO and they *examined* me!"

Mr. Anonymous, Jr., described his memories of touring the space craft, and he drew sketches of the entity and features of the space craft.

Other attendees. Each participant had fascinating stories to tell the group, including Carl and Margery Higdon of Rawlins, Wyoming (now living in Texas). Carl had experienced a loss of time (see Chapter 2) while hunting elk south of Rawlins[2]. Also, Pat and Wanda McGuire (see Chapter 2) had experienced many UFO encounters on or near their ranch north of Laramie, Wyoming.

Many people traveled from other states, and foreign nations, to visit the ranch and view the water well. Pat had been featured on various TV docu-

---

2. Sprinkle, 1979.

mentaries while describing cattle mutilations and UFO sightings on the ranch. He also described being "picked up," many times, by alien entities who gave him various instructions, including the task of digging a water well on the ranch.

Despite the variety of reports from participants, there was a general agreement among attendees that UFO activity was occurring, and groups of ETs were working with humankind toward the twin goals of planetary rejuvenation and human evolution. Those views were summarized well by two persons, Ann Canary and Ida Kannenberg.

S. Ann Canary. Ann was raised in a Christian family (Southern Baptist). In 1947, when she was four years old, she and her family watched a strange "star" that hovered over some oak trees, off and on, for several weeks. Later, Ann was spanked when she claimed that she had talked with a "moon man," because her mother thought that Ann was lying.

In 1966, Ann experienced a near-death experience, as if her soul was taken from her body and transported to another dimension. Compassionate beings communicated with her about a special mission before she returned to her body. In 1971, she was taken to a space craft for an examination of mind and body, including a genital examination. In 1977, she had another encounter with ET entities.

Ann talked about ET encounters with many persons and assisted them to ease their fears about these encounters. She described her 1980 interpretation of these phenomena as follows:

Changes Brought About in the Inner Me as a Result of This Experience:

S. Ann Canary

After my experience, I knew that I had been privileged with a glimpse at something infinitely wondrous and profound. My inner consciousness had undergone a complete and staggering metamorphosis. Those truths I had been taught through the years by my church, family, parents, and teachers no longer were valid to me. Those beliefs had been replaced by an understanding of the process we call creation, and I knew our Earth science and education were not yet beginning to suspect the universal laws that govern the creation of worlds within our Universe. The following is a synopsis of the changes brought about in the inner me as a direct consequence of my experience:

1.   I have embraced a faith of cosmic dimensions. I know the Creator as sexless and all creation as a material manifestation of mind extended into matter. Love is the governing factor behind all experiences in life as we know it—love and caring. I have no allegiance to any church. My experience opened the door to my inner spiritual awareness, and I have established a pattern of ceaseless learning, growth, and profound inner wonder at the possibilities all of us have for growth as individual souls.

2.   I no longer have allegiance to any particular form of earthly government, political system, race, economic or social structure. I prefer life on Earth under a political system which allows freedom of thought and expression. Now I view myself as a resident of Earth, a Citizen of the Galaxy, and an immortal soul who is evolving intellectually, physically and mentally according to a master plan that is progressively uplifting no only Earth, but the entire Universe. My only allegiance is to my Creator and I am totally committed in my service to the Cosmic Christ.

3.   I have continued to be obsessed with an expanded desire for truth and understanding of Earth's and man's evolutionary progress from pre-history through, and including, present and future evolutionary patterns.

4.   I have studied the mind and altered state of consciousness as they are taught and explained by parapsychology. I feel man's mental and physical evolution are intricately connected with spiritual evolution for each man must learn inner self-government, and collectively we must learn it as a species before we will be allowed to venture into more advanced worlds. We are in our infancy here, and it is vital we learn self control as individuals and as a planet.

5.   We are responsible for what our minds manifest around us. I feel our lives reflect the state of our attitudes, thoughts, and inner reaction that become physical actions directed at the material world around us.

6.   I have strived to balance myself in the three major areas so as to improve my self-awareness and heighten my awareness of the world around me. I have tried to evolve physically, mentally, and spiritually into a balanced human being.

7.   I have tried to live my principals and moral laws within myself, as well as without in such a way as to be able to help others help themselves. I do not judge—I do not condemn. I feel man is his own ultimate judge and therefore metes out his own punishment.

8.   I have vowed to serve the Universal Law and those principals that are uplifting and true, and I try to live and feel the law of love for others.

9.   All life is *one*. We are part of the *stars*, oceans, all creation. We are only one dimension in a multi-dimensional Universe. We are not the Lords of Creation. We are only a small group of children drifting on a sea of ignorance, and we may sink our boat before we reach the point of maturity whereby we can protect ourselves from our own self-destructive tendencies.

10.   I have no fear of death. Death is the laying aside of one's physical body. Life is eternal—mind is eternal. Earth is a school wherein mind can learn how to govern matter and physical actions through proper mental thoughts and attitudes.

11. My mission is to Earth's citizens and environment in so far as I can assist the thinking of those who live here…. Unless the consciousness of humankind is raised, the planet will not evolve beyond its present immaturity and we will ultimately destroy the work of eons, ourselves, and the present environment of our world.

12. Man is facing a crucial period in his evolution as a species. He must consciously choose change or face destruction. Man must have social, economic, and religious progression on a planet wide basis.

13. I believe in a Father-Mother God, a balanced interchange between the creativity of both sexes. This is necessary for the establishment of all things material and physical, as well as producing a "healthy" world. It begins with the union of male/female for the reproduction of a species, but the same principal governs the formation of matter and creation of worlds. Man is not the ruler of this world. Man's present social/material creations reflects his own weaknesses and the weakness will only be corrected when man corrects his narrow perspective of his own power and sense of importance. He must acknowledge and embrace the female half of himself spiritually and mentally as well as physically.

14. (I have the) knowledge that we are unknowing participants in a living universe that is founded upon unchanging governing natural laws of cause and effect. There are other life forms, other worlds, other dimensions.

15. (I am experiencing) loss of interest in the accumulation of material "things."

16. Basically I have become a pacifist. War depletes—it does not enrich. I would die in defense of a certain truth—but never be an aggressor. I must be a defender only.

17. (I have the) knowledge that the world's fuel must be water. (I feel a) total disagreement with any government or business or society that pushes the use of nuclear fuel, or weapons. Man is following a path of foolish ignorance and danger when it comes to properly dealing with the atom. We can or will destroy ourselves in our *ignorance* of what we are tampering with. Our science is not advanced enough to protect us from the consequences of our science's mistakes—and those mistakes will be made.

18. Within myself (I experience) the consummation of science with religion.

After many years, I now realize and know that my own transformation was not and is not a single experience here on Earth. There are literally hundreds, if not thousands, of people who are or have experienced this metamorphosis. Our numbers are growing yearly and we are beginning to locate and communicate with each other.

An alien invasion has already occurred upon Earth. The conquering power is not military or technological/economic superiority. It is a revolution in consciousness, and spiritual knowing that has been implanted within the minds of thousands of people all over the world.

The future of this world is passing into the hands and minds of these people. Those of us who have been contacted no longer serve the old orders. We fear nothing—least of all the threat of death or physical deprivation. We are *here—now*! We walk among you daily—we pass you on the streets, stand next to you in the elevators, and you see little of what is moving daily closer to completion. We are among you—and our force is the force of mind governed by morality and an ethical code that upon Earth is incomprehensible.

Ida M. Kannenberg. With both clarity and courage, Ida has described her experiences in three books: *UFOs and the Psychic Factor, Alien Book of Truth,* and *Project Earth.*[3] Her ET encounters included childhood events, as well as a 1940 encounter in the California desert.

In 1980, Ida traveled to Wyoming for hypnosis sessions, so that she might recall more about her 1940 "on-board" experience, including the memory of "implants" for communication with ETs. In 1968, she was frightened by telepathic messages and she was hospitalized. However, the physicians who examined her declared her to be without psychopathology. (Now, she jokes about being "certifiably sane.") In 1978, the "voices" began again, and Ida began to record the messages.

She continued to question the purpose of ET encounters; once, she asked: "Into what are we being initiated?" Her mentors replied: "Into a worldwide organization dedicated to the purpose of helping peace and justice return to the world." Ida summarized her experiences as follows:

Ida M. Kannenberg
April 23, 1980

In a hypnosis session with Dr. Leo, I have been made aware that my contacts with UFO people have been a lifetime, indeed a before lifetime thing, though I was quite unaware of its extensiveness.

In many months of actual telepathic contact, I think I have run through every known emotion in response to them, from aversion, disgust, anger, fear, to total acceptance and even—gratitude. For I feel the longgoing experiences have been for one overall purpose—to develop me as a useful "outer" person, and to give guidance to my evolutionary progress as an "inner" person, for that seems to lie behind the point of their contacts in our lives. They have said, "We come to rejuvenate the Earth and to aid in the evolutionary development of man."

This is the Great Plan with which they collaborate, but they have themselves many needs and wishes of their own, their own personal axes to grind. They ask bluntly that we exchange our help for theirs.

---

3. Kannenberg, 1992, 1993, 1995.

Since we are left exactly in the dark as to these intents and purposes, and of our before-lifetime dedication, we feel we have been invaded or imposed upon without justice or apparent reason (and sometimes without mercy).

Their methods to make contact were meant to emphasize their realness, to make us aware they were actually there, that they have powers we have forgotten, and to make us above all *think*. Mostly they have succeeded in scaring us to death by their abrupt methods without explanations. My own first overt contact with them in 1968 landed me in the state hospital, one scared-to-death kid!

Ten years later, in 1978, began the months of telepathic contact, writing as dictated by them, explaining many things. My skepticism stood firm, though I wrote avidly. I frequently referred to them as liars, not understanding how their various pieces of information fit together. To me there was no fit, but it was only because I lacked enough of the right pieces to make them fit.

After a hypnosis session with Dr. Leo in April, just past, my skepticism abated, so I am not kicking or squealing at every idea they try to impart.

I would say the events they put us through are meant to develop us through experience, the only way to true actual development. Each of us is taught what is uniquely "our thing." When enough contactees come forward with their complete stories, some of which they do not now remember, for they are timed to remember, then corroborations and coincidences will become apparent, and an overall pattern will emerge which may be utilized to make sense to our kinds of minds. We will understand what they are trying to say with their kinds of minds. Actually, the kinds are the same, for both are human, but there are some slight evolutionary differences, and some very large cultural and environmental differences.

When all contactees come forward and share their experiences, we can then see the underlying principles that hold it all together, and then it will become believable and understandable. We will see that we are not invaded, that we are but extended in experience and knowledge.

That is my personal conviction.

A Statement from Hweig (UFO Entity)

Our subject is proper alignment of factors to reveal the greatest amount of understanding of UFOs, and their makers, occupants, designers, correspondents, etc.

In other words, this outline will show how to put together all your garnered facts in order to get the most informative material. A comprehensive viewpoint from *cause* is needed.

Comprehensive Viewpoint from Cause of the UFO Phenomenon

—THE PLAN

The Plan is the rejuvenation of Earth and its inhabitants

A. Rejuvenation through collaboration of UFO people with Earth's inhabitants.

    I. Teaching—Leading into new discoveries

    II. Drawing out of potentials and developing latent abilities

        a) Contactee reports—methods of reception

    III. Organizing and extending knowledge

    IV. Modifying present social structures

    V. Resolving current conflicts and threatening dangers of all categories

B. Rejuvenation through application of special knowledge and abilities of the UFOs

    I.Technological

    II.Scientific and Medical

    III.Psychical

        a) Mode of being

        b) Psychic abilities

C. Rejuvenation through Cultural exchange

    I. Language

    II. Intercommunication of ideas

    III. Friendship and marriage

    IV. Art and literary inspiration

D. Rejuvenation of people through rebirth of nonmaterialistic values

    I. Spirit of helpfulness

    II. Desire to be useful

    III. Reconstructed work ethic

    IV. Attitude of cheerfulness

    V. Cooperation and sharing

E. Rejuvenation of Earth through extension of knowledge of the physical earth and new sense of values concerning the physical earth

    I.Physical

        a) Land—cooperate with natural forces

        b) Forests—replenish and use wisely

        c) Water supplies—find substitutes for and new sources

        d) Plants

        e) All natural resources—value and replace

        f) To improve upon nature and help her along with some of her destroyed or hindered plans

    II. Sources of energy

        a) To rebuild areas which have been depleted of deposits—oil, gas, coal, etc.

        b) Find easier, less expensive sources of energy

        c) Find new ways to accomplish things that do not require such extensive uses of energy

    III. Animal life

a) Restore dwindling species

b) Breed healthier animals

c) Control better living conditions for animals

F. Infiltration. No government can stop this kind of mental invasion by passing laws against it. It must be recognized that it exists, discover how it exists, and above all, *why* it exists.

I. Reconstruction of man and his institutions from the inside out

II. Attain positions of influence and power

Eventually, this will be extended in great detail. Its purpose now is to evaluate what and why our contactees are undergoing certain disciplines and being led to specific discoveries.

You have among the members of this study-conference several members who can find their own fields within this outline. Let them be assured that their work is of major value and importance to the entire world, for no one on Earth is doing precisely the same research as they, and each of these categories or studies *must be done*!

Signed
Hweig, Amorto, and Jamie

Characteristics of UFO Contactees

Most of the conference attendees could relate to the characteristics and self statements of other UFO experiencers, as presented (page 5) in my introduction[4] to the 1980 proceedings:

1. They seem to be average, normal people in their social and psychological functioning.

2. They seem to be highly susceptible to hypnotic suggestion.

3. They seem to experience many psychic phenomena and/or possess some psychic abilities.

4. They exhibit loving concern for all humankind.

5. They often report a feeling of being monitored or experiencing continued contact with UFO entities.

6. They sometimes report a feeling of having been "chosen" or selected as a UFO contactee.

7. They act as if they have an important mission or task in life.

8. They sometimes express anxiety about the "state of humankind," and they may warn others of the possibility of future catastrophes.

---

4. Sprinkle, 1980.

9. They often express the feeling that they are not only planetary persons, but also cosmic citizens.

10. They sometimes feel as if their real "home" is beyond Earth.

Summary. I summarized our conference as follows:

Like summer in Laramie, Wyoming, the contactee conference was short but sweet. According to the comments of participants, the conference was very successful: individual levels of trust, confidence, and enthusiasm were much higher at the conclusion of the sessions.

I will not attempt to summarize each participant's views of the significance of the conference; I will describe my own reactions which, to a large extent, are based upon the verbal and nonverbal communication of participants. My one disappointment was that Gayle Bever, Catherine Fisher, Kim Lenz, and Lucille McNames were unable to attend the conference. However, they participated through their written statements, as well as their years of courage and communications.

According to immediate criteria, the conference was successful, Participants were good natured, open, and honest in describing their UFO experiences and sharing their information with others. There was a sincere attempt to search for patterns of UFO experiences, although we all recognized that our sample of cases is small, and that the ABCs of UFO phenomena (Absurdity, Bizarreness, Confusion) prevent an easy integration of all aspects of UFO encounters. Most participants had decided to "go public," or to allow videotaping of their presentations. The discussions were not smooth and polished—in fact, the camera (darn it!) captured us as we are—common people talking about our uncommon experiences.

According to short-range criteria, the conference seems to have been successful. Friendships were initiated, with proposed collaboration on tasks of mutual concern and interest. Some participants gained a sense of "recognition" as they met other participants with similar experiences. Some participants stated that the main effect of the conference was to confirm the reality of their UFO encounters; others stated the effect was to reaffirm the significance of their work. We all seemed to feel a humbling of ourselves, personally, and an ennobling of ourselves as participants in a planetary plan.

According to long-range criteria, the conference may or may not be successful. There are so many doubts and so many questions:

• Will our participation lead to personal and interpersonal changes in our lives?

• Will other UFO contactees respond favorably to our statements and presentations?

• Will similar conferences be established?

• If other conferences are established, will similar information emerge from presentations and discussions?

- If these conferences are videotaped or filmed, will there be public interest in viewing these films?
- And (big question!) will there be funds to compensate participants for their time, travel, and travail?

The answers to these questions may determine the measure of social success of the conference.

From a scientific or scholarly viewpoint, there are many questions about the long-range significance of the conference:

- Will scientists and scholars regard these statements as pseudoscience and pseudoreligion? Or as nonsense? Or as naughty words? Or as knotty lines to untangle?
- Will some physicist or engineer puzzle about the "cylinders" described by the 83-year-old Bud Hooper, and the "cylinders" described by the 18-year-old Mr. Anonymous, Jr.? Or the "black box" described by Kim Lenz and the "black box" described by Mary Sewall?
- Will some biologist or physician puzzle about the marks on the skin of Gayle Bever, Ann Canary, and Kim Lenz?
- Will some psychologist or sociologist puzzle about the personality patterns of participants, or the "survival plans" of Ann Canary, John Williams, and the Anonymous Family?
- Will some parapsychologist or theologian puzzle about the "mental messages" received by UFO contactees and the claims that UFOLKS have come to "rejuvenate the Earth" and to "assist humankind" in our social and spiritual development?

The answers to these questions may determine whether there is any scientific significance for the conference.

Perhaps the UFO phenomenon will go away, leaving a trail that only historians can discern—and describe as perceptual anomalies and social aberrations. Perhaps UFOs are space craft, piloted by intelligent beings who are preparing humankind for catastrophic Earth changes, physical and political. Perhaps UFOs are sophisticated holograms displayed by intelligent beings so that Earth people will become interested in time and space travel and in building "flying saucers" and becoming "flying saucer occupants." Perhaps the UFO display is a "spiritual lesson" to determine which *observers* are willing to become *witnesses*, to demonstrate the intellectual and spiritual strength needed to speak the truth as they know it to be. Perhaps the UFO display is a "battle": a struggle of "good guys" and "bad guys," galactically; or a conflict of "the forces of light" and the "forces of dark," psychically; or the whimsey of ghoulish gods, "soulsuckers," who are heaven-hopping while they harvest their cosmic crops!

The reader may have a favorite fantasy (or fear) about the UFO phenomenon. I am aware that emotional reactions are more important than intellectual considerations in determining the form and content of human belief systems. Thus, I commend to you the exercise of imagining your foulest fears, and highest hopes, about the purposes and programs of UFO people. Then, if you desire a UFO display, meditate upon the question, "What can I do for UFOLKS, in exchange for UFO sightings?" Be careful about your wish, you may receive it!

The Rocky Mountain Conference on UFO Investigation was a significant event in my life. Because of the efforts of many good persons who paid their own way with the twin currencies of cash and courage, I have realized a favorite daydream: a conference where the "real" UFO experts describe their "investigations." (Now, I shall hope for the other daydreams to come true: The wish to participate, full-time, in a center for UFO research, and the wish to participate in a formal, and public, face-to-face encounter with UFO people!)

I believe that the contactee conference also was a significant event in the lives of all the participants, including those who were unable to attend the meeting. I have watched many of these persons face their conscious worries and their subconscious memories of abductions, examinations, and instructions. I have watched (and wept) while they relive their UFO encounters— once again experiencing the anger, anxiety, doubt, fear, humiliation, and pain. Their tears and trauma, however, seem to be the outcome of "experiments" rather than "torture," of lessons being learned rather than bodies being abused. These persons may have come into contact with "devils," but they have responded by demonstrating greater love and concern for all humankind.

I do not know if these short statements by these remarkable people will have an appreciable influence on the current direction of UFO research. However, my sincere hope is that these statements will provide encouragement for other UFO abductees and contactees to come forward and share their experiences. Perhaps a pattern of information can emerge which will help us to learn, to understand, and to accept, the significance and meaning of the UFO experience in the lives of UFO contactees. If so, then we shall face the bothersome question of whether the experience of the UFO contactee is a prelude to the educational, moral, social, and spiritual rejuvenation of humankind. Would it not be ironic if our fears were well founded, that UFO phenomena represent some horrible happening in our lives? And, most terrifying of all, what if each earthling must face an alarming prospect: neither being food for someone's table, nor being cannon fodder for someone's war, but just enduring the agonizing change that makes us a better person?

Past/Present/Future Studies

I have had my solutions for a long time.
But I do not yet know how I am to arrive at them.

—*Karl Friedrich Gauss*
Mathematician

Introduction

This chapter provides a brief summary of some studies that I have conducted, or in which I have participated. The general purpose of these studies has been to explore various characteristics of UFOErs (UFO experiencers). These studies sometimes are compared with other studies by other researchers.

Master Degree Studies

Over the years, various graduate students have asked me to assist them in serving as instructor for their independent study courses. Sometimes the topics were conventional (e.g., personality theory, counseling theory, hypnotherapy, etc.) and sometimes the topics were unconventional (e.g., past life therapy, UFO experiences, etc.). Usually, the graduate students were enrolled at the University of Wyoming. However, on occasion, the students were enrolled in other programs.

Lorraine Davis. Ms. Davis completed her Master's degree at J.F. Kennedy University, in 1985. She requested and received, from Dr. June Parnell and me, the names and addresses of potential participants. Her study was entitled, "A Comparison of the Near Death Experience and the UFO Experience as Vehicles for Spiritual Evolution." She went beyond the medical, physiological, and psychological aspects of NDEs, as studied by such notable researchers as Raymond Moody, M.D., Ph.D., and Michael Sabom, M.D., et al.

Based on inventories by Kenneth Ring, Ph.D., professor of psychology, University of Connecticut, Ms. Davis compared NDErs and UFOErs on their "religious" and "spiritual" attitudes. She confirmed what others had observed: Both NDErs and UFOErs, as groups, did not rate themselves as showing an increase in their "religious" views (conventional church affiliation or dogmatic beliefs); however, after their experiences, they viewed themselves as increasing their "spiritual" awareness and their connection with the cosmos or universe.

Scott Flor. Mr. Flor conducted a study of UFOErs, including some participants at the 1988 Rocky Mountain Conference on UFO Investigations. He hypothesized that UFOErs were more likely to demonstrate psychical awareness than non-UFOErs. Those of us who participated in the study were asked to "guess," or intuit, the location of concealed targets: Behind which squares were there hidden images of UFOs?

The difficulty in the methodology, in my opinion, was that an experimental mode was used for what might be an experiential process. (Someday, I hope, UFOErs and experimenters can cooperate—as have persons like Uri Geller; Ingo Swann; Hal Puthoff, Ph.D.; and Russell Targ—in order to incorporate the "personal" as well as "professional" aspects of experimental protocol.)[1] The results of Scott Flor's study were at the "chance" level of probability.

Other Studies

Ken Ring, Ph.D. Dr. Ring came to the Rocky Mountain Conference on UFO Investigations in order to invite interested attendees to participate in his study, "The Omega Project." (I admire Ken because he demonstrates so many of the values that characterize the ideal scientist: courage, curiosity, and compassion—with true humility in his willingness to participate emotionally with UFOErs. Like so many good folk, including Rich Boylan, Ph.D.; Edith Fiore, Ph.D.; Richard F. Haines, Ph.D.; Jim Harder, Ph.D.; Linda Moulton Howe; C.B. "Scott" Jones, Ph.D.; Jim and Coral Lorenzen (both deceased); John Mack, M.D.; Frank Salisbury, Ph.D.; Bert Schwarz, M.D.; Michael Swords, Ph.D.; et al., Ken has a deep commitment to seek "scientific" truth, but he also is willing to listen to others who express their "personal" truth.)

Ken's book, *The Omega Project*, is a model presentation of a complex study so that the general reader can grasp the statistical results of his comparison of NDErs and UFOErs on a variety of inventories.

---

1. Someday, perhaps, UFOErs and UFO researchers can cooperate—as have persons like Uri Geller, Ingo Swann, Keith Harary, Ph.D., Hal Puthoff, Ph.D., Russell Targ and others, in order to merge both "personal" and "professional" aspects of experimental procedures for remote viewing and other parapsychological studies.

I was pleased to note that some attendees at our Laramie Conference were willing to modify their views about "cold" and "uncaring" scientists after they had the opportunity of becoming acquainted with Professor Ring. They saw him as a person who was rigorous in his methodology design, but friendly in his interpersonal style and seeking a meaningful context for studying the characteristics of NDErs and UFOErs.

The study by Ring and Rosing (1990), in the *Journal of UFO Studies* (JUFOS), is among the few empirical studies of the personality characteristics of UFO abductees/contactees. Other studies or surveys include: Bloecher, Clamar, and Hopkins (1985); Bartholomew, Basterfield, and Howard (1981); Ballard (1987); Fiore (1989); Hopkins (1981,1988); Jacobs (1992); Parnell (1987); Parnell and Sprinkle (1990); Rodeghier, Goodpaster, and Blatterbauer (1991). In my opinion, the study by Parnell (1987), and by Bloecher, Clamar, and Hopkins (1985), establish the observation that most UFO experiencers are "normal" in their responses to personality inventories and psychological assessment procedures.

Further, the results of these studies are supported by the results from two excellent studies by Ring and Rosing (1990) (R&R); and Rodeghier, Goodpaster, and Blatterbauer (1991) (RGB). Another excellent study was conducted by Bartholomew, Basterfield and Howard (1991) (BBH), who concluded that "fantasy-prone personality"—rather than psychopathology—is the best hypothesis for explaining UFOEs.

However, in my opinion, the conclusion of the BBH study was flawed because of the viewpoint that psychic phenomena are not "real." The BBH study is based upon inventories that were developed by Barber and Cherry, who worked with 47 persons, mostly young females; reports of psychic phenomena, spirit visitations, etc., were considered to be "fantasy" experiences.

If one takes the position that, at some level of reality, spirit visitations occur, and ESP phenomena (clairvoyance, telepathy, precognition, and psychokinesis) occur, then persons who report these events might not necessarily be "fantasy-prone" personalities.

In my opinion, the BBH study is a step forward from the conventional opinion that UFOErs are experiencing psychopathological conditions (neurotic or psychotic or crazy). However, the RR and RGB studies go beyond the BBH study in considering the extent of "fantasy" in the responses of participants. Their results do not support the hypothesis that UFOErs are fantasy-prone personalities.

Yet both teams of researchers have somewhat different interpretations of their results. Ring and Rosing suggest the possibility that "abductees" are experiencing alien contacts in the "imaginal" world (midway between our consensual physical reality and the controversial spiritual or psychical reality). Rodeghier et al. imply that UFO abductions are occurring in the consensual reality that we "know" (or claim to know) as the "real world."

Question: Could all three groups of researchers be correct? Could UFO abductions/contacts be occurring at a physical level? At a psychical level? Both levels?

Robert A. Rerecich, Jr. During the 1993 UFO Conference on the Campus of the University of Wyoming, Bob Rerecich invited interested "abductees" to participate in his study. Bob was a graduate student in the department of psychology, University of Idaho, State University, Pocatello, Idaho. (His major advisor was Dr. Jane Harris, who—some years earlier—was a graduate student in the department of psychology at the University of Wyoming. She conducted her doctoral study at the University of Montana with John [Jack] Watkins, Ph.D., who is internationally known for his work with hypnotic phenomena.) Bob found that Ps scored like persons who are "normal" in terms of psychopathology, but are similar to persons who have experienced high levels of stress or "post traumatic stress disorder" (PTSD). Once again, the hypothesis of "fantasy-prone personality" does not seem to account for claims of UFO/ET encounters.[2]

Back to the Future

In 1986, I completed a small study of "future forecasting," based upon the good work of a psychologist, David Loye, Ph.D. Loye[3] developed a brief inventory to assess what he calls the HCP Profile (Hemispheric Consensus Prediction Profile).

Loye learned that both groups of persons, who either are characterized as "left brained" (using analytical and logical processes) or as "right brained" (using intuitive and emotional processes), are successful in predicting possible future events. Further, Loye found that, by pooling results from both groups, their predictions can be even more accurate.

I compared three groups of conference participants: 36 Elder Hostel members (retired persons); 55 UFO investigators (UFO Conference); and 122 counselors and psychologists (ACD: Arizona/Nevada Association for Counseling and Development). The 213 participants were asked to complete the HCP Profile (see Table 9-1) and then to respond to three items:

(1) Will there be a nuclear war before 2000 A.D.?

(2) Will President Reagan be re-elected—or complete his term in office?

(3) Imagine a U.S. (or U.N.) official announcing public contact with UFOLKs while holding a colored plastic clip. What color is the plastic paper clip? Red? White? Blue? Green?

---

2. Rerecich, 1994.
3. Loye, 1978, 1983.

Results of the study indicated that there were no significant differences between the responses of groups on the items about nuclear war and President Ronald Reagan.

However, the UFO Conference participants and the ACD Conference participants, who were characterized as more right-brained in their future forecasting processes, responded differently than the retired persons on the item about possible formal contact with UFOLKS. Approximately 40% (rather than the expected 20-25%) of participants at the UFO Conference and ACD Conference selected the option of a blue plastic paper clip. (Each color was considered to be "encoded" in the mind of the researcher as a time frame of five years: red = 1985 - 1990 A.D.; white = 1990-1995; blue = 1995 - 2000; green = 2000 - 2005.) Thus, if one accepts the methodology and the results, one could speculate that either the right-brained participants were resonating, telepathically, to the mind of the researcher; or else they were sensitive, precognitively, to possible future events about public contact with ETs; or both. Thus, the results could be an indication that some participants are "tuned in" to future events.

However, good left-brained researchers have pointed out some other possible explanations for the results: blue is a very popular color, which may account for the larger number of right-brained participants who selected that color. Also, "red, white, and blue" is a frozen metaphor (e.g., USA flag), which may account for higher percentage of participants who selected the color blue.

If a researcher had the money and the motive, then he/she could conduct a similar study, using other (less popular) colors for embedded codes for the years between 1995 and 2005. Or, we can wait a few years to learn if Leo's study was "lucky" as an indicator that 1999(?) is to be the year that formal contact is announced.[4]

Forward to the Past

In 1989, I presented a paper, "A Comparison of Possible Other Life Impressions from UFOErs and Non-UFOErs," at the Second International Conference on Paranormal Research.[5]

A total of 123 persons had participated in five reincarnation workshops during 1987. The written responses of 59 participants at the UFO Conference (UFOErs) were compared to those of 64 persons (non-UFOErs) who had attended other reincarnation workshops. (See Appendix G.)

4. Or you can read Swann, 1993.
5. Sprinkle, 1989.

The results indicated that there were few differences between the two groups, although UFOErs tended to explore more distant time periods (past and future) than did non-UFOErs.

Psychological Resonance: A Pilot Study of PRIMING Procedures

From January 1985 through June 1986, 250 persons participated in a pilot study of PRIMING Procedures. PRIME is an acronym for Psychological Resonance Impressions of Mutual Experiences.[6]

After completing arrangements for a fee and appointment, each participant sat quietly while I audiotaped my verbal impressions of the person. Afterward, in the "sitting sessions," each participant discussed reactions to the session. (See Appendix H for a copy of the rating form.)

In the "long distance" sessions, the audiotape cassette, with information and evaluation form, was mailed to each participant. With the expert assistance of Dr. Steve Bieber, University of Wyoming, group ratings were analyzed. (See Appendix I: Pilot Study.)

The results showed no significant differences between the groups on the basis of gender, however, the sitting participants rated the items somewhat higher than the long distance group.

The results support the holographic model of mind, and they support the hypothesis that resonance procedures can be used at a distance to share information.

An Experimental Study of PRIMING

As outlined earlier (Chapter 6), an experimental study of PRIMING procedures was conducted with the able assistance of Ted Chapin and Lori Russell. (Now, Dr. Ted Chapin and Dr. Lori Russell-Chapin live in Peoria, Illinois.)

The results of the experimental study were disappointing to me. About half of the 50 Ps were able to identify the videotaped session that was conducted for them; the other half did not.

Our attempt was to obtain "psychic impressions," or a "life reading," of each participant while he or she was sitting elsewhere (in another room in the same building, or at "long-distance" in another town or city). After each session, the videotape was submitted to each participant, along with a videotape of a session with another participant.

The task for each participant was to identify the videotape of "self" rather than the "other" participant.

The results could be summarized as follows: there was no statistical support for the hypothesis that the experimenter (Leo) was able to provide ver-

---

6. Sprinkle, 1985b.

balized impressions that were selected by each participant as "similar" to his or her self characteristics.

However, the interpretation of results was more difficult for me. The "scientist" and "professor" aspects of Leo were accepting of the results: The experimental method had been followed; the results were not significant beyond "chance"; the hypothesized process had not been observed.

Yet, the "therapist" and "counselor" aspects of Leo did not accept the results. I "knew" that the process was observable, because I had worked with hundreds of persons who were satisfied, even pleased, with their audiotapes of "sitting sessions" (SS) or "long-distance" (LD) sessions. Many of those persons had written and/or verbalized their satisfaction with the "life reading" as a significant event in their path of self-understanding and spiritual development.

Were we deluding ourselves? Or was the experimental study conducted in a way that prevented us from obtaining results that were similar to those of the initial field study?

As I reflected on (rationalized?) the findings of the study, I also recognized the possibility of a flaw in the experimental design. Perhaps we eliminated the emotional aspects that were present in the field study, and that provided the psychic connections between experimenter and participants.

Ted and Lori and I were so concerned about sensory and social "leakage" of information from Ps that we placed very tight controls on the information available to me. Right before each videotaped session, I was told that a person was sitting in another room; however, I was not told if the person was male or female. I was distracted by this lack of information, and perhaps I allowed my uncertainty to affect my behaviors.

In the field study, I might not know the participant, but I knew the gender In the field study, I might not know the participant, but I knew the gender and name, or initials, of the person. For example, one psychologist, a professor at another state university, had given me some information about a client who had not responded to traditional psychotherapeutic procedures; indeed, the client's symptoms were difficult to diagnose by the psychologist and his colleagues. When we conducted a "long-distance" (LD) session, I was provided information about the gender and initials of the client. (Thus, it was not likely that I could travel to another state, within a few days, and locate an unknown person who lived in a town other than that of the professor. Even if I could have located and talked with that person, it is not likely that I could learn more about the psychological condition of that person than the other psychologists who knew that person.) Yet, the verbalized impressions of the audiotaped session were viewed, by both client and psychologist, as helpful to them in their work together.

Of course, "coincidence" could be an explanation for results that indicate similarity between self-ratings and ratings of the verbalized impressions.

However, after hundreds of sessions, the process, procedures, and productions must be taken seriously by any fair-minded observer.

Thus, I wondered what would have happened in the experimental study if Leo were told the gender and initials of each participant? Would that information have made a difference in his level of confidence and his ability to "merge" with each participant? If so, would that procedure have provided a richer result in terms of individual scenarios? If so, would that outcome have assisted more participants to identify the videotaped session? Or would an audiotaped session be more helpful—and less distracting—than a videotape of an old bald guy who was waving his hands and talking about possible other lives?

Perhaps, some day, there can be funding for another experimental study.

A Field Study of Life Readings

An eight-year field study was conducted between 1985 and 1992 in order to test the hypothesis that Long Distance sessions would be as effective as Sitting Sessions by participants in psychological resonance procedures. (See Appendix I.)

Over the years, more and more participants described these sessions as a "life reading," á la Edgar Cayce. Now that I am in private practice, and more concerned about my clients than my colleagues, I also call these sessions Life Readings.

After these sessions, each participant was given an evaluation form, with a stamped return envelope, and asked to complete and return the form, with any comment about the Life Reading. Each session was audiorecorded and the cassette tape was given to the participant. (See Appendix H for copy of the evaluation form.)

Results of the Field Study

Approximately 500 Long Distance and approximately 500 Sitting Session Life Readings were evaluated by more than one thousand participants. Long Distance sessions were rated, in general, as effective as Sitting Sessions.

The majority of participants were satisfied (and many were pleased) with the personal significance of the verbalized impressions and they rated the comments as similar to their self-perceived characteristics and their spiritual development. However, some participants who participated in both SS and LD sessions said that they preferred the Sitting Session so that they could discuss the significance of the verbalized impressions.

Note. In psychical research studies, the term "cold reading" refers to a session in which one person (a psychic or medium or charlatan) provides information to another person (a client or customer or sucker). The information may focus on significant events in the life of the participant; to personal characteristics; and/or to relationships with other persons.

Accuracy of information, as confirmed by the participant, may be attributed to the psychical intuitiveness of the provider and/or spirit guides, or the accuracy may be attributed to the skill of the provider in noting verbal and non-verbal cues, including body language of the participant.

The skeptical investigator may seek methods of minimizing sensory and perceptual cues in the procedures. Many "believers" (positive) accept the hypothesis that some providers can give accurate information; many "believers" (negative) reject the hypothesis that some providers can give accurate information. Those who are "skeptics" are not sure if some providers can give accurate information. (I remain truly skeptical of my own abilities, so I do not think of these sessions as providing "knowledge"; I call these comments "impressions," and allow the participant to evaluate the significance of the comments.)

If the reader is skeptical about these results, then the reader can consider several hypotheses to explain the results. However, we cannot rely on the hypothesis of "coincidence" or "chance"; there are many participants in the study, and the correlation of agreement is very high. We cannot rely on the hypothesis of sensory cues to explain the results; the Long Distance sessions were conducted without the presence of the participants—and without telephone discussion of the session: no dialogue occurred during the sessions, except between Leo as "Self" and Leo as "Participant."

The only hypotheses that seem to be relevant are: (A) Leo is engaged in a hoax and he is falsifying data; (B) participants in these sessions are very gullible and easily persuaded to accept the verbalized impressions as directly related to their self perceptions; (C) the results are indications that, somehow, Leo and Participant are able to merge psychically and to generate verbalized impressions that are perceived by the Participant as similar to his or her self views.

Hypothesis A (Hoax) could be checked by reviewing data sheets (evaluation forms) and checking for signs of tampering by Leo.

Hypothesis B (participants as gullible) is based on a very cynical view of human nature; however, it probably is the best hypothesis for any scoffer to accept.

Hypothesis C (Resonance between Leo and participant) may be difficult to accept by a skeptical reader, but it seems to fit the procedures and the data.

The only other "reasonable" hypothesis is that Leo is being aided with information about participants from spirit guides. I accept this hypothesis; however, I am unable to describe, adequately, this process.

A Field Study of Scientific Opinions of UFOErs

As the reader must know by now, one of my pet peeves is the misuse of the word "scientific," especially if the word is overused by someone who is not investigating phenomena but is criticizing someone else who is investigating. And one of my pet biases is the "fact" (an observation) that UFOErs are experiencing "true" as well as "real" events. Thus, the reader should not be surprised to learn that an attempt has been made to compare the "scientific" opinions of UFOErs and non-UFOErs.[7]

Since 1990, I have been collecting some data from interested persons who respond to background items and two brief survey forms: *Scientific Opinion Survey* (SOS) and *PACTS Survey* (based on the *PACTS Model*, Sprinkle, 1988). (See survey forms in Appendix K.)

Between January, 1990 and June, 1992 (two-and-one-half years), data were collected from nine groups of persons who were attending workshops or conferences in California, Colorado, and Wyoming. (See Appendix L.)

Results of Ratings of "Scientific Opinions." In general, we can interpret the ratings as an indication that UFOErs and non-UFOErs differ in their responses to items about "credible evidence" for various phenomena. (Apparently, credibility—like beauty—is in the eye of the beholder!) Also, UFOErs and non-UFOErs differ in their claims about ESP experiences and UFO encounters, and in their level of personal belief in the concept of reincarnation. These UFOErs, as a group, tend to agree with the statements that there is credible evidence for various phenomena of "new science." For example, in a pilot study of 228 participants, there were 122 UFOErs and 106 non-UFOErs. Among the non-UFOErs, there were 35 (33%) who expressed a belief in reincarnation; among UFOErs, 91 (75%).[8]

PACTS Survey. If participants claimed to be UFOErs, then the instructions requested that they also respond to the *PACTS Survey*. Ratings were tallied for each topic: Preparation; Abduction; Contact; Training; and Service.

The majority of UFOErs indicated that the topics, and related comments, were similar to their own experiences. The results provide some support for the hypothesis that UFOErs perceive themselves as going through an "initiation" or vision quest or shamanic journey, which eventually leads to a mission or duty to serve or assist others.[9]

---

7. Sprinkle, 1993.
8. Sprinkle, 1991b.
9. Special thanks are extended to Sally Marriott, MSPH, *Research Consulting*, Salt Lake City, Utah. Sally and her colleagues were most helpful in their consultation and computer analyses of data from the Life Readings. *Scientific Opinion Survey*, and *PACTS Survey*. Apologies are extended to Sally for not following her excellent suggestions for a detailed and precise report of the findings from these studies.

UFO Researchers who focus primarily on the UFO abduction experience may question whether these other topics are relevant. An interesting study could be conducted on the number of years (and level of maturity?) between "abduction" and "service" for the average UFOEr. When does a UFOEr focus on "abduction" (*being taken away from* Earth) and when does a UFOEr focus on "adduction" (*being taken toward* the Stars)?

UFOErs and New Science. If these results from two small groups of Ps are reliable, then we can consider some interesting implications.[10]

The traditional researcher, of course, could argue that we cannot generalize these findings; in other words, we should not expect that other groups UFOErs would respond in the same way to the SOS and the *PACTS Survey*.

However, for the sake of informed speculation (see Chapters 11 and 12), I am assuming that other UFOErs will tend to score like this group of UFOErs. I am assuming, based on more than 30 years of correspondence with thousands and thousands of persons, that UFOErs usually are in agreement with the outline of "new science": the study of physical sciences, biological sciences, psychosocial sciences, *and* spiritual sciences. (Or, if you like "old reality": the study of Nature, Body, Mind, *and* Soul.)

If further study reveals similar results, then we may be able to establish a "line in the sand" or the "shibboleth" that separates UFOErs from non-UFOErs: UFOErs tend to minimize a belief in a model of science that is merely mechanical and materialistic; UFOErs tend to maximize a belief in a model of science that also includes the study of metaphysics and mysticism.

Conclusion

Various studies of UFOErs have led me to the tentative conclusion that UFO experiences are "forcing" Humankind to emphasize a model of "new science" that not only allows, but also demands, the study of human consciousness and spiritual development. In Chapter 10, we explore various models of human experience for a framework in which we can compare the possible connections of reincarnation and UFO experience

PART THREE: Summary and Conclusions

Since 1961, I have conducted several formal studies of UFO experiencers, and I have participated in some studies of other UFO researchers.

These surveys have provided some information about the personality characteristics of some UFOErs. Further, my "thinking" and evaluation of the results of these studies have provided me with the tentative conclusion that many UFOErs are changing their philosophy of science from a materialistic

---

10. Sprinkle, 1994.

model to a model of science that is both physical and psychical, or based both on materialism and mysticism.

The combination of empirical and experiential evidence from UFOErs, including persons who participate in the Rocky Mountain Conference on UFO Investigation, influenced my perspective that UFOErs not only are involved in individual initiations with ETs, but also are gathering in families, groups, and organizations.

PART FOUR provides my "feeling" about the significance of reincarnation and UFO activity: Humanity is evolving from Planetary Persons to Cosmic Citizens.

PART FOUR

Social Synthesis of Reincarnation and UFO Activity

Who sees not God Everywhere, sees God truly nowhere.

—Ken Wilbur, Eye to Eye

*I did not arrive at my understanding of the fundamental laws
of the universe through my rational mind.*

—Albert Einstein

In Parts One, Two, and Three, I have been describing what I experienced when I was "sensing" UFOEs, "intuiting" POLs, and "thinking" about the results of various studies of persons and their impressions of POLs and UFOEs. Now, in Part Four, I have the opportunity to describe my "feelings" about connections of these phenomena. Perhaps the tough-minded, or left-brained, reader may wish to avoid, or discount, these last three chapters as being too "soft", or overly speculative. So be it. However, these chapters represent a personal effort to synthesize, or to merge, the psychological functions of gathering and evaluating information about UFO activity and the process of reincarnation or soul development.

Chapter 10, A Model Chapter, provides a brief description of mental models about "personal", "interpersonal", and "transpersonal" patterns of human behaviors. I like these models as indicators of how we humans learn and how we interact with others around us.

Chapter 11, Some Speculations, provide some tentative guidelines for the psychical analysis of UFO experiences. If the reader is willing to regard the guidelines as a game, then he/she can evaluate or interpret any UFOE as an indication of his or her level of soul development and his/her readiness for ET contact.

Chapter 12, Some Implications, summarizes my views about the meaning and significance of reincarnation and UFO activity, not only in terms of personal and interpersonal behaviors, but also within a transpersonal perspective. I argue that—to some degree—we can choose, individually and collectively, what our response shall be to the scary stimulus of UFO activity. These tentative conclusions may be incomplete or wrong, but I hope that they provide some encouragement for the reader to seek some corrective responses or better choices.

A Model Chapter

Introduction

The purpose of this chapter is to present some models of human behaviors. The models are arranged in three general sections: individual, interpersonal, and transpersonal behaviors. However, the alert reader will notice that these models show much overlap between those patterns of behaviors that might be characterized as *individual, interpersonal,* and *transpersonal.*

Also, the discerning reader will recognize—and accept?—the principle that any model may or may not be an accurate description of human nature and human activity. Thus, the reader is cautioned that these models may not be useful. (Usually, in the philosophy of science, a theory is not viewed as "right" or "wrong," "true" or "false," but as "useful" or "not useful" for further exploration.)

Further, if a model is viewed as useful for further exploration, then the reader should be aware than merely adopting, or endorsing, the model, does not guarantee further personal or spiritual development: that knowledge and growth comes from within the Self. (The Kingdom of Heaven is within.—Jesus of Nazareth)

However, within these limitations, I hope that the general reader may find something of value within this chapter of many models.

Some Models of Individual Human Behavior

Individual Mental Health: I like myself as I am, but I am dissatisfied with my achievement (self-esteem *plus* self motivation).

Individual Psychological Functions: Carl Gustave Jung, M.D., Swiss psychoanalyst and colleague of Alfred Adler, M.D., and Sigmund Freud, M.D., developed a model of four psychological functions: sensing, intuiting, thinking, and feeling. (See Prologue.)

Self-Reinforcement of Behaviors. David Premack, Ph.D., experimental psychologist, developed a model of positive reinforcement, concluded: "Reinforcement results when a Response of a lower independent rate coincides, within temporal limits, with the stimuli governing the occurrence of a Response of a higher independent rate."[1] (See Appendix M: Some Models of Human Behavior.)

Another way of stating the Premack Principle is: any response (A) can reinforce any other response (B), provided that A is more likely to occur than B, and provided that B is made contingent upon the occurrence of A. (Honestly, folks, that's the way some psychologists talk!) And what does that sentence mean, in everyday language? It means, "If…, then…!"

Everyone knows the *if/then* contingency: If I sweep the floor, then I can drink a glass of orange juice. If I finish my piano lesson, then I can play tennis. If I complete my college degree, then I can get a job. Etc. In other words, if B occurs, then A can occur, so that B is reinforced and, thus, occurs more often.

Dr. Premack, when he was at the University of Missouri-Columbia, worked with both human and animal subjects. He learned that he and his students could modify the behavior of monkeys and boys. (Are there many differences?) Monkeys could be taught to turn a knob so that they could open a door and move a lever, or they could move a lever in order to open a door and turn a knob. Boys could be taught to play a pinball machine in order to obtain a candy bar, or, they would eat a candy bar in order to play a pinball machine. The contingency of behaviors was dependent upon the level of occurrence of each behavior.

Contingency Management. One can manage personal behavioral changes by the use of self-contingencies, i.e., the use of "covert operants." (A covert operant refers to a "hidden function" or "covered act of learning." In much of adult human behavior, there are little self-statements that are quietly spoken or silently repeated to oneself.) Homme[2] suggested that these self statements can be reinforced by use of the Premack Principle, e.g., "I can learn to control my anxiety…," reinforced by a deep breath.

---

1. Premack, 1959, p. 219.
2. Homme, 1966.

In May 1966, I listened to Dr. Homme, as he presented a paper on the methods of self reinforcement at a meeting of the Rocky Mountain Psychological Association, Albuquerque, New Mexico. The meeting was held in a long narrow room; my friends and I were sitting in the last row, far away from the speaker. At one point in the lecture, Dr. Homme showed his wit with a terrible pun. Some members of the audience laughed; some groaned. One man in front of us was incensed: he leaped to his feet, waved his arm, and yelled, "Don't reinforce him!" I leaned forward and whispered to the man, "You just did!"

Over the years, many of my clients have benefited from the practice of the Premack Principle, using Homme's examples for self reinforcement. Some of my clients have asked the question: "Is this like the power of positive thinking?" I reply, "Yes, but it is more powerful. This is the power of positive thinking *plus* the power of positive reinforcement of that positive thought."

I encourage them (sometimes in the first session) to practice a specific procedure: take a deep breath, hold the breath, mentally repeat a positive self statement (e.g., "I can learn to control my anxiety," "I can learn to like myself," etc.), then exhale, releasing the breath, and thereby reinforcing the further occurrence of the positive self statement. While the client is engaged in repeating the positive self statement, the client is less likely to be engaged in self-pity or self-anger (the two major self-destructive or self-defeating behaviors.)

Self-Defeating Behaviors (SDBs) The activities of self-pity and self-anger are engaged in by most people, at one time or another. However, many clients have become "experts" in self-pity (Why does my God/society/family/ Higher Self wish for me to suffer so?) and/or self-anger (Damn me! I am so stupid/ugly/crazy/useless!). The level and extent of these self statements can be a factor in the level and extent of SDBs in interpersonal or social behaviors, and, thus, a factor in one's level of happiness as well as one's productivity. (See Appendix M)

It is *natural* to experience some self-pity and/or self-anger whenever one commits an error. However, if a person engages in prolonged self-anger, or self-pity, then one's energy is wasted on self-criticism or self-punishment. Thus, in the long run, it is more efficient to engage in positive self-reinforcement (Premack Principle) and use one's energy to move closer to the desired objective and personal goal.

Note: Every golf shot (except a hole-in-one) is an "error." The good golfer adapts to each "error" in such a way that she/he is able to minimize the number and kind of errors. In the same way, the creative person does not deny his or her handicaps or failures, but uses the lessons from life as a means of developing a greater level of self-confidence and a more productive manner of reaching personal goals.

A Model of Human Behaviors: Professor Gordon Allport provided three models of "man" or human beings: reactive being, reactive being in depth, being-in-the-process-of-becoming.[3] At the time, his article was an advance over the conflict between behavioral and psychoanalytic models of human nature. Now, of course, the controversy can be expanded to another level.

Four Psychological Models of Human Beings

1. Humans seen as beings in spiritual emergence: wholism, psychicly complete, spiritually enlightened, "transpersonal psychology."

2. Humans seen as beings in-the-process of becoming: holism, orthopsychology, personalistics, "existential psychology."

3. Humans seen as reactive beings in depth: psychoanalysis, psychodynamics, "depth psychology."

4. Humans seen as reactive beings: natural positivism, behaviorism, operationalism, physicalism, "scientific psychology."

These four models of human behaviors can be compared to the ancient model of human reality: nature, body, mind, soul.

Interpersonal Models of Human Behaviors

Timothy Leary, Ph.D., provided a model of interpersonal behavior that is based upon two dimensions: self attitude and attitude toward others.[4] (See Appendix M.)

The model indicates that anyone can perceive oneself as "dominant" or "submissive" (self attitude), and one can perceive other persons as "friendly" or "hostile" (attitude toward others). Further, the model indicates that one can predict the patterns of behavior that can occur in various interpersonal interactions. Thus, if one chooses, one can "control" the patterns of behaviors that occur in interpersonal situations. The model indicates that "dominant" behaviors by one person tend to pull more "submissive" behaviors from another person. Further, "friendly" behavior by one person tends to pull more "friendly" behavior from the other person; "hostile" behavior from one person tends to pull "hostile" behavior from another person.

Thus, if I exhibit "submissive/friendly" behaviors, then I am more likely to pull "dominant/friendly" behaviors from another person. If I exhibit "dominant/friendly" behaviors, then I am more likely to pull "submissive/friendly" behaviors from another person. If I exhibit "dominant/hostile" behaviors, then I am more likely to pull "submissive/hostile" behaviors from another person. If I exhibit "submissive/hostile" behaviors, then I am more likely to

---

3. Allport, 1962.
4. Adams, 1964.

obtain "dominant/hostile" behaviors from another person. (See Appendix M for a similar model by Dreikurs.)

Of course, in any interpersonal interaction, the other person may have a preferred mode of behavior; the person may or may not respond to my manipulations or my pattern of interpersonal interactions. (As psychiatrist Harry Stack Sullivan, M.D., stated: "Nothing makes life difficult except other people and one's own inadequacies for dealing with them.")

A Model of Suffering

If the reader does not enjoy the *game* of human life, and regards human existence as nothing but suffering, then a model of suffering may be more appropriate. (See Figure 2) This model is based upon the notion that suffering can occur at several levels: *natural, normal, neurotic,* and *creative* suffering.

Soul — Creative Suffering (Anguish of the Soul)

Mind — Neurotic Suffering (Misery of the Mind)

Body — Normal Suffering (Pain of the Body)

Nature — Natural Suffering (Hardships in Nature)

FIGURE 2. *A Model of Suffering*

The model of suffering is based upon a model of reality (or evolution) that includes four levels of consciousness (or evolution of consciousness). The model combines the concepts of several writers.[5]

Soul	Intuiting	Spirit	Spiritual Evolution
Mind	Thinking	Thought	Psycho Social Evolution
Body	Feeling	Life	Biological Evolution
Nature	Sensing	Matter	Physical Evolution
Ancient Model	Jung	Teilhard	Huxley

FIGURE 3. *A Model of Reality and Evolution*

Willis Harman, Ph.D., the late president of the Institute of Noetic Sciences, presented a model of science and reality. He described science as a four-level enterprise: physical sciences, life sciences, human sciences, and transpersonal sciences.[6]

5. Huxley, 1953; Jung, 1933; Teilhard de Chardin, 1961; Sprinkle, 1985b.
6. Harman, 1988.

In my opinion, Harman and other "new science" writers have provided a basis for maintaining the "old science" philosophies of rationalism and empiricism, while paving the way for the next stage: experiential science.

Some Models of Transpersonal Behaviors

There are many models of transpersonal (religious and spiritual) behaviors. I am unable to understand many of the models, and there are many religious traditions with which I am only vaguely familiar. Thus, this section is only a sketch of several transpersonal models.

Some sources that have influenced my views and philosophy are these: *The Holy Bible* (Judaic Old Testament and Christian New Testament), *The Book of Urantia*[7]; *OAHSPE*[8]; *The Keys of Enoch*[9] by Dr. Jim Hurtak, and various interpretations of the teachings of ancient Sumeria, Lemuria, Atlantis, Egypt, Greece, etc. For example, Zecharia Sitchin's books, about the relations of humans and gods, are most instructive.

Also, I have been influenced in my views of religious traditions by Head and Cranston, and other writers, who have argued that every major religion, and every major culture, has presented some view about the concept of reincarnation.

Reincarnation. The question about the reality—or nonreality—of reincarnation is much too large for me to answer.[10] However in my view, a wise and efficient God (He? She? They?) would make use of souls, over and over, so that the individual lessons learned in one life could be effectively applied in another lifetime. According to this interpretation of reincarnation, "justice" could be sought "within" the soul rather than imposed from "without" the soul. This philosophy would support the notion of compassion (freedom of choice) as well as the notion of efficiency—in the long run, that is!

Thus, the ethics of reincarnation, as well as the efficiency of reincarnation, could be two important factors in any argument about the Grand Plan of the universe.

Another argument in favor of reincarnation is that the recycling of souls also could be conducted for the purpose of extending consciousness to "higher," or "wider," levels of cosmic activities. For example, if souls continuously recycle, their efforts could be used to further the evolutionary process at several levels: physical, biological, psychosocial, and spiritual. This model indicates that the goal of God, or Creation, is one of "becoming"—a model of a universe that is not static but dynamic. (In other words, rather than claim

---

7. *Book of Urantia, 1955.*
8. Newbrough, 1882.
9. Hurtak, 1977.
10. The reader is referred to Part Two for commentary about the experiences that have led me to accept the concept, in some form, that the soul returns, again and again, to the physical plane in a biological body for psychosocial tasks on a spiritual journey.

that "God is dead," or claim that "God is omnipotent," one could argue that "God is growing—and I helped!")

Many current cosmologists argue for a Big Bang theory about the origins of the known universe. They may be correct. Certainly, I recognize the limitations of my intellect when I try to read their writings. Yet, I wonder if they are correct, or if the ancient traditions are more accurate?

Ancient traditions describe the "breath of Brahma" (the Creator breathing in and breathing out) as cycles of expansion and contraction of the universe. Is it possible that the Big Bang observations are merely views of one segment of much larger cycles of creation and consciousness?

A Day of Creation. Paramahansa Yogananda, a yogi of great intellectual and psychic powers, described his view of astrology: "Its message is a prod to pride; the very heavens seek to arouse man's determination to be free from every limitation."[11] He went on to describe the calculations of his teacher, or guru, Sri Yukteswar, in regard to the Ascending Arc and the Descending Arc, each of 12,000 years: "The 3600-year period of *Treta Yuga* will start in A.D. 4100; the age will be marked by common knowledge of telepathic communications and other time-annihilators."[12]

If the traditions are correct, then we have a long road behind us and a long road ahead of us, cycle after cycle, not only for our individual souls, but also for the collective souls of humanity.

Doubts about Reincarnation. Some of my friends scoff at the notion of reincarnation. They argue, that the belief of "many lives" is too easy; thus, the lazy soul, or amoral person, can coast along, without effort, without concern for the next life, and without concerns about the decisions and deeds of this lifetime.

However, that argument assumes (A) that there is little connection between the conditions and choices of one lifetime and the conditions and choices of another lifetime; and (B) there is only one level of human tasks, rather than several levels of increasingly difficult tasks for the soul.

If it is true that the soul moves from one level to another level of tasks, then the lessons of one lifetime may be connected—and significant—for learning the lessons of another lifetime. Then, "cause and effect" (science, karma) may operate continuously.

In my opinion, the argument that humans experience "extinction" after one lifetime is an argument for an "easy" existence. (Almost anybody can handle one lifetime!) What is more difficult, in my opinion, is a sense of responsibility to oneself, others, humanity, and God, not only in serving well during one lifetime, but serving well in many cycles, many families, and many cultures.

---

11. Yogananda, 1971, p. 173.
12. Yogananda, 1971, p. 193.

How does one learn to maintain coherent personal and interpersonal values when one is living with a family in a society where the family members are regarded by others to be pariahs? Paupers? Predators? Protectors? How does one learn to handle the twin tasks of personal achievement and interpersonal charity?

A Model of Psychic Communication. Gardner Murphy, Ph.D., former president of the American Psychological Association, wrote an excellent book, *Challenge of Psychical Research.*[13] Earlier, he provided a model of psychical communication, in which he discussed the implications of denying, or resisting, one's own intuition. In this model, psychical communications are occurring at all times; however, one's own internal resistance often prevents awareness of those communications.

Thus, his model suggests that, if we wish to listen and hear what other persons are "sending," then we must meditate: be "still," go "inside," and become "aware" of the inner information that is available to our conscious self. Inner resistance to our own information is the barrier, or the difficulty, rather than the other person.

A Model of the Journey of the Soul. In my opinion, the best model of the journey of the soul is the model that has been presented by George Meek.[14]

Meek argues that the purpose of life is continuous mental, emotional, and spiritual growth. The proven path for individual self-development, taken from the teachings of Buddha and Jesus, et al., is as follows: seek first the consciousness of God, the Creator; learn to know your true self; love others; show compassion; radiate kindness; practice patience; share with others; continue to grow mentally; serve others.

Meek's model is similar to that of Edgar Cayce, the "sleeping prophet."[15] Cayce was a mystic who developed the ability to speak in the trance state about the body/mind/soul health of other persons. He provided *health readings*, then *life readings*, for persons who experienced body ailments, emotional conflicts, and/or spiritual concerns. Cayce was a conscientious person, who read the Bible at least once a year. When he began to provide readings to other persons, he was surprised—and experienced guilt—at his expressions of information about former lifetimes. Then, in reading, and re-reading, the Christian teachings, he recognized the purpose of various parables, as well as the significance of the process of reincarnation.

Cayce described a vision (precognitive?) of himself, as a boy, possibly living in Nebraska, on a sea coast, (East or West?) in 2005 A.D.; long-haired

13. Murphy, 1961.
14. Meek, 1980.
15. Cerminara, 1967, p. 226.

scientists, in air ships, traveled with him to the locations where he had lived his former life as Edgar Cayce.

Perhaps, in another decade, some readers will be able to confirm, or disconfirm, the accuracy of that vision about earth changes and about the soul's journey of the man we knew as Edgar Cayce.

A Model of Reincarnation. A model of reincarnation that appeals to me is similar to the model of evolution:

Spiritual—Tasks of Integrating Evolving Civilizations

Psycho-Social—Tasks of Increasing Technical and Ethical Knowledge

Biological—Tasks of Diversifying Levels of Consciousness

Physical—Tasks of Colonizing Planets/Galaxies

FIGURE 4. *A Model of Evolution and Reincarnation*

Thus, the model suggests that we humans are preparing (co-preparing?) ourselves for moving off the Planet Earth and extending our civilization and our consciousness to other civilizations of other planets and galaxies. (Yikes! There goes the neighborhood!) This presumed process may be happening on many planets, in many galaxies, where other intelligent entities are wondering: "Who am I? Why am I here? What is the purpose of life? Where shall I go to find the answers to my questions? I wonder if there are other worlds and other entities out there in the stars? Hmmm! I wonder."

Common or unique? I recall the day when Marilyn gave birth to our first child, Nelson. (The birth of each of our children was very exciting: Eric's cry, which sent a chill of remembrance through me; Matthew's delivery, by a gracious mother and a tolerant physician who allowed the presence of a very nervous father; and Kristen's arrival, like a princess, to provide courtly—and comedic—consultation with the queen mother!)

When Nelson arrived, both Marilyn and I knew that the human birthing process had been happening for thousands and thousands of years. Yet, it was such an exciting event for us that I wished for others to acknowledge the significance of the event! Soon after Marilyn returned from the hospital, we took a short stroll around the campus of Stephens College, Columbia, Missouri. Pushing the baby carriage, I spotted the approach of a fellow professor, who was both left-brained and laconic. I hailed him and proudly announced that Marilyn and I had a new baby! The professor bent over, peered into the carriage, straightened up, and with a deadpan expression, said: "Yep! That's a baby."

I can imagine the attitude of those invisible beings who channel information through humans about the many civilizations and levels of consciousness beyond Planet Earth. During the next few years, as we humans struggle through our transformation, we finally shall become a "new age" of what? Infancy? Childhood? Adolescence? Maturity? Perhaps the invisible beings will smile and offer a tolerant, perhaps indulgent, comment: "Yep! It's another new age." I wonder if this new age will be as good as the previous new age?[16]

Models of UFO Activity

The best model of UFO activity, in my opinion, is that by Dr. James Deardorff. (See Chapter 12 for information about the model.) Another excellent model of UFO activity, in my opinion, is the model by Morris K. Jessup, astronomer and early UFO researcher, who wrote several books on his investigations, including a book on *Flying Saucers and the Bible*.[17] Jessup argued, like Charles Fort and others before him, that humanity is being influenced by extraterrestrial entities.

Shepherds, sheep, and sheep dogs. Jessup argued that UFO activity is an interaction between three groups: Higher Forces, humans, and extraterrestrial entities (ETs):

(Angels/Gods)—Higher Forces Are the Shepherds

(Earthlings)—Humans Are the Sheep

(ETs)—Aliens Are the Sheep Dogs

FIGURE 5. *A Model of Human and ET Interaction*

Jessup argued that interactions are based upon a simple thesis: If we (sheep) follow the Higher Forces (shepherds), then all is well. If we do not, then the aliens (sheep dogs) come after us and nip our heels! And it hurts!

Thus, this model indicates that we humans are influenced by outside forces in either or both of two ways: we are pulled, positively, by the powers of the gods; or we are pushed, negatively, by the actions of the little grays, or clones. The task of the Higher Forces is to "herd," or "harvest," the souls of humanity; the task of the little ETs is to assist the Higher Forces by providing lessons or missions for humans, in order to hasten our evolutionary growth toward the soul harvest.

The model suggests that ETs are not interested, exclusively, in our human environment; there are other planets where they could live. Also, ETs are not

---

16. Sitchin, 1993.
17. Jessup died under mysterious circumstances. Some people said that he died in the act of suicide; others said that he had help from unknown persons who were agents of the U.S. government.

interested exclusively, in the "meat" of our bodies, or the genetics of our race. Obviously, they could grow meat more quickly on cattle, and they could take a few sperm and egg samples—or skin tissue samples—and reproduce whoever they wish to reproduce. Further, the model suggests that ETs are not interested, exclusively, in the "minds" of humans, because robots and computers could be manufactured more efficiently for developing intelligence. Thus, it seems that ETs and Higher Forces are more interested in us humans because of our "souls," or our psychic powers, for communal meditation and social enhancement.

The big question is: Are we being herded and harvested in order to share our souls for expanding human consciousness? Or are we being herded and harvested for expending human consciousness? Are we at the "end" of our human existence, or are we at the "beginning" of another level of human existence?

A Model of ET Entities. A model by Nancy Cooney indicates the possibility that there are many ETs who are being used by Higher Forces (whoever the Heaven they are!) to influence us humans. Ms. Cooney states that her reading of the UFO literature has suggested the thesis that specific UFO entities are associated with specific activities or interactions with UFO experiencers (UFOErs).[18]

If her hypothesis has merit, then we can speculate that various scenarios are being presented to UFOErs for various purposes. (See Figure 10-13.) The big question, if this model accurately describes UFO activity, is: Are these activities, and scenarios, presented to humans for the benefit of the ET entities? UFOErs? Humanity? Or all three?

Activities	Entities
Clinical Observation	Short, Cloaked Entities
Religious Activities	Apparitions, Marian, JC, etc.
War	Robots
Expanded Consciousness	Insectoid (tall, thin)
Other Life Forms	Light Beings
Technology	Gray Skinned
Ecology	Tall Blondes
Philosophy	Old, Bearded Men
Reproduction	Half Humans

FIGURE 6. *A Model of UFO Entities*

18. Sprinkle, 1988b.

There are many, many hypotheses about the significance—and nature—of UFO phenomena. In this section, the bias is on those models that emphasize an educational and transformative evolution of humankind.

The CSETI Model. There are many concepts and observations on the possible purposes of UFO entities and why they mutilate cattle, abduct humans, etc. In my opinion, many of these concepts tend to be static rather than dynamic, reactive rather than proactive.

The work of CSETI is an excellent exception. Initiated by Steven Greer, M.D., the Center for the Study of Extraterrestrial Intelligence provides its members with the opportunity for field experience, and possible interaction with ETs, which is based upon principles of self awareness, diplomacy, and cooperation with various levels of human and ET groups. However, some CSETI members act as if they were guiding ETs to field locations through chanting, flashing lights, and mentally communicating contact coordinates. In my opinion, the ETs also are guiding CSETI members, so that we can assist other persons to prepare for eventual formal contact.

PACTS Model. The *PACTS Model* provides a model of UFO experiences as viewed from the perspective of the UFOEr.[19] Whether the UFOEr views the model as a description of "personal," "interpersonal," or "transpersonal" behaviors may be dependent upon the UFOEr and the level of self awareness; the level of acceptance of the "reality" of UFO experiences; and the level of acknowledgment by the UFOEr that his or her experiences are part of an educational or conditioning program.

If a person is experiencing the levels of preparation and abduction, then he or she probably views these experiences as "personal." If a person experiences contact and training activities, then he or she probably views these experiences as "interpersonal" (especially if family members and friends doubt or scoff at the reality of these experiences). However, once a person completes the training stage, there is no doubt in the mind of the UFOEr that service is "transpersonal" in scope and purpose.

Spiritual—Message: Cosmic Consciousness Conditioning
Psycho-Social—ETs as Messengers to Humankind
Biological—ETs as Biological/Interdimensional Entities
Physical—Space/Time Craft

FIGURE 7. *A Model of UFO Activity*

The model indicates that craft are physical phenomena; ETs are biological entities (when they wish to be); ETs are messengers to humankind; and

---

19. Sprinkle, 1988a.

the spiritual message is CCC: Cosmic Consciousness Conditioning. Further, the model suggests that the tasks of humanity, collectively as well as individually, are to focus, gradually, on each level of activity. First, human interest would be focused on the physical space/time craft and their functions and powers. Second, human interest would be focused on the genetic and sexual aspects of ETs. Third, human interest would be focused on the mental and cultural characteristics of ETs. Fourth, human interest would be focused on the psychic and spiritual aspects of ET communications.

If that interpretation of UFO activity is appropriate, then we could conclude, tentatively, that the human task is half-way completed. In my opinion, the vast majority of humankind is aware of UFOs as physical craft. Further, a majority of humans is aware of ETs as UFO occupants.

However, in my opinion, many of us humans are resistant to our subconscious awareness that ETs are "messengers." And, certainly, most of humankind is resistant to the awareness that changes are necessary within us before we shall be ready to comprehend and acknowledge the ET message! (Hint: UFO activity can be viewed as a *mirror* for human activity!)

Perhaps it is best that most of humankind continues to slumber—at least for a little while longer? Perhaps it is best that a majority of individuals go through the process of "remembering" our UFO connections—before we deal with our ET communications?

Chapter 11 provides the interested reader with a procedure for exploring his or her UFO experiences. Someday, if enough individual persons (critical mass?) accept the notion that our individual UFOEs are significant, then we can anticipate a political recognition that UFO activity requires not only a "personal," but also an "interpersonal," response.

Eventually, I believe, we can anticipate a "transpersonal" perspective for an awareness, acceptance, and acknowledgment of the reality and message of UFO activity.

Some Speculations

We throw our hands before our eyes and cry that it is dark.

Most people are willing to change,
not because they see the light,
but because they feel the heat.

Inquire within.

—*Anonymous*

Introduction

Over the years, many persons expressed their doubts and frustrations in these terms: "Leo! I am tired of all the fear and anger that is being expressed about ET abductions and UFO encounters! Help me to learn about the significance of my encounters so that I can ease my negative reactions and develop more positive steps for personal and spiritual development."

The interested reader is encouraged to play the game of psychical analysis of UFOs.[1] *Exploration*, not necessarily *explanation*, is the goal of the game. The UFOEr determines, in the long run, whether there is some personal significance in the possible explanation of a UFOE. Humankind, in the long run, will determine if there is social significance in a possible explanation of UFO activity.

Psychical Analysis of UFO Experiences

Physical analysis of a UFOE can be conducted by attending to any physical and biological evidence, e.g., metallurgical analysis of a UFO fragment; photographic and radar records of UFO activity; soil samples of UFO landing

---

1. Sprinkle, 1992. The game of psychical analysis of UFOEs has been developed from the observations of many persons, especially John A. Keel; Frank A. Salisbury, Ph.D.; Jacques Vallée, Ph.D.; Dan and Aileen Edwards; Matt Graeber; and Ida M. Kannenberg, 1992. Paula Marlatt was helpful by asking me to formalize the general procedures for analyzing UFO experiences.

traces; medical examinations of abduction body marks, implants, and other physiological conditions of UFOErs; etc. The evidence is perceived to be "external" to the UFOEr.

Psychical analysis of a UFOE can be conducted by attending to any psychological and parapsychological evidence, e.g., personality characteristics of the UFOEr; personal interpretations of the significance of UFOEs; dowsing for subtle energies that are associated with UFO landings and/or ET entities; scrying or channeling information from ETs (extraterrestrial intelligence, UFOLKS, Spirit/Space Beings, time travelers, alien visitors, intruders, interdimensional entities, star persons, angels, aliens, et alia). The evidence is perceived to be "internal" to the UFOEr.

Problem. Most UFOErs are puzzled, and some are traumatized, by their UFOEs. Sometimes, UFOErs attempt to confirm or validate their experiences by comparing their reports with other UFO reports. For example, UFO investigators often are asked questions that are similar to the following: "Has anyone reported a UFO that is shaped like a boomerang?" "Have you heard of UFO abductees who have unexplained scars on the inside of their knees?" "Have you talked with a contactee who channels information from the Ashtar Command?" Etc.

The major difficulty for employing psychical analysis is the "morality" of conventional scientists, who fear that being "subjective" is tantamount to being "unscientific." However, if a UFO investigator is willing to confront the inner doubts and the anxieties (emotional resistances) about losing "objectivity," then psychical analysis can be employed to explore the possible personal significance of a UFOE.

Method. There are several methods for psychical analysis of UFOEs, including:

- Individual hypnosis sessions with a hypnotherapist.
- Group support and/or discussions with friends and family members.
- Pendulum technique for exploring subconscious memories of UFO/ET encounters.[2]
- Self-hypnosis and/or dream analysis procedures for exploring memories of UFOEs.[3]
- Channeling information from ETs.[4]
- Intuitive or psychical methods of scrying, dowsing, and/or assessing the significance of UFOEs.

2. Fiore, 1989; Sprinkle, 1976a, 1978/1979.
3. LeCron, 1964.
4. Klimo, 1987.

The most difficult question, in my opinion, is that of personal versus transpersonal significance, or individual versus social meaning of UFOEs: Which aspect of a UFOE is important to the participant and which aspect of a UFOE is important to society?

Factors

There are many factors involved in the psychical analysis of UFOEs, perhaps as many as there are UFOErs. However, basic factors can be grouped under the acronym STARs (Space, Time, Activity, and Ruminations).

Space. Consider the possible significance of the location of the UFOE. If it occurs indoors, then reflect on the size, shape, and possible symbolism of the building or facility; if it occurs outdoors, then consider the terrain, climate, weather conditions, etc. For example, if the UFOE occurs inside a car, or a small room, then the location might represent an "egg" or "fetus," ready for "birth."

Time. Consider the possible significance of the timing of the encounter; contemplate the year, month, week, day, hour, minute of the encounter; consider the seasonal significance (holiday or special event) of the encounter; reflect on the life development (physical, biological, psychosocial, and spiritual growth) of the UFOEr. For example, if the UFOE occurs at night, then the UFOEr may be "in the dark," not yet conscious of the possible significance of the scenario, until he/she "sees the light."

Activity. Consider the possible significance of the UFOEr's life style and concurrent activity; note the activities as occupational or recreational; consider the prevailing conditions of the UFOEr in educational, marital, philosophical, religious, sexual, social, and vocational activities. (Occupational: position or job; vocational: the "calling" or "true work" to which the UFOEr is attracted.) For example, if the UFOEr is engaged in her/his "regular duties," then the UFOE might represent the task of integrating the significance of the UFOE into "everyday" philosophy of life-style.

Ruminations. Consider the possible significance of the mood of the UFOEr: emotional and spiritual mood, including feelings, thoughts, and attitudes about self and others; optimism and/or pessimism about self, others, humankind, planet, universe; and any altruism or desire to assist and heal humankind and the planet. For example, if the UFOEr has (consciously or subconsciously) been wishing to be of service to God or to society, then he/she may be "volunteering" for an encounter, for a mission to assist in the merger of "science" and "spirituality", or for contacts between humankind and ET civilizations.

Analysis

With the various factors of STARs as "backstage," or background, now consider the "front stage," or foreground, of the UFOE.

Assume that the unusual *light* or *object* is representative of the soul or inner self of the UFOEr. If there are several lights or objects, then consider the lights or objects as representative of significant others.

Assume (or pretend!) that the UFOE is both "real" and "true." In other words, consider the possibility that the UFO(s) is a physically solid object, which is showing the UFOEr an important aspect of the inner self: an encounter with one's own soul, a dramatic display that portrays the UFOEr's inner world.

Using the techniques of psychological analysis of Earliest Recollection[5] and the techniques of dream report analysis[6] continue to explore the possible connections and mental associations of self and other within the scenario(s) of the UFO encounter(s). Consider the possibility that the UFOE is an externalized version of internal patters of self.

Analysis can be continued along these lines:

A. Using the visual field as an internal "map," note the directions, movements, speeds, disappearances, reappearances, and other activities of the object(s).

B. Note the stated (and inferred?) feelings and emotions of the UFOEr about the initial appearance, actions, changes, shapes and eventual disappearance of the object(s). If the UFO is reported as a "light," then consider the brightness of the UFO as a possible indication of the brilliance or the enlightenment of the soul or higher self.

C. Contemplate the UFOE, and any pre and post events, as a guide to past, present, and future development, as well as an indication of the "direction" in which the life of the UFOEr is moving. (Ancient Chinese proverb: If we do not change our direction, then we may end up in the very place that we are headed!)

D. View the UFOE as an educational guide, not only for self discovery, but also as a communication with the higher self and/or spirit guides. If the UFOE includes ETs or UFO entities, then view the entities as players or actors for the various scenarios.[7]

E. Compare the UFOE with the model of UFO abductions by Bullard: Capture; Examination; Conference; Tour; Journey; Theophany (manifestation of a deity); Return; and Aftermath of the abduction experience.[8]

---

5. Adler, 1958.
6. Hall, 1966.
7. Cooney, 1990.
8. Bullard, 1987.

F. Consider the relevance of possible past-life memories and possible future life dreams.

G. If the reader is confused by these various guidelines, then consider this possibility: Imagine that the UFOEr is located in a huge experimental laboratory for the exploration of ESP or psychic phenomena. Imagine that the experimenter is some Wizard of Odds (ET); imagine that the UFOEr is the participant or co-researcher in the experiment. Then, imagine that the goal of the experiment is to stimulate the UFOEr to reflect on her/his physical, biological, psychosocial, and spiritual levels of soul development. After the initial shock of "seeing" one's level of soul development (Yikes!), the UFOEr—eventually—can be educated for future space/time travel and for communication with other intelligent beings throughout the galaxy. (Shall we assume that the program is similar to a drivers' education course for cosmic citizens?)

H. Remember the ancient aphorism: if you seek enlightenment, then lighten up! Spiritual development is hard work. It involves many lifetimes, so the task is to relax and learn many lessons of love!

Some Case Examples

If the reader has accepted (or tolerated) these assumptions and guidelines, then she/he can explore the use of these guidelines by applying them to "simple" UFOEs. These guidelines should not be used to evaluate the possible significance of a UFOE—except by the UFOEr.

Most experts of dream-report analysis agree that the best interpreter of a dream is the dreamer. Likewise, the best interpreter of a UFOE is the UFOEr. However, a UFO investigator can be of assistance to a UFOEr in exploring the possible significance of the UFO report.

Here are several case examples that briefly describe the personal evaluations of UFOErs. In each case, I followed similar methods. First, I listened carefully to the UFOEr, not only to the content of the report but also to the manner and mood of the participant. Second, we discussed the apparent physical (or "real") aspects of the UFOE, including the doubts and anxieties about the reality of the UFOE. Third, the participant and I explored the apparent psychical (or "true) aspects of the UFOE. Finally, we mentally "merged," or we combined our mental activities in discussing and proposing some possible interpretations of the personal meaning—to the UFOEr—of the encounter.

Father and Son. A man and his middle-school son reported the family experience, some years earlier, of their sighting of several nocturnal lights that appeared over a Wyoming mountain, near their hometown. After several "up and down" movements, the lights rose quickly and sped away in a southeast direction. Then, as we discussed the possible personal significance of the observations, both father and son recognized the possibility that the four (or five?) lights could represent the financial "ups and downs" of the family, which led to their decision to move the four family members (later, five, with the addition of another child) to the southeastern United States where their situation, economically, "rose quickly." Now, they have relocated in Wyoming, where they feel good about their family situation; also, they were pleased about their courage in reporting their UFO sighting.

Mother and Children. A businesswoman, with university training in biological sciences, described her nighttime UFO observation: She was riding in a car, which was driven by her husband, who is a professional person with training as an attorney. She tried to direct his attention to some bright lights that seemed to be pacing their car as they traveled south from Wyoming to Colorado. However, her husband was unable to see the lights before they disappeared from her view. She described the lights as one large, glowing, round light, followed by three smaller lights.

As we conferred, we moved from a sensory description of the sighting to a perceptual analysis of the possible significance of the experience. However, she was unable to arrive at any satisfactory interpretation of the personal meaning of that event. Then, several years later, the woman telephoned and declared, in a rather flat and resigned tone of voice: "Leo, I now know the meaning of that UFO sighting. I have divorced my husband, and I'm moving to Colorado with my three children." She interpreted the sighting as a precognitive display of future events: the divorce, and her relocation of self and three significant others.

College Student. In a small group discussion, a young woman volunteered information about her own UFO experience, and then she agreed to play the "game" of analyzing the possible significance of the UFOE. I pretended to be the college student; then, I retold her story, somewhat as follows:

> I am a seventh-grade pupil, riding in a car that is being driven by my seventh grade music teacher. The teacher's infant son and her dog are in the back seat of the car. As we drive north and east over the prairie toward the Wyoming/South Dakota border, we notice a bright light in the night sky. As the car gets closer to the light, we notice that the lights seem to become bigger and more intense. Finally, as the car is underneath the light, the teacher stops the car. We get out; we look up at the huge, brilliant light; there is no sound; I'm excited and scared; the baby is crying; the dog is barking; we are afraid; we get back into the car; she speeds away, but the light pursues us! At last, the light goes away as we drive into the city of Hot Springs, SD.

I then interpreted—tentatively—the UFOE as a "map" of the future; and I suggested that, someday, "I" (as the seventh grade pupil) would go to a place of "great light" or great knowledge, like the University of Wyoming! (She smiled, as if to indulge my bit of humor.) Then, I continued, not only would this light or knowledge be exciting and scary, but also this knowledge would pursue me! Finally, in ending the possible interpretive comments, I asked her to help me by discussing her mental associations with the name "Hot Springs." Did she think of the name in association with Native Americans? Or with healing procedures? Suddenly, a puzzled look appeared on her face; then she gasped, "Oh! Do you know what I've been thinking recently? I've been thinking that I should change my major (field of study) to music therapy so that I can go out and help American Indian kids!"

She recognized the possibility that the UFOE was a significant scenario for her professional plans, as well as for her current academic activities.

Colorado Housewife. A middle-aged woman (who was among those who urged Ruth Montgomery to write her 1985 book, *Aliens Among Us*) talked openly about her UFO encounters to her family and friends. She became interested in the (taboo) topics of ESP and reincarnation. She puzzled about the daytime scenario, recalled during our hypnosis session, in which she walked from her car, climbed through a barbed wire fence, entered a landed space craft, and was subjected to a "medical examination." Lying on a table and surrounded by several figures who wore surgical masks and gowns, she cried out in pain and anger as the "surgeon" jerked her body. Later, in another session, impressions were gained that indicated a possible past life in which the soul of the woman was in the body of a male surgeon. The male surgeon was rough and he "jerked around" his patients. The farmwife, who now is a strong but compassionate person, recognized the possibility that the UFO scenario not only was physically "real" but also a quick karmic lesson: "Be careful how you treat other persons. In another lifetime, you may receive the same treatment." She interpreted the UFOE as a reminder for herself, as well as a lesson for others who might accept her report, that there is both physical and spiritual significance in UFO activity.

Young White Man. A young Caucasian male, a student at the University of Wyoming, asked to talk with me about a puzzling array of symptoms, e.g., "loss of time," unusual dreams, a compulsion to read about science and religion, an obsession with UFO reports, etc. I suggested to him the possibility that he was a UFO contactee, but he denied any UFO sightings. I smiled and discussed with him the possibility that he may have repressed or forgotten any memory of a UFO encounter. He replied that he had his doubts, but he was willing to explore his subconscious memories for any earlier encounters.

We conducted relaxation procedures and I gave suggestions for him to explore memories of his adolescent and childhood experiences. I was puzzled when he reported no impressions of childhood or infant encounters.

Then, I asked him about his attitude toward reincarnation. He shrugged his shoulders and said, "Oh, I suppose that it's a possibility." He was willing to explore POLs, and I suggested that he explore any POL that may be connected to his interest in UFO activity. Then, when he relaxed deeply, he described himself as a young male, a Native American, who was hiding in some bushes and watching a huge object slowly descending toward the Earth. He reacted with strong emotions as he described the bright lights and the hovering object. Then, he described an opening in the object, and a feeling of compulsion to enter the object. He sat inside, talking to a strange little man who said to him, "You won't remember this event until another lifetime when you will be a white man."

The young man grimaced, twisting in my office chair, while he gasped, "White man! Who wants to be a white man?" (It's a dirty job, but somebody has to do it!)

As we discussed his reactions to the session, we each recognized our skepticism about the other participant in the interaction! However, each of us was aware of the strong feeling that the memory was "true."

Idaho Woman. A woman from Idaho (a friend of Ann Canary Brooke) described her conscious memories of her UFO sightings, and her concern about a scar on her shoulder. Her grown daughter, during a sunbathing session, had asked her about the strange scar. When the woman talked with her family physician, a dermatologist, he was surprised and puzzled about the scar. It was a small circle, about 3/8" in diameter, with lines like spokes of a wheel.[9]

During individual hypnosis sessions, each woman described a similar UFO encounter when the daughter was a child. Also, the mother described an abduction from her apartment by a strange entity who took her to some nearby woods. They were in a strange "building." (Later, when the woman investigated that area, she did not locate any building.) The ET took hold of an instrument (like a dentist's drill) and then touched her shoulder. The woman cried out during the session as she seemed to reexperience a painful burning sensation on her shoulder, which she described as the same area where the scar was located.

We agreed to meet later for further exploration; meanwhile, she showed me her personal library, including many books on Jewish culture. Although the woman professed a belief in traditional Christian teachings, she described her deep interest in Judaic traditions.

Later, in Laramie, she and a friend visited my office so that we could explore further her memories of the ET abduction and examination. When she expressed puzzlement about her obsession with Jewish culture, I suggested that she recall the significant event that she associated with her interest. She groaned, gasped, and almost fell out of the chair; she described with great

---

9. See the article about "Rachael Jones," 1977, *APRO Bulletin*, November, 26, No. 5.

anguish a scenario that was reprehensible to her. She viewed herself as a teen-aged German lad, in a Nazi uniform, with rifle, who was herding branded Jews into cattle cars for shipment to a concentration camp. There was no doubt in her mind, afterward, that the scar was a reminder to her of her involvement in those activities. She accepted her interest in UFOs, and in education, as a means by which she could assist others to develop more compassion for each individual person, as well as for humankind.

Denver Psychotherapist. A professional hypnotherapist, Mary Brinkopf, sought hypnotherapeutic sessions to explore her memories of an encounter with alien entities. She had served, for several years, as a chan-neler of ET communication; however, she puzzled about a strange episode that occurred in April, 1991. She awoke with pain over her right eye; she examined her eyebrow in a mirror and noticed two puncture marks, like an insect bite. Within two days, her face was very swollen and very painful. When she removed a small object from that area, the swelling subsided. She preserved the object, and she hopes that a physical scientist can determine if it is "unusual"—or, as she suspects, if it will be viewed as non-evidence of her ET contact. Her memory is that she was beamed aboard a space craft by unseen, but friendly, entities. She felt herself on a table, looking up at the entities who surgically cut a spot on her right eyebrow and then inserted the small object into the cut.

During the hypnosis session, January 13, 1992, Mary and I "merged" psy-chically, and we channeled information about her POLs. One scenario indi-cated a lifetime as a priestess in Ancient Egypt, when she served as a "seer" and prophet of future events, but her work was threatened by the sting of a large insect over her right eye.

Mary does not know if the scenario is "true," in the sense of whether she served as a priestess in Ancient Egypt during a past life, but she knows that in this lifetime, she "always" had experienced a deep fear of insect bites—as well as the recent anxiety that the facial swelling might threaten her work as a channeler of ET communication. Now, she expresses a greater confidence in herself and in her work. She views the event as a "test." She now perceives herself as more "right" (right eye) in what she "sees." I commend Mary Brinkopf for her courage in exploring her subconscious memories, and I appreciate her permission to use her name.

Discussion

This model of psychical analysis of UFOEs is presented as a "game," and as an approach for individual UFOErs to learn more about the possible per-sonal significance of their UFO encounters.

Obviously, this approach will not be satisfying to (or utilized by?) those UFO investigators who only are "nuts and bolts" in their approach. Perhaps this approach will be rejected by those persons who are convinced that

UFOEs are evil and Satanic, or that ETs are manipulating and controlling humankind for their own devious motives. (One UFOEr, who expressed amazement and fear after his hypnotic session on his "missing time" and abduction experience, asked me, "Leo, do you think that this is war?" I replied, "I don't think so; I think that it is worse." He gasped, "Worse?" "Yes," I said, "I think that it is education!")

Perhaps, during the next few years, we shall continue to explore the possible purposes of UFO activity. Perhaps some of our worst fears (war, rape, slavery, social control, or destruction of body/mind/soul and society and the planet!) will come to pass. Perhaps the MIBs Men in Black[10] will reveal themselves as representatives of sinister civilizations who are engaged in a silent invasion[11] in order to continue their domination and control of humankind, including any genetic engineering program.[12] Maybe so; maybe not. Maybe a UFOE is meant to be a puzzle.[13]

It may be that these various scenarios (environmental and physical games; sexual and biological games; political and psychosocial games; and psychical and spiritual games) are designed to stimulate society for further evolution.[14] Perhaps the purpose of UFO activity is to force us humans to confront ourselves! Perhaps, as Walt Kelly's hero, Pogo, has proclaimed: "We has found the enemy, and the enemy is us!" Perhaps the rash of investigations and stories[15] is a surface indication of what is happening within our collective unconsciousness: mind at large.[16]

Perhaps, someday, we shall know if UFO activity is as old as stories of the Bible.[17] Perhaps we shall learn if UFO activity is "cosmic consciousness conditioning," helping us to evolve from planetary persons to cosmic citizens.

Summary

This chapter is an attempt to establish tentative guidelines for conducting psychical analysis of a UFO experience (UFOE). Both background factors (space, time, activity, and ruminations) of the life-style of a UFO experiences (UFOEr) and foreground factors of the UFOEr's current situation are considered to be important in any interpretation of the personal significance of a UFO encounter.

It is assumed that the UFO, whether a "light" or an "object," represents the inner self or soul of the UFOEr. If there are several lights or objects, then they may represent significant others. By use of dream report analysis, earliest

10. Giannone, 1992.
11. Crystall, 1991.
12. Hopkins, 1981, 1987; Jacobs, 1992a, 1992b.
13. Ring, 1992.
14. Royal and Priest, 1992.
15. Blum, 1995 and Sheldon, 1995.
16. Grosso, 1985.
17. Deardorff, 1992; Sitchin, 1990; and Thompson, 1993.

recollection, and/or meditative techniques, the UFOEr (with assistance from a UFO researcher?) can analyze the UFO "display" as an external or physical manifestation of internal or personal patterns and processes.

Psychical analysis is a "game." Exploration, not necessarily explanation, is the goal of the game. The UFOEr determines, in the long run, whether there is or is not some personal significance in the possible explanations of the UFOE.

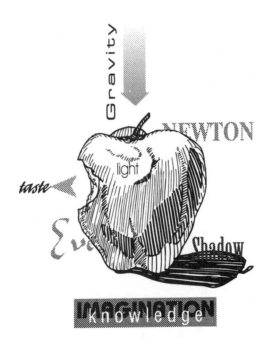

Some Implications

*The plan of the soul is sacrificial service to
the plan of evolution, which, as far as humanity
is concerned, is the spiritualization of matter. Our
task is to spiritualize matter...the path of evolution
is the growing awareness of what the soul is, wants, and
is seeking to express through the man or woman in incarnation.*

—Benjamin Creme
Consciousness, Jan/Feb 1993

Introduction

This chapter concludes Part Four, which provides my "feelings" about these various explorations into reincarnations and UFO activity. The chapter offers both general and specific implications of the journey of the soul as suggested by the stimulus of POLs and UFO experiences.

If these views have some merit, then we have before us a thesis about a possible connection between reincarnation and UFO activity: cosmic consciousness conditioning.[1]

Both physical analysis and psychical analysis of UFO and POL experiences can be conducted in order to test the hypothesis that UFO activity is an educational program for enhancing the evolutionary development of humankind.

Embargo Hypothesis of ET Strategy

The best hypothesis about ET strategy, in my opinion, is that of James W. Deardorff, Ph.D., Professor Emeritus, Atmospheric Sciences, Oregon State University, Corvallis, Oregon. Dr. Deardorff argues that a possible ET strategy for Earth is an embargo on direct communications about their presence.[2]

---

1. Sprinkle, 1976b.
2. Deardorff, 1986.

However, the embargo is *leaky*. (With the name of Sprinkle, I am fascinated with a leaky embargo theory!) Thus, according to the Deardorff hypothesis, some information about UFO/ET phenomena comes through to the general public by means of books, movies, newspapers (and television beer commercials?) However, physical evidence is withheld, in order to minimize any early interest that might be shown by conventional scientists and by conventional governmental officials.

Then, gradually, after the general public becomes aware of the ET presence, more and more evidence is gradually introduced that might become more interesting to the conventional scientist and to the conventional official. In this manner, the dominant culture remains unaware, initially, of the ET presence. (Also, panic is more private and personal, rather than collective and communal.)

Ethics and UFO Activity

If the Deardorff hypothesis is correct, then there are several implications that follow:

First, the ET ethics are of a very high order. Not only do the ETs minimize their initial (renewed?) intervention with humankind, but they also are aware that Earth societies must learn to deal slowly with the ET presence. (If the ET presence has been with humankind "forever," then the task is to renew—gradually—the connection at a level of awareness that is appropriate for us as "modern" humankind.)

Second, the current institutions of Earth societies must be modified in order for humans to learn how to detect and to accept the ET presence.

Third, each individual human must struggle with the challenges and changes that are needed for adapting to the ET presence, whether that person is "pro" or "con" to the hypothesis of extraterrestrial intelligence. (As Deardorff points out, a few "weird" and "wrong" UFO contactees can be "helpful," because their claims minimize the interest of conventional scientists and, thus, the embargo is protected and prolonged.)

Fourth, the process of change must be both efficient and effective. The process must be slow enough to minimize social chaos, but sufficiently suitable for engendering a planetary ethos.

Some beginning UFO investigators (young souls?) often ask the basic question about ETs or SBs (Space Beings or SOBs!): "If they are so smart, then why don't they land and contact me/us/the White House, et al.?"

As a counseling psychologist, I often have heard a similar question from many beginning clients: "If you are so smart/advanced/educated, then why don't you tell me how to run my life?" Of course, if we as parents/teachers/counselors fall into the trap that is proposed by children/pupils/clients, then we soon learn that the arrangements may be somewhat efficient, temporarily, but the method—in the long run—is not effective.

The best method is to serve as a guide, and to encourage the learner to experience errors as well as successes, suffering as well as joy, fear as well as hope, etc. Then, together, both guru and chela, teacher and pupil, parent and child, counselor and client, can face their fears and doubts, angers and hates, and learn how to grow in their trust and love for one another.

Can it be any different with ETs/humankind and their interactions?

Fifth, the movement from a smaller group to a larger organization requires some kind of initiation or rites of passage. Those persons who claim that "gangs" of adolescents are "bad" are wrong, in my opinion. Adolescent development demands "gangs" or groups into which the individual can adapt to social expectations. The task for adults is to encourage organized groups of Scouts and Explorers rather than to allow organized groups of violent armed youth.

Similarly, I believe that UFO activity is serving both as individual initiation and social stimulus, so that Earth governments minimize their tendency to act like armed and lawless gangs, and begin to cooperate as a planetary community.

Individual Initiation in UFOEs

Various writers have described the process of "initiation" that UFOErs suffer or enjoy.[3]

Apparently, the "UFO display" is presented to various individuals in order to puzzle and prod them toward some solution of their own personal UFO mystery. Of course, the individual task is a "mission impossible." Thus, the individual UFOEr must decide—eventually—whether to risk ridicule (or marriage or job) by confiding in other persons about his or her UFOEs and the resulting angers and anxieties, doubts, and fears.

Interpersonal Aspects of UFOEs. Gradually, as more individual UFOErs confide in other persons, then families and friends must decide whether to accept or reject the claims of the UFOErs. The doubts and fears of the UFOErs, thus, may become the doubts and fears of families and friends. Some persons react in a supportive and helpful manner; some react in a manner of denying and rejecting the messenger as well as the message!

Gradually, groups of persons turn to scientists and mental health practitioners for answers to their questions. Some scientists and practitioners are supportive and helpful; some are denying and rejecting of UFOErs as well as their claims. (Indeed, some UFOErs are treated as if they were causing flatulence in the pews of the Cathedral of Science. Some are hushed and punished, like a child who claims to be molested by Uncle ET!)

---

3. Salisbury, 1974; Thompson, 1991; Kannenberg, 1992.

Some UFOErs, because of their intolerance of ambiguity, or their personal philosophy, claim to "know" the true purpose of UFO activity, whether that purpose be good or evil, scientific or theological, military or social, etc. Then, the average person of rationality and good will is puzzled. Because there are so many conflicting claims by various UFOErs, and conflicting conclusions by "experts" (scientists, mental health practitioners, and governmental officials), the general public may become confused and distrustful both of UFOErs and conventional authorities.

Societal Aspects of UFOEs. Eventually, according to this "grassroots" hypothesis, all established institutions are challenged by the implications of the ET presence. (The False Memory Syndrome could be seen as a necessary protection for the larger society to delay increased levels of awareness—not only of childhood memories of human abuse, but also childhood memories of ET encounters.) Thus, economic, educational, military, political, religious, and scientific institutions are challenged and gradually changed so that the human community can accept and adapt to the increased awareness of the ET presence.

National Implications of UFO Activity. My feeling is that political scientists soon will be analyzing the possibility of ET presence as a factor in the ongoing political process. Probably, that analysis will not begin seriously until there is an easing of governmental secrecy about the evidence of UFO activity by military observers.

My wife, Marilyn, tells me that what I believed to be a clever comment had been stated by someone else before I stated it. However, I claim that the idea was "new" to me when I said it. At our June 1992 UFO Conference in Laramie, during a discussion about the implications of UFO secrecy by the U.S. government, one anxious woman raised the question, "What can we do about ending the secrecy?" I responded, "This fall, there will be a national election. If you wish for change, then vote for more female politicians. First, they will clean the House. (The woman gasped at my apparent sexist comment.) Then, they will clean the Senate. (She smiled in appreciation.) Then, they will clean the Oval Office!" (She laughed!)

International Implications of UFO Activity. I have experienced an internal "knowing" for many years that any public announcement about formal contact with ETs would come from U.N. officials. I believe that any solution to the UFO problem is contingent upon international cooperation for study and research, as well as any invitation for public contact with ET representatives. I continue to be impressed by the good work of many individuals and international groups of persons who exchange information about UFO activity.

The United Nations SEAT serves as a forum within the international community in the study of parapsychology and ufology.[4] Perhaps, someday, the armed conflicts between regions of Earth will become ancient history, and then the international community can deal directly with the question about the ET presence: threat or promise?

Sociologists tell us that there are two methods for developing a sense of communal spirit: "Rally around the flag!" Or, "It's us against them!"

Will the U.N. flag be a sufficient symbol to rally the communal spirit of humankind? Or must the ET presence be viewed—temporarily—as a threat to the welfare of the planet? Are there good guys and bad guys among the ET civilizations?[5] If so, does humankind join forces with the good guys in order to defeat the bad guys?

Planetary Implications of UFO Activity

Many UFO contactees receive messages that there are two purposes for UFO activity and ET intervention: to assist in the rejuvenation of planet Earth, and to encourage the continuing evolutionary development of humankind. Of course, some UFOErs have been poor spokespersons for their cause, and some have been criticized for their methods as well as their messages.

However, the questions remain. What if these messages come from ET entities? What if these messages are true? What if UFO activity, and the ET presence, is for the purpose of planetary rejuvenation and human evolution? If so, then, we should anticipate at least two general implications: (A) more and more persons shall become interested in the well-being of Mother Earth; and (B) more and more persons shall become interested in ESP and human potential for evolutionary development.

Thus, we might be puzzled—but not necessarily surprised—that the ET strategy could provide humankind with opportunities for several lessons, minor mysteries that offer some partial pieces to the solution of the UFO puzzle. For example, there are worldwide reports of paranormal phenomena, including Big Foot and other "manimals"; cattle mutilations; crop circles or agriglyphs; earth changes and climate changes; Men In Black; martian monuments; past-life memories; visions of religious figures (Marian apparitions, et al.); and all kinds of silly/serious games: physical and military games; biological and sexual games; psychosocial and governmental games; spiritual and healing games. The spiritual games include mental messages being channeled through UFOErs, apparently from ET entities, offering information about the ABC's of reality (absurd, bizarre, and crazy information!). UFOErs are being bombarded with information about ancient wisdom and future knowledge, including claims about *time* and *space*, *matter* and *light*, the plight of the planet, the evolution of humankind!

---

4. Society for Enlightenment and Transformation; Room S-1755, UNCG; P.O. Box 20; New York, NY, 10017.
5. Andrews, 1993.

These games are bothersome to many persons, especially those without a sense of humor! And these games are especially upsetting to persons who are wedded to a dogmatic view of the universe—whether that viewpoint be a righteously rigid religiosity or a seriously sanctimonious scientism![6]

Religious Implications of UFO Activity

There are many books that in my opinion provide a basis for grasping the religious implications of UFO activity.[7]

In a recent article, Dr. Barry Downing has focused on Exodus as a paradigm for UFO strategy.[8] Earlier, Downing had analyzed historical scenarios of the Old Testament and New Testament that could explain the angels of God as ET representatives, and the "chariots of fire" and "clouds from Heaven" as UFOs or spacecraft.[9] Dr. Richard Thompson compares the modern UFO literature with that of ancient writings about the Vedic traditions, and—surprise?—he finds many similarities.[10]

Dr. Deardorff has provided excellent contributions to the history of Judaic-Christian traditions. These contributions are not yet recognized and appreciated by Biblical scholars, but perhaps the contributions shall be recognized someday. Deardorff has analyzed the translations of an ancient scroll that described the life of Jmmanuel (Jesus of Nazareth). As Deardorff points out, there are many difficulties in accepting the information as evidence about the Christian traditions. However, there are many reasons for viewing the Talmud Jmmanuel as a source for further investigations by biblical scholars.[11]

If there are other copies of the ancient scroll, and if those copies became available in the public domain, then other translations could be conducted. Perhaps someday the claims about the teachings of Jmmanuel can be compared to the claims of traditional Christian doctrines. If the document is an accurate description of the life and teachings of the man from Nazareth, then there are several important implications for humankind, including: (A) there is a continuing relationship between humankind (Earth) and ET representatives (Heaven); (B) the story of Christianity is also a story of UFO activity; (C) the human spirit is developed through the experiences of many lifetimes, or reincarnations![12]

Whether the work of Deardorff shall or shall not point toward a newer version of Christian tradition is a question that can only be answered through future Biblical studies. However, there is no doubt in my mind that

---

6. Pursglove, XXXX.
7. Downing, 1968; Deardorff, 1991; Thompson, 1993.
8. Downing, 1994.
9. Downing, 1968.
10. Thompson, 1993.
11. Deardorff, 1992, 1994.
12. For other implications, see Winters, 1994.

modern UFO activity already has affected, and shall continue to influence, religious institutions and religious authority.[13]

Victoria Alexander recently conducted a survey among 1,000 ministers/ priests/rabbis to obtain their views about the reactions of their congregations to any confirmation of contact with an advanced civilization.[14] On the basis of 23% return (230 surveys), she concluded that these theologians do not feel that their faith and the faith of their congregation would be threatened. There are questions about the methodology and conclusions, but the survey is an interesting example of dealing with the assumed religious impact of public information about UFO/ET contact with humankind.

Astrological Implications

In my opinion, the greatest influence of UFO activity is the slow but certain change in patriarchal institutions and masculine domination. Those readers who are interested in astrology, and who wish to prepare themselves for the changes in the next few years, may wish to review the work of Dan Ward, Ph.D.[15] Dr. Ward is a physicist and astrologer who has presented many interesting papers, including "Initiation, the Descent into Hades," and "Astrology According to the Goddess." Ward presents his analysis of the argument that the assignment of Aries as the rising sign of the zodiac was a patriarchal attempt in the second millennium B.C. to reduce the power and influence of the goddess culture, and to impose a male-god bias upon astrology and society.[16] Ward considers the implications of returning Taurus to the Ascendant in astrological charts, including the balancing of astrological houses and planetary rulerships; the resulting equality between the feminine moon and the masculine sun; the more rational incorporation of the unseen (subconscious) planets; revised interpretations of the meanings of the twelve astrological houses; and the potential for a necessary return of Taurus to the Ascendant.

If Ward[17] is correct in his analysis, then by May 3, 2000 A.D., we shall all be aware of the changes that have led to the "return of the goddess" and the balancing of God and Goddess, patriarchy and matriarchy, masculinity and femininity. (Hint: I believe that the changes are occurring already!)

Scientific Implications of UFO Activity

Every student of the philosophy of science is aware of the principles that empirical investigations, as well as rational thought, are important for scien-

---

13. For an historical interpretation of the effects of human and ET interactions, see Freer, 1987.
14. Alexander, 1994.
15. Dr. Ward is a physicist and astrologer who has written papers on cycles and legends, including "Initiation, the Descent Into Hades." (He also is known as Daniel Nightwolf.)
16. Ward, 1992.
17. Ward, 1992, p. 270.

tific research. We note, with pride, that we modern students of science are not like some students of Aristotle, who accepted (without question?)) that great scientist's claims about various natural phenomena, e.g., the number of legs on insects and spiders. And sometimes they were wrong!

Now, in modern science, we follow "new" evidence—not the authority of "old" scientists—in determining what topics may be studied, which hypotheses and methods should be followed, and which data to interpret for our tentative conclusions about various phenomena.

Or do we?

Thomas Kuhn, along with other philosophers and historians of science, has outlined the pattern of shifts in "normal scientific endeavors." We all are influenced by the Zeitgeist, the spirit of the times, the paradigm or model of science that prevails in each generation of scientists.

During the Middle Ages, the prevailing "scientists" were the Church officials. Their view was that of Rationalism: they "knew" how many planets revolve around the sun. Thus, when Galileo presented them with his telescope, they were confounded. They feared, and rejected, his new empirical methods of observing the "known" universe. Galileo was told to recant his "error" and was placed under house arrest. (He was fortunate in comparison to Bruno, who was burned at the stake for his statements about intelligent life in the Heavens.)

However, more and more observations, by more and more observers, eventually led to a worldview of science that is based upon a combination of rationalism and empiricism. Most young scientists, often males, have been instructed to go out and explore! They are encouraged to seek, through rational and empirical methods, what objective and material truths can be discovered about Mother Nature.

But now, the previously prevailing winds are shifting. Just as the dogmatic Rationalists (the Church officials) were confounded by the empirical methods of Galileo and others, so now the Establishment Empiricists (the academic priests) are confounded by the "new" internal meditations of Experientialists.[18] The work of many scientists, including investigators of transcendental meditation, are demonstrating the individual benefits as well as the social benefits of deep meditation. Experientialists are using meditation like a "microscope": to look within the world of the meditator. They also are using group meditation like a "telescope": to observe the social effects of coherent thought.

Modern Scientists. We modern scientists, like UFO contactees, are facing our own "mission impossible." The dilemma of modern conventional scientists is that the UFO mystery cannot be solved by clinging exclusively to

18. Aron and Aron, 1986; Davenport, 1992; Dossey, 1982, 1989; Harman, 1988; Russell, 1992.

rational and empirical methods. Thus, current conventional scientists must either admit to ignorance (sin! sin! sin!) in resolving the UFO mystery, or (taboo! taboo! taboo!) modify the morality of science from our limited rational and empirical methods to a more expanded approach of rational, empirical, and experiential methods.

In the last five decades, many conventional scientists have attempted to dismiss the UFO message, as well as the messengers—both ETs and human contactees. However, the UFO phenomena continue, and the methods of rationalism and empiricism have not been adequate to resolve the mystery.

In my opinion, the UFO puzzle cannot be solved until experiential sciences are developed and utilized in UFO research. Thus, the current chore of conventional scientists is to consider an "immoral merger": the taboo task of merging rationalism and empiricism within the emerging experiential sciences.

I claim this viewpoint despite my respect for the work of many UFO researchers, e.g., Jerome Clark, who stated, "Ufology ought never to be confused with or, worse, think of itself as a branch of paranormal study."[19]

I share the wish of ufologists that ufology be considered part of science, and I share the wish of parapsychologists that parapsychology be a part of science. However, I do not share the viewpoint that ufologists and parapsychologists should consider themselves as separate from or in competition with other scientists.[20]

Indeed, I hope that ufologists and parapsychologists recognize the opportunity that is being presented: a merger for the benefit of humankind as well as for science. Will the emerging experiential sciences become the focus of the next generation of female/male scientists? If so, will the structure of science resemble the MAPS Model of Sciences? The MAPS Model of Sciences presents some implications and suggestions about possible changes in the methods, approaches, phenomena, and specialists in science. The model suggests an historical shift from rationalism, empiricism, and experientialism, to transtemporal explorations. (See Appendix M)

Peter Russell, in his 1992 book, A White Hole of Time, presents an analysis of the shift of focus in science from space/matter to a focus on time/light. My feeling is very strong that the next generation of scientists shall look back at our pre-space/time travel and spirit communication period as a very provincial and isolated era for science.

Further, I believe that humankind may be developing a readiness for a science that emphasizes the precepts of healing rather than harming, teaching rather than threatening, counseling rather than controlling, and evolving rather than ruling. An integrated model of science/spirit could lead to a view of human nature that is more compassionate than arrogant, more gentle and

19. Clark, Sep/Oct 1993.
20. Sprinkle, 1991a.

generous than angry and violent. Perhaps a balance of science and spirit shall reflect the ancient balance of God and Goddess.

I do not know if the new version of science will reflect the various models of physics and metaphysics.[21] However, my tenuous grasp of Peter Russell's viewpoint and my many hours of listening to UFO contactees, who describe their experiences in "time travel" and dimensional explorations, provide me with a glimpse of possible future directions of the scientific enterprise in the "world of light."

Empirical science has helped us, via the telescope, to look out to the heights of the macrocosm and, via the microscope, to look into the depths of the microcosm. Far out and far in! Now, experiential science is helping us to explore (through group meditation) the collective unconscious, just as we explore (through individual meditation) our individual subconscious.[22]

Perhaps, someday, art and music can rejoin science, along with the renewed partnership of astronomy and astrology.

Implications of "Secret" UFO Information

Many UFO researchers have written and spoken eloquently about the implications of any public announcement of formal contact between humankind and ET civilizations. For example, Stanton Friedman, a nuclear engineer and UFO researcher, has outlined several reasons for Earth governmental officials to maintain secrecy about UFO activity. Friedman includes the interest of officials in learning more about the UFO propulsion systems; the competition between nations in weapons and defense systems; the political problems in the international community; the religious problem; the economic difficulties; and the possibility of psychological panic.[23]

However, my feeling is that the general public already is being prepared for the "shock" of an official announcement about the ET presence.[24]

In my opinion, the major difficulty is not that of *telling* the public what is known about UFO activity. The main difficulty is "talking" about the implications of UFO activity for our collective conscience. Humankind must face many issues of learning how to be ethical and responsible not only for our own growth, but also in our relations with other sentient creatures. We must learn to become cosmic citizens. I wonder: Which politicians are willing to face their voters with a chat about these implications? Ouch!

I doubt that any astute politician would issue an individual public statement. My guess is that international groups will serve as temporary links between individual nations and the United Nations.

---

21. Harman, 1988; Van Flandern, 1993.
22. For an artist's beautiful and awesome visual display of these worlds, see Gray, 1990.
23. Friedman, 1991, pp. 12-60.
24. For example, see Carey, 1991; Essene and Nidle, 1994; Royal and Priest, 1993.

In this scenario, representatives of scientific agencies and "think tanks" could be consulted for their evidence and opinions. Then, gradually, the information about "past" secrets could be released, so that governmental officials could be seen as responsive to public "demands" for an end to secrecy, while maintaining political authority and social stability. Then, gradually, more information could be released.

Within this scenario, governmental officials could be waiting now for more public demonstrations to end the cover-up of UFO evidence. It may well be that the "mission impossible" for governmental officials is to maintain some secrecy on the one hand and, on the other, prepare the public for the inevitable announcement.

Of course, with the many social changes that have occurred recently and the many changes that are occurring now, it may be that the general public already is aware, at the subconscious level, that ET/human contact shall soon be announced. (And, meanwhile, we are angry and anxious about that future announcement!)

Ahh, well, what do I know?

I do know that more and more persons are impatient with the perceived arrogance of scientists and officials. The current difficulties of locating the MARS Observer (Fall, 1993) is another example of the questions that UFO contactees ask about official policy: Was the probe truly lost? Or was there a cover-up by officials, so that the "face" of Mars can be photographed without public awareness of results?

I wonder if the "error" in the Hubble telescope was merely an expensive mistake that is now corrected, or whether the "shortsighted" lenses were a means by which officials and scientists could study, quietly, some other phenomena?[25]

Implications of Reincarnationism

Most of my friends who are UFO researchers are impressed with the social implications of governmental release of UFO information. However, I am more impressed by implications of possible public acceptance of the concept of reincarnation.

If further data were obtained in support of the reincarnation hypothesis, and if the kinds of evidence were considered to be sufficient for scientific and public acceptance, then the implications are more mind-boggling than "aliens among us." Indeed, the implications would not only be mind-boggling, but soul-boggling as well.

Reincarnation and Human Nature. If reincarnation were accepted in some conceptual or theoretical form, as a model of the process of soul devel-

25. For informed speculation about Planet X, see Sitchin, 1990.

opment, then several implications would follow from that belief. First, many of us, especially in the United States, would face the challenge of changing our views about ourselves and others. Our sense of reality, fashioned mainly by sensory and materialistic considerations, might be augmented by our intuitive and emotional considerations.

Second, our views of our human potential would be greatly expanded. Socially and educationally, we might focus not only on physical and biological conditions for enhancing growth, but also on psychosocial and spiritual concerns for growth.

Third, our ethical concerns might expand beyond property and possessions to personhood and potentials. Our attorneys and political scientists might consult as often with theologians and parapsychologists as with physicians and psychiatrists.

Fourth, the specialty of "psychology" might truly become the "study of the soul." (Or will we devise another term for what the ancient Greeks meant by "psyche-ology"?)

Fifth, the quarrels between groups of activists, e.g., the pro-abortionists and anti-abortionist groups, might shift from a focus on the body and mind to a focus on body/mind/soul. Then, for example, interested persons could argue about the best interests of the unborn "baby" as well as the "parents" of the fetus, whether the parents be the biological and/or the social parents of the fetus. We could have many more creative arguments than the current arguments about the tissue issue![26]

Sixth, more arguments could occur between the proponents and opponents to the death penalty for criminal acts. There could be some fascinating discussions about the question of which is more beneficial as a lesson to the soul of a person in a criminal body: public execution or life imprisonment as a community servant?

A minor implication: newspaper and television items about funeral arrangements might reflect the difference between the "body" and the "person." For example, the news item might state that Mr. Jones left the body on January 15; the body will be buried on January 18th.

Seventh, there could be many more arguments about "suicide": When is that act a "crime" against society, and when is the act a "choice" of the person to realign her or his ongoing relationships with the community of souls?

The biggest implication, in my opinion, might be the willingness of scientists and the general public to explore the conditions of spirit attachment and spirit releasement.[27] If the concept of karma (cause) and multiple life-

---

26. Woodhouse, 1996, pp. 404-411, has provided cogent and compassionate comments on the arguments about abortion—from the perspective of reincarnation.
27. Baldwin, 1993; Fiore, 1989; Hickman, 1994.

times were accepted by a majority of humankind, then various changes might occur in the interactions between individuals.

In my opinion, the most significant effect could be a positive one: We might be more kind and more gentle with one another! (After all, if I believe that as I sow, so shall I reap, then it is to my own material and spiritual advantage that I treat others with respect as well as compassion.)

However, I recognize that for some persons there could be a negative change: More conflicts could occur, especially in regard to issues about marriage, family, education, and individual development.

If one becomes one's own spiritual authority (rather than being subject to the authority of Parent/Judge/Pope/God), then what prevents one from choosing suicide, homicide, cheating, lying, etc., as methods to achieve one's current goals? The person who fears chaos could raise the question of "what if?" What if everyone believes that he or she is responsible for his or her own development and refuses to listen to the advice of peer and parents, family and friends?

Of course, the cynical observer could raise the question: So what else is new?

Yes, it is now true that there are many persons who engage in violent or self-destructive behaviors in order to achieve short-range goals. Would a social ethics that included the concept of reincarnation prevent these behaviors? Perhaps not.

However, if the general public, and political leaders specifically, believed in karma, then we might become more tolerant of persons who are considering anti-social or suicidal acts; we might provide formal procedures by which a person could petition for permission to leave the body.

If public officials, and parents, believed that their major task was to educate and nurture those for whom they feel responsible, would they become more competent and more compassionate? Would we, as members of our community, experience less guilt and less self-blame if a citizen decided to leave the body through suicide? Or if an infant "died" from Sudden Infant Death Syndrome? Would we meditate more often and learn to assist the soul to move on to new lessons, or to enter a new body and review the old lessons?

I am unable to answer these and other social questions. However, I do know that the principles of karma and reincarnation are very valuable to me, both personally and professionally. My work with clients is enhanced whenever we focus on the questions of personal values and spiritual options. The persons with whom I participate in soul explorations are able to increase their feelings of efficiency and effectiveness when they accept the principles that they are here in this lifetime, by choice; their relations with family and friends are lessons for self-acceptance and self-forgiveness, as well as opportunities for further growth and service to others.

Most of my clients not only learn to ease their personal fears and doubts, but they also learn to appreciate the sanctity of souls around them. Further, they usually enhance their zest for living when they recognize and accept the "game" of living in the body. It's the opportunity of a lifetime! It is an opportunity to ease the pain of the past (sometimes perceived as anger or depression), to minimize the fear of the future (sometimes perceived as anxiety), and then receive the present: the gift of living in the *now*! It is an opportunity to learn through both suffering and joy, an opportunity for further love and sharing.

Personal Implications. If there are more lifetimes for me to continue Leo's lessons, then I hope that my current lifetime is helpful in several ways:

First, to earn another opportunity to be with Marilyn. What a truly marvelous soul! (And beautiful babe!)

Second, to be associated, somehow, with the souls of our children and our friends. What talented and creative personalities!

Third, to minimize or end my direct association with a few of the repressive and fearful personalities of my former colleagues. If we are associated in another lifetime, perhaps I can learn how to cooperate with them so that they shall be less fearful and less repressive of my own ethical choices to explore taboo topics.

Nevertheless, if there is a future choice between conformity and comfort versus challenge and change, then I plan to choose challenge and change. Perhaps, in a future lifetime, we can learn to forgive ourselves for our petty quarrels; perhaps we can learn to cooperate with others as humankind deals with the task of lifting off the planet, in space/time travel and exploring other planets and other dimensions of reality. If necessary, we may find ourselves— with the rest of humanity—rising up from our bodies while the planet is being destroyed! Yikes!

If that is our prospect, then we may face the task of settling another planet and going through the long process of human evolution again! Ugh!

If that occurs, I wish us well! My hope is that the majority of souls now on the planet Earth are willing to face our angers and fears, learn to deal with them with less violence, then—using our inner resources and assistance from ET civilizations—develop new ways of seeking and reaching our hopes and dreams.

Within the ethics of karma and reincarnation, my hope is that we can learn to modify our old views of human nature, develop a model of science that is rational and empirical and experiential, and establish a world community that is based on self-control and cooperation with others.

Each day, I pray that—with the blessing of God the Creator, and with the help of my spirit guides—I can work with many others to assist in the merger of Heaven and Earth.

Implications for Humankind

The important questions, in my opinion, are the question of "who" is being selected for further cosmic consciousness conditioning (CCC)? And "how" are these souls being selected for further CCC?

There are at least three models or scenarios that might illustrate the results of the reincarnation process and the pressures of UFO activity: the "masculine" or testing model; the "feminine" or nurturing model; and the "integrated self" or self-selecting model.

A. *The Testing Model.* This scenario suggests that individual souls must be tempered and tested, in order to demonstrate merit. If the soul is purified and strengthened through the rites of initiation, including acts of courage and competence, then the soul is judged to be good and is chosen for further development.

B. *The Nurturing Model.* This scenario suggests that the relationships between souls are tested and tempered, in order to demonstrate merit. If souls are tempered and tested, through acts of compassion and cooperation, then families and/or groups of souls are judged to be good and are chosen for further development.

C. *The Self-Selecting Model.* This scenario suggests that both individual souls and groups of souls are tempered and tested, in order to provide opportunities for self-acceptance and service to others. Thus, selection for further development is a process of self-selection, in cooperation with others, so that both individual and group tasks are honored and enhanced.

If we perceive ourselves, as humankind, to be bright and brave, then we could hope that ETs and SBs select us to survive and to go on to the task of "seeding" the next planet. And, within this scenario, the implication follows that those of us who are not so bright, and not so brave, shall not survive. (We would not be "keepers"; we would be thrown back for a couple of thousand years until the next harvest!)

If we perceive ourselves, as humankind, to be compassionate and cooperative, then we could hope that ETs and SBs select all of us to nurture the next generation of humans, whether that generation be located here on this planet, or whether that generation be on a "new" planet.

If we perceive ourselves to be a newly emerging level of humans, then we could select ourselves as "ready" to use our past performance and our future potentials as reasons for further development. Thus, as a somewhat advanced society, we could decide our physical environments, our biological and genetic directions, our psychosocial and political mores, and our spiritual goals. We could decide when we are morally prepared and ethically responsive to the demands of dealing with other civilizations within the "galactic federation" and/or the "ultra-dimensional federation."

It may be that our tasks are all of the above: to prepare ourselves individually and collectively for welcoming and interacting with extraterrestrials and spiritual beings. Thus, in my opinion, it is a bit premature to quarrel among ourselves about "good" and "bad" ETs. Those arguments remind me of the discussions of middle-school pupils about "good" and "bad" teachers. If the discussions are about specific personnel, then those perceptions can change as children become adolescents, and adolescents become adults. If the discussions are about which pupils shall learn and graduate, then the discussions can focus less on the powers of the teachers and more on the potentials of the pupils.

Perhaps, humankind is provided with a variety of individual, group, and social tasks. Perhaps, each of us can choose—within certain limits—which of the these tasks are appropriate for us individually; then, collectively, with assistance of higher forces, we choose the next step for our species.

Doom-and-Gloom Scenarios

If the fate of humankind is to experience a violent destruction of the planet, and a mass extinction of our souls, then we can prepare for that outcome in several ways:

A. Wail and whine about the injustice of the cosmos; then, passively wait for the end of consciousness. (Sigh.)

B. Gnash our teeth and rage about the injustice of the cosmos and aggressively attack those "leaders" around us who, apparently, have failed us. (Arggh!)

C. Celebrate the past and current achievements of humankind; joyfully praise ourselves and others for previous efforts to survive and to raise the level of civilized awareness and behaviors. (Yahoo!)

Conspiracies and Control Scenarios

There are so many current theories about conspiracies by various ET groups and governmental officials that it is difficult to list them, much less analyze them.

Some UFO researchers are convinced that there are "bad guys" (e.g., grays, reptoids, Dracons, Zeta Reticulans, Trilateral Commission, international bankers, and various levels of military and governmental officials— along with Satan, et al.) These alleged conspiracies range from withholding UFO information to mind control, so that humankind is unable to remember our past and unable to develop our potential.

The implication of these themes is that we may never discover and understand the purposes and powers of ETs and SBs, unless the "good guys" rescue us from the "bad guys," or unless we learn to rescue ourselves from these conspiracies and control systems.

The interested reader can obtain current information about UFO theories from *UFO Magazine* and *FSR Review*. (See Appendix O.)

My own bias is to minimize the significance of the doom-and-gloom scenarios, and to minimize the significance of the conspiracies and control systems scenario. I choose to maximize the significance of the human potential scenario. Why? Because it feels better to me, that's why! (Way to go, Leo!)

Further, there is ample evidence that most human cultures have accepted a duality of "gods": good guys and bad guys, e.g., angels and demons, forces of light and forces of darkness, or higher forces and lower forces, et al.

Many prophets and spiritual teachers have been quoted by their followers on the purposes of various levels of gods, e.g., OAHSPE;[28] *The Book of Urantia*[29]; books by Zecharia Sitchin; *Talmud Jmmanuel*[30] and *Celestial Teachings*.[31]

My bias is to accept the view that the human spirit can learn and evolve from various interactions with both good and evil entities, both angels and devils. In my opinion, the human spirit can be strengthened through each of these kinds of interactions. (Christians can recall the story of Jesus in the desert being courted by Satan: Jesus did not turn away from temptation but faced it, and then rejected temptation through informed choice.)

In my opinion, the "educational approach" by ETs, cosmic consciousness conditioning, can account for the apparently inconsistent activities of good/bad guys, as MIBs, ETs, SBs, tricksters and funsters, silly and serious, profane and profound.

I am reminded of a minor event, in 1952, when I was a "draftee" in the U.S. army, Camp Chaffee, Arkansas. Around 2:00 A.M., one dark chilly morning, we were rousted from our cots by several cadre staff members. The were yelling, "Piss call! Piss call!" They herded the drowsy young men toward the latrine. One young farm boy was slow to get out of his cot; the staff member overturned the bunk bed, and yelled again, "Piss call!" The young man, lying on the floor, shook his head and complained, "But I don't need to go to the toilet!" "Yes, you do!" "Why?" "Because we say so!" The young recruit asked, "Why do you say so?" The reply: "Because we've got you by the balls!" The young man sighed, nodded his head, and replied, "OK! OK!" He rose and headed toward the latrine, apparently understanding and accepting the principle that he was to comply with the instructions, no matter whether the orders were meaningful or not!

In my work with UFOErs, I have noticed that so many persons are able to go through the initiation stage quickly, because they accept and acknowledge the apparent absurdity of the process. Possibly, because of their past-life expe-

28. Newbrough, 1882.
29. *Book of Urantia*, 1955.
30. Rashid, 1992.
31. Deardorff, 1991.

riences, many UFOErs are aware of their close connections with ETs and SBs. Thus, they view most ETs as star brothers and sisters. They recognize the probability that they have chosen to be in the human body during an important cycle of human history, and they are prepared to serve on this planet during a very difficult and challenging period for humankind.

And the task? Although individual tasks may vary, the main mission is to serve as a vessel of love and light, providing compassion and competent assistance to others through advising, counseling, guiding, healing, and teaching. Some UFOErs are parents to "star children"; some are educators, entertainers, medical and mental health practitioners, law officials, speakers, writers, et al. Many UFOErs view themselves merely as friends and neighbors, quietly but effectively helping others by listening to them and talking with them about their doubts and fears, angers and anxieties, hopes and expectations for themselves and for the planet.

In my work as psychologist and UFO researcher, I have met so many of these good souls. Sometimes, when I talk with a client or UFOEr, I feel a sense of "homecoming," as if the other person and I are brothers or sister and brother. We share a resonance of trust and compassion and, somehow, we "know" that our work together is significant, not only for ourselves, but also for humankind and creation.

The important question, in my opinion, is not whether there are "good" and "evil" forces, positive and negative energies, matter and anti-matter, etc. Of course there are!

The important question in my mind and soul is the relationship between these forces and the individual soul. Is the struggle occurring in outer space? Inner awareness? Both?

If there is a struggle for individual souls, is the struggle between friends or foes? Do angels and devils report to the same commander? Are the forces of light and the forces of darkness merely players in a great cosmic contest? If there is a struggle for individual human souls, and if both good and evil entities are engaged in that struggle, then I believe that the human spirit shall continue to grow. If we are important enough for "someone" to send demons after us (or hounds from Heaven), then we possess something of significance, or we are of significance.

Thus, from a pragmatic point of view, each person can assume that he or she—as a good soul—shall continue, regardless of the death of the body. Then, the question remains: what is the duty, or destination, of humankind?

Perhaps the next step for humankind is to develop space/time travel for exploring various planets in other solar systems: the outer space mission. Perhaps the next step for humankind is to develop states of consciousness for exploring various dimensions of intelligence: the inner time mission. Perhaps the next step for humankind is to join with other galactic civilizations in mutual explorations of outer space and inner time.

In each of these scenarios, there are many tasks that require our increased competence and our increased compassion. Perhaps by the turn of the century, we shall obtain some glimpses of the tasks before us. Truly, this is a scary but exciting era to be in the body and with other courageous souls around us.

Hurry Up and Wait

Anyone who has experienced military training is familiar with the term: Hurry up and wait!

Often, the personnel are ready before the signal is given to commence the march or to begin the operation. So, while we wait for the new century to arrive, and the new age to dawn, I offer some suggestions to any reader who is bored or bothered by the current chaos:

Nature/Environment: Consider joining an environmental protection group; each day, at noon, meditate for one minute on world peace; recycle used material; minimize use of harmful chemicals and EM fields, etc.

Body/Health: Assume more responsibility for personal health by taking MEDS: Meditation; Exercise; Diet; and Sociability. Consider joining groups to end violence in home or street; to end public smoking; and to utilize resources and energy programs that are less polluting and more healthy for all.

Mind/Communication: Consider the possibility of listening to others around you about their fears and hopes for the planet and humankind; then sharing with others your fears and hopes for the planet and humankind.

Soul/Consciousness: Consider the suggestion to meditate daily on your task or mission in this lifetime; listen to your "inner guides" or higher self. Be on the lookout for "coincidences" or synchronicities that inform you of your communications with ETs or SBs or angels or higher forces.

If the inner guidance causes you to question your relationships with other persons around you, then follow the advice of the columnist, Ann Landers. Ask yourself: Am I better off with or without these fearful persons? Then, with gentle compassion, choose to continue—or to end—these relationships on a personal, interpersonal, and/or social level.

Self-Forgiveness and Self-Growth

There are many procedures that can be followed in order to cleanse and purify the body/mind/soul. Some persons prefer to pray alone, some with others. Individual and group mediations can create conditions that facilitate helping and healing. Some persons engage in body work and massage, some in sweat lodge ceremonies and vision quests; etc.

In past-life therapy, many clients learn that an important procedure is to explore the memories of possible other lives (POLs) in which we played the roles of victim and persecutor. Usually, when we experience symptoms of body pain and/or mental turmoil, and/or spiritual anguish, we can recall POLs as "victim." However, when we seek the "earliest" memory of the source of our discomfort, we often recall a lifetime when we played the role of "persecutor."

When we learn to forgive ourselves as persecutor, then we can move from the role of victim and persecutor to the role of the "rescuer." The game of rescuer is more fun and more satisfying (to me) than the games of victims and persecutors. However, the role of rescuer is dependent upon the opportunities to interact with victims and persecutors—and to be influenced in those interactions. Thus, rescuers often turn out to be victims and/or persecutors themselves—or, at least, very tired rescuers!

The most satisfying role, I believe, is that of "guide." A guide can serve, at times, as victim/persecutor/rescuer. However, the main task of a guide is to be aware, to accept, and to acknowledge the essence of the other person. (The God in me salutes the God in you.)

Thus, each social encounter, or interpersonal interaction, is both art and science: the science of knowing self and other; the art of evolving that relationship for the benefit of self and other.

While we are awaiting the turn of the century, and the dawn of a new age of science and spirituality, we can practice our roles of guides with our brothers and sisters of humankind.

Then, when we are ready, we can welcome among us the representatives of space/time civilizations. We can then minimize our reactions as victims, persecutors, and rescuers for them, as they minimize those roles in their interactions with us.

Both humankind and ETs can serve as mutual guides, as learners and teachers for all.

PART FOUR: Summary and Conclusions

My "feeling" about the evidence for reincarnation and UFO activity is an emerging belief that we humans are evolving from planetary persons to cosmic citizens.

There are many implications in our growing awareness of the process of reincarnation and soul development, and the educational programs of UFO experiences. These implications range from our roles as individuals, members of groups, and members of humankind. We seem to be readying ourselves for space/time travel as well as further communication with many levels of consciousness.

Evidence is increasing that, during the next few years, we humans will become involved in formal public communication with physical entities from other planets, as well as spirit entities from other dimensions.

I am anxious, and excited, by the education, personal, social, scientific and spiritual challenges that we face as cosmic citizens of many cosmic cultures.

Epilogue

I sat on the edge of the exercise bench, sobbing and sobbing. I continued to sob for a minute or two; then I lifted my head from my hands, and I tested my left hand.

The pain was gone!

I glanced at the clock; the time was a few minutes after 6 A.M. (6 November 1995). I had completed three sets of bench presses; one arm curls; and one arm presses.

A few minutes earlier, I had rested briefly before continuing the exercises for back lifts and leg lifts.

While resting, I contemplated the chronic pain in the joint of my left hand. I reflected deeply on the source of the pain.

Huffing and puffing, and sweating, and trying to "see" the thumb joint, I reexperienced the mental images of my memories of a possible other life (POL) as a Christian crusader.

* * * * *

During the past four years, while working every month with Judy Ginnity, RN, and her husband, John, Reflexologist, (and with Dr. Kent Nelson, DO, Chiropractor), I had learned to ease and then to end the chronic pain in my tailbone, left hip, left shoulder, and neck. The only remaining sources of chronic pain were my feet and left thumb.

I had learned, earlier, to ease some of the pain in my feet and left thumb by exploring my memories of another POL: I reviewed a scenario where I saw myself as a Roman soldier who was on guard duty during a bitterly cold night. The guard decided to leave his post (an offense that was punishable by death) in order to learn why there were no replacements for him and the other guards.

The guard went to the tent of their leader. He found the leader in bed with a woman. Enraged, the guard tried to throttle the leader; however, he restrained himself from doing so because of his sense of loyalty to the leader.

Later, the guard was declared guilty of leaving his post and, thus, was executed. The guard, out of loyalty, would not speak the truth that might have found the leader to be guilty of neglecting his duty to his men.

Remembering, accepting, and releasing the "morality" lesson in that POL had been helpful in recalling the lifetime as a Christian crusader.

I had viewed myself as a young crusader, eager to serve God and Crown, and willing to pledge loyalty to his leader. Two vows were made by the crusader: to fight to victory; and to return safely to his wife and young children.

However, during battle, the crusader was severely injured. His left arm dangled, without shield, because of repeated blows to the left shoulder. He used his left shoulder as a shield, while continuing to wield the sword in his right hand. Eventually, he slipped from the saddle of his horse and fell heavily to the ground. He attempted to rise and return to battle; however, the left arm was attached by only a tendon. The crusader was dying, and he agonized not only from pain, but also from shame and guilt: the social shame of knowing that he had failed to continue fighting, and the personal guilt from not fulfilling his vow to return home to wife and children.

I had reviewed that scene, several times, while lying on Judy Ginnity's massage table and sobbing with tears of remorse. I had recognized aspects of those vows in my current lifetime, as I tried to serve as a loyal proponent of "new science," as well as a faithful husband and father. Yet, the continuing pain in my thumb and feet were a continuing source of frustration.

* * * * *

And then, while sitting and sobbing on the exercise bench, I recognized and released the source of pain in my left thumb: Once more, I view the battle scene; I see the form of the leader who leans from his horse and peers through his visor at the fallen soldier. Without a word of compassion, or a word of commendation, the leader turns away from the dying crusader. At that moment, I--as the soldier--am enraged. My wish is to throttle the leader!

By recognizing my rage, and by releasing that wish to throttle the leader, I forgave myself and forgave the leader for that moment in that lifetime.

By forgiving the leader for his lack of commendation, and by forgiving myself for my lack of achievement, I increased my compassion for both leader and follower. I forgave myself (again) for the attack on the (same?) leader of the Roman guards, and I forgave the (same?) leader for insisting that the guard show his loyalty by maintaining silence about that long delay in the changing of the guards.

Also, I knew that I could learn to forgive a certain University of Wyoming administrator who seemed compelled to persuade or pressure various directors of student services to leave their posts for other positions--as if his leadership style required that he "change the guards" on a regular basis.

While writing this section, I continue to flex my left thumb, and I continue to marvel at the lack of pain. Also, I "know," intuitively, that I am learning to heal the chronic pain that I have experienced in my feet for many years. I am reminded of the wisdom of an excellent scientist, Dr. Borysenko; she wrote: Pain is the teacher; the lesson is love.

* * * * *

I began writing the introduction to PART ONE with a comment about the characteristics of the "ideal" scientist. In my opinion, the ideal scientist displays the training, ethics, and procedures of the conventional scientist; also, he or she displays courage by exploring unconventional topics; creativity in the new methods for systematizing new knowledge; and compassion for sharing with others the results--regardless of the personal sacrifice.

There are many good examples, including David R. Hawkins, MD; Paul R. Hill; Michael Newton, Ph.D.; and Rupert Sheldrake, Ph.D. (See Appendix G.)

Paul Hill (1995) has presented his physical analyses of UFO phenomena: *Unconventional Flying Objects*. His training and former activities as a NASA engineer are impressive, but he showed courage in continuing his investigations despite denial and pressure from administrative officials about his work.

Michael Newton, Ph.D., (1994) has assisted many clients to explore "between lifetimes" for lessons that are important to them in their current soul development. He has proposed a model of levels of soul development (p. 103, *Journey of Souls*).

Rupert Sheldrake, Ph.D., (1981, 1988) has contributed to science in general, as well as biological science, in his analyses of genetic changes and his theory of morphic resonance. Now, in his 1994 book, *Seven Experiments That Could Change the World*, he provides his readers with elegant but inexpensive methods to explore puzzling natural phenomena. He invites skeptics as well as skeptical conventional scientists to test various hypotheses about the world around us.

On the Sunday afternoon before the 6 November 1995 exercise routine, I had completed my reading of the 1995 book by Hawkins, *Power versus Force*.

I marveled at the efforts of Dr. Hawkins, and others, who have developed an approach for the scientific study of human consciousness. Using the technique of "applied kinesiology" (muscle testing), Hawkins has provided a summary of results from his survey of thousands of participants and millions of questions.

His claims, if read and replicated by other researchers, may revolutionize our view of ourselves as "spirits" as well as "scientists."

As I reviewed the "map of consciousness" (p. 52), I was reminded of the description by Saint Augustine of two roads for the human journey, one descending and one ascending. Hawkins indicates that we humans can descend from Courage to Pride, Anger, Desire, Fear, Grief, Apathy, Guilt, and Shame. Or, if we choose wisely, we can ascend from Courage to Neutrality, Willingness, Acceptance, Reason, Love, Joy, Peace, and Enlightenment. His studies suggest that as a collective community we humans are able to increase the level at which we operate; individual "masters" or teachers are able to serve as examples for us as we explore and enhance our spiritual journey.

As I continued my "sensing," "intuiting," "thinking," and "feeling" of the implications of the research by Hawkins, I contemplated his claim that every person "knows" how to seek truth at the level of collective consciousness. However, our individual biases and our cultural filters can block and/or distort our awareness of truth!

I pondered the question of whether muscle testing is another variation of indeomotor responses, pendulum techniques, or dowsing techniques. (According to my preliminary testing, the answer is in the affirmative!)

I wondered if conventional scientists would learn to use these methods to obtain responses from UFO experiencers, and UFO investigations, and to explore the realities of UFO activity, as well as the Federal governmental cover-up of the ET presence.

According to a recent newspaper item, approximately one-half of the USA adults agree with the statement: "Some Americans feel that flying saucers are real and the Federal government is hiding the truth from us."[1]

However, in the long run, I believe that the cover-up will become irrelevant. When public information about the ET presence becomes pervasive, then the relevant questions will focus on the powers and purposes of cosmic civilizations. To whom can curious persons turn for reliable information: Governmental representatives? ET representatives? UFO experiencers? Themselves?

Can internal dowsing and external dialogue be combined by investigators to check on the honesty of governmental documents and the integrity of ET representatives? Can we increase our technical and ethical competence in order to communicate with various levels of cosmic consciousness?

Can we illuminate our soul samples and enlighten the path of our soul journeys?

This is a time of change and challenge. May we all experience more--

Love and Light,

—Leo

---

1. (See the summary of a Scripps Howard News Service and Ohio University survey, "Flying Saucers Real? Many believe so." *The Arizona Republic,* July 8, 1995, pp. A1-A16.)

Summary of 1961-62 Study

The results of the 1961-62 study[1] are summarized as follows:

Summary

A questionnaire survey was conducted among three groups: 26 Ph.D. faculty and graduate students in a Psychology Department (Psychology); 59 graduate students enrolled in an NDEA Guidance Institute (Guidance); and 259 members of an organization which is interested in "flying saucers" or Unidentified Flying Objects (UFOs), the National Investigations Committee on Aerial Phenomena (NICAP). It was hypothesized that there would be no differences between the scores of the three groups on the *Personal Attitude Survey*[2] and the *Scientific Attitude Survey*[3].

The results showed significant differences (P<.001) between the three groups with respect to their mean scores on both inventories, with the NICAP groups scoring higher on both "dogmatic" and "scientific" inventories, followed by the Guidance group and the Psychology group, respectively. Also, the survey showed differences in regard to social status and education. Psychology and Guidance subjects received an *Index of Social Status*[4] which would classify them in the Upper Middle Class, while NICAP subjects would be classified mainly in the Upper Middle and Lower Middle Classes. The average years of education were tabulated as follows: Psychology, 18.8 year; Guidance, 17.2 years; and NICAP, 14.0 years).

The results suggest that the NICAP group is more "dogmatic" and more "scientific" than the Psychology and Guidance groups. There are two feasible interpretations of these results: 1) The *Scientific Attitude Survey* (Sprinkle, 1962) is not useful in assessing "scientific" attitudes, and/or 2) the two inventories have assessed the tendency of the three grops to exhibit the "Yeasay-

---

1. Sprinkle, 1969.
2. Rockeach, 1960.
3. Sprinkle, 1962.
4. McGuire & White, 1955.

Naysay" pattern[5]. The latter interpretation indicates that there may be more "yeasayers" (those with an agreeing response set or a readiness to affirm) in the NICAP groups, followed by the Guidance group, and Psychology group, respectively.

---

5. Couch & Keniston, 1960.

UFO Report Form

IUR
Institute for UFO Research
1304 S. College Ave.
Fort Collins, CO 80524
970/482-3731

UFO Report Form

(Unusual UFO Observations and Impressions)

This questionnaire is designed to gain information in several specific areas: self-information about each participant; a self-description of each participant's views about his/her psychic abilities; a self-description of each participant's views about UFO phenomena; "loss of time" events; and impressions obtained by each participant about the possible origins, powers, and purposes of those who control UFO phenomena.

Please Note: On the last page, there is a section for your signature and the date of completing the questionnaire. Also, each participant is asked to indicate whether his or her name may be used in connection with any publication or results from this study. The personal information will be handled in a confidential manner, and no names of participants will be used in any publication unless participants permit their names to be used.

This is an abbreviated form. Please take additional paper to answer the questions fully, if you intend to fill out the form.
Thank you very much for your cooperation and willingness to complete this questionnaire.

R. Leo Sprinkle, Ph. D.
Counseling Psychologist

209

I. Self-Information: (Please complete the following items.)

  1. Name (Please Print)_____

  2. Address: _____

  3. Telephone (_____)_____

  4. Date of Birth: _____

  5. Check one: Male_____ Female_____

  6. Age: _____

  7. Please circle the number which represents the total number of years of your formal education or its equivalent:

  1 2 3 4 5 6 7 8 9 10 11 12 13 14 15 16 17 18 19 20

  8. Please list any special diploma, certificate, degree, or educational award or achieve-ment:_____

  9. Check one: Married_____, Divorced_____,

     Never Married_____, Remarried_____,

     Spouse is deceased_____. No. of Children_____.

  10. Title of present occupational position:_____

  11. General duties of your present position:_____

  12. Other occupational positions which have been held prior to present position:_____

  13. Psychic Interests and Abilities: (Please complete the following items. If you wish, you may use the back of the page for additional comments.)

  A. Do you believe that you have some ability to gain extra-sensory perceptions (ESP) of thoughts and feelings of other people (telepathy)?

     Yes_____No_____Not sure_____

  B. Do you believe that you have some ability to gain impressions of events or objects which are outside your usual environment (clairvoyance)?

     Yes_____No_____Not sure_____

  C. Do you believe that you have some ability to gain impressions of future events (pre-cognition)? Yes_____No_____Not sure_____

  D. Do you believe that you have some ability to influence the physical environment around you (psycho-kinesis or "mind over matter")?

     Yes_____No_____ Not sure_____

  E. Have you ever participated in a scientific investigation of your ESP abilities? Yes_____No_____

  F. Have you participated in a seance or group meditation to demonstrate your ESP abilities? Yes_____No_____

  G. Do you gain some of your psychic impressions through any of these processes?

     Dreams Yes___ No___

Communion with other persons Yes___ No___
Visions Yes___ No___
Communion with other spirits Yes___ No___
Prayers Yes___ No___ Other Processes: _____
Meditations Yes___ No___

H. Through what process do you gain most of your psychic impressions?
_____

I. Have you experienced a spiritual event or religious "rebirth"?
Yes____ No___

J. Do you consider your knowledge of parapsychology (study of ESP) to consist mainly (check one or more) in the areas of: personal interest in ESP events of every day life____; magazine and newspaper accounts of ESP events____; empirical investigations of alleged ESP events____; experimental investigations in the laboratory of ESP processes____.

K. Have your psychic interests and abilities decreased____; increased____; or remained the same____ since your UFO experience(s)?

L. Have psychic experiences decreased____, increased____, or remained the same____ since your UFO experience(s)?

III. UFO Phenomena: (Please complete the following items. If you wish, you may use the back of the page for additional comments.)

1. Have you seen a UFO (Unidentified Flying Object)? Yes____ No____

2. If you have seen a UFO, please give the date, location, number of objects seen, and your opinion of what you saw.
_____

3. Are you a member of any organization which gathers information about UFO reports? Yes____ No____ If "yes," please list the organization(s): _____

4. Do you believe that most "Unknown" sightings can be explained by the hypothesis of "Misinterpretation of Known Phenomena"? Yes____No____

5. Do you believe that most "Unknown" sightings can be explained by the hypothesis of "Psychological Phenomena?" Yes____No____

6. Do you believe that most "Unknown" sightings can be explained by the hypothesis of "Lies or Hoaxes"? Yes____No____

7. Do you believe that most "Unknown" sightings can be explained by the hypothesis of "Governmental Secret Weapons"?Yes____No____

8. Do you believe that most "Unknown" sightings can be explained by the hypothesis of "Extraterrestrial Space Craft"?Yes____No____

9. Have you observed a UFO sighting during which you experienced a "loss of time"? If so, are you now aware of the possible events which occurred during that "loss of time" experience? Please describe your impressions of the event and possible association with a UFO observation: _____

10. Have you used self-hypnosis or sought hypnotic sessions in order to remember any "loss of time" events? Yes____No____

IV. UFOLKS: (Please complete the following items.)

1. Have you experienced a UFO sighting which included the observation of a humanoid or UFO occupant? Yes____No____

If "yes," please give the date, location, number of UFO occupants seen, and your opinion of what you saw:_____

2. On the back of this page, please draw a figure or figures to represent the UFO occupants, or UFOLKS, whom you observed.

3. Have you communicated, directly or indirectly, with UFOLKS?
Yes____No____

If "yes," have you communicated through writing_____, speech_____, or through "mental communication" _____?

4. If you communicated by speech, could you notice lip movement of the UFOLKS? Yes____ No____

5. Was the speech conducted in English? Yes___ No____. Other language?_____

6. If you communicated in writing, do you have any written material given to you? Yes____ No____

7. If you communicated through "mental communication," were you told by UFOLKS how this process was conducted? Yes____No____

8. Were any apparent devices (microphones, earphones, etc.) used in the communication by UFOLKS? Yes____No____

9. What information did you give?_____

10. What information did you receive? _____

V. Life Changes: (Please use a page to describe the changes, if any, which have occurred since your UFO experience[s] in your personal, social, scientific, and spiritual attitudes.)

Please circle the number that corresponds to your current attitude about the concept of reincarnation[1]:

0 1 2 3 4 5 6 7 8 9
DisbeliefUncertainBelief

VI. <u>Additional</u> <u>Comments</u>: (Please use this page to describe, in detail, your own psychic impressions of UFO phenomena, including your own impressions of the possible origins, powers, and purposes of UFOLKS or those who control UFOs.)

Signature _____

Date _____

_____ You may use my name with any publication of this information.

_____ Please do not use my name with any publication of this information.

---

1. This item was added many years later, at the suggestion of James W. Deardorff, Ph. D.

Results of Study of Psychic Impressions of UFO Phenomena

Results of Initial Study[1]

Results of the *Adjective Check List* (ACL) profiles indicate that the scores of the 63 participants were similar to those scores of US men and women, with the highest average score on the Intraception Scale (expressed need for psychological awareness) and the lowest average score on the Succorance Scale (expressed need for assistance):

TABLE 1. Mean Scores on the Adjective Check List[a]

#	Name of ACL Scale	Code	Males	Females	Total
1	Number Checked	(No Ckd)	52.21	58.17	54.48
2	Defensiveness	(Df)	49.85	52.83	50.98
3	Favorable Items	(Fav)	49.10	57.25	52.21
4	Unfavorable Items	(Unfav)	49.08	44.08	47.17
5	Self Confidence	(S Cfd)	50.10	56.04	52.37
6	Self Control	(S Cr)	48.23	52.92	50.02
7	Lability	(Lab)	52.82	53.17	52.95
8	Personal Adjust-ment	(Per Adj)	47.69	53.71	49.98
9	Achievement	(Ach)	52.36	54.00	52.98
10	Dominance	(Dom)	49.79	53.54	51.22
11	Endurance	(End)	53.25	52.54	52.98
12	Order	(Ord)	53.05	52.88	52.98
13	Intraception	(Int)	55.89	57.13	56.37

1. Sprinkle, 1976a.

215

TABLE 1. Mean Scores on the Adjective Check List[a]

#	Name of ACL Scale	Code	Males	Females	Total
14	Nurturance	(Nur)	50.07	53.42	51.35
15	Affiliation	(Aff)	47.46	50.67	48.68
16	Heterosexuality	(Het)	46.07	50.92	47.92
17	Exhibition	(Exh)	49.59	50.25	49.84
18	Autonomy	(Aut)	51.33	51.88	51.44
19	Aggression	(Agg)	49.21	49.88	49.46
20	Change	(Cha)	49.26	51.00	49.92
21	Succorance	(Suc)	47.10	43.75	45.83
22	Abasement	(Aba)	48.03	45.83	47.19
23	Deference	(Def)	47.46	46.92	47.25
24	Counseling Readiness	(Crs)	52.05	50.54	51.48
Number of Participants			39	24	63

a. These obtained scores are based upon standard scores, with an average (mean score) of 50 and a standard deviation (SD) of 10

TABLE 2. Mean Scores on the SVIB-Male Profiles, (N=39)[a]

Group	Description of Occupational Group	Scores
I	Biological Sciences and Professional	35.87
II	Physical Sciences	31.44
III	Production and Military Officer	22.03
IV	Technical and Outdoor	23.82
V	Personnel Services	26.21
VI	Esthetic Occupations	37.36
VII	Business Detail & Office Work	19.44
VIII	Sales and Business Contact	24.62
IX	Verbal Occupations	36.10
SL	Specialization Level	47.10
OL	Occupational Level	57.23
MF	Masculinity-Femininity	40.18
AACH	Academic Achievement	56.03

a. These Obtained Scores are based upon standard scores, with an average (mean score) of 50 and a standard deviation (SD) of 10.

TABLE 3. Mean Scores on the SVIB-Female Profiles, (N=24)[a]

Group	Description of Occupational Group	Scores
I	Music Occupations	32.00
II	Artistic and Verbal Occupations	29.13
III	Professional and Social Services	27.88
IV	Life Insurance Saleswoman	20.63
V	Business Occupations	26.54
VI	Teacher and Housewife	28.33
VII	Nurse and PE Teacher	31.25
VIII	Medical Occupations	29.67
IX	Math, Science, and Engineering	30.17
FM	Femininity-Masculinity	50.79
AACH	Academic Achievement	52.17

a. These Obtained Scores are based upon standard scores, with an average (mean score) of 50 and a standard deviation (SD) of 10.

About three-fourths of the participants (26 males and 20 females) described themselves as having "some" ability for extrasensory perception (ESP). Only 17 participants (13 males and 4 females) described themselves as having "no" ESP abilities. About one-half of the participants (15 males and 16 females) described themselves as having a high interest in the study of ESP, including participation in scientific investigation or group demonstration of their ESP abilities; 32 participants (24 males and 8 females) described themselves as persons who are not interested in the study of ESP and have not participated in scientific investigations or group demonstrations of their ESP abilities:

TABLE 4. Classification of Claims of ESP Interests and Abilities

	Males	Females	Total
Average Years of Education	13.82	14.29	14.00
Standard Deviation	3.23	2.97	3.12
Have "no ability" for ESP (telepathy, clairvoyance, precognition, or psychokinesis)	13	4	17
Have "some ability" for ESP (telepathy, clairvoyance, precognition, or psychokinesis)	26	20	46

TABLE 4. Classification of Claims of ESP Interests and Abilities

	Males	*Females*	*Total*
Have "high interest" in ESP, including participation in scientific investigation and/or group demonstration	15	16	31
Have "no interest" in ESP, including no participation in scientific investigation and/or group demonstration	24	8	32
Total Number of Participants	39	24	63

TABLE 5. Classification of Claims of UFO Observations

	Self-Description of UFO Observation	*Males*	*Females*	*Total*
A	Has not seen a UFO	8	4	12
B	Has seen "nocturnal wandering light" (V)[a]	1	0	1
C	Has seen "unusual object" moving continuously through sky (IV)[a]	3	1	4
D	Has seen "unusual object" stationary or with discontinuous flight (III)[a]	8	3	11
E	Has seen "cloud cigar" in the sky (II)[a]	0	0	0
F	Has seen "unusual object" on or near the ground (I)[a]	8	4	12
G	Has not seen a UFO but has experienced communication with UFO occupants	4	5	9
H	Has seen a UFO and has experienced communication with UFO occupants	5	6	11
I	Has seen UFO occupants and has experienced communication with UFO occupants	1	0	1
J	Has seen UFO, been inside UFO, and has experienced communication with UFO occupants	1	1	2
	Total Number of Participants	39	24	63

a. An attempt was made to classify the statements of UFO observations within the system presented by Vallée, J. and Janine. *Challenge to Science: the UFO Enigma.* N.Y.: Ace Star Books, 1966, pp. 225-226.

TABLE 6. Classification of Psychic Impressions of Possible Motives of UFO Occupants

	Possible Motives of UFO Occupants	Males	Females	Total
A	*Hostile*, to invade the Earth or destroy humankind	1	0	1
B	*Alien*, unknown extra-dimensional mind	0	0	0
C	*Curious*, to study humankind	23	6	29
D	*Prevenient*, to prevent destruction of Earth	2	2	4
E	*Nurturant*, to assist development of human-kind	2	4	6
F	*Hostile* (see above)[a]	0	0	0
G	*Alien* (see above)[a]	2	1	3
H	*Curious* (see above)[a]	8	6	14
I	*Prevenient* (see above)[a]	0	3	3
J	*Nurturant* (see above)[a]	1	2	3
	Total Number of Participants	39	24	63

a. Has experienced communication with UFO occupants: F, G. H, I, J

Most of the participants were willing to describe their impressions of possible motives of UFO occupants. Classification by the investigator indicates that the impressions of participants range between "hostile," "alien," "curious," "prevenient," and "nurturant" motives. (if a participant did not specify his or her impression of the motives of UFO occupants, his or her response was classified in the category labeled "curious.") Of the 40 participants who claim that they have not experienced communication with UFO occupants, 29 participants (23 males and 6 females) describe impressions which suggest a "curious" motive on the part of UFO occupants. Of the 23 participants who claim that they have experienced communication with UFO occupants, 14 participants (8 males and 6 females) describe impressions which suggest a "curious" motive on the part of UFO occupants. Thus, 43 participants (31 males and 12 females) describe impressions which suggest a "curious" motive on the part of the UFO occupants. See Table 6 for information on the impressions of possible motives of UFO occupants.

Table 7 presents selected correlations which indicate significant statistical relationships between certain variables of the inventory scores and descriptions of participants. These correlations are of interest to the extent that they reflect some expected relationships; however, none of the correlations is so high that it could be used with confidence to predict the relationship which might be obtained through future observations. In general, the higher correlations probably are obtained because of similarity of items or overlapping characteristics of the participants.

TABLE 7. Selected Correlations of Participant Characteristics

#	Variables	Males	Females	Total
1 & 37	Years of Education and SL (Specialization Level) of the SVIB-Male	+.430		
2 & 3	Survey of UFO Observations and Level of Psychic Impressions	+.705		
2 & 3	Survey of UFO Observations and Level of Psychic Impressions		+.534	
1 & 19	Years of Education and Heterosexuality Scale of ACL		-.426	
1 & 30	Years of Education and Group III, Professional Occupations of SVIB-Female		+.565	
1 & 19	Years of Education and Academic Achievement Scale of SVIB-Female		+.528	
2 & 3	Survey of UFO Observations and Level of Psychic Impressions			+.635
3 & 6	Level of Psychic Impressions and Favorable Item Scale of ACL			+.352
	Number of Participants	39	24	63

Results of Second Survey

Since the completion of the initial study, the investigator has attempted to learn about other persons who have experienced psychic impressions of UFO phenomena. During the past few years, another 19 persons have responded to the request that they complete the questionnaire and inventories. Most of these persons also completed two other psychological inventories: the 16 PF Test (*Sixteen Personality Factors Test*) and the MMPI (*Minnesota Multiphasic Personality Inventory*).

These persons usually became known to APRO investigators because of unusual UFO sightings, including experiences which suggest that the participants had experienced "mental communication" with UFO occupants. In some cases, the participants claimed that they were engaged in a continuing series of telepathic communications with UFO occupants.

The limitations of this phase of investigation were similar to those of the initial study; the questionnaire method of obtaining data; the question of representativeness of the sample of respondents; and the biases of the investigator.

Results of the *Adjective Check List* (ACL) indicated that the obtained scores were similar to those of US men and women, with higher group scores

Results of the *Adjective Check List* (ACL) indicated that the obtained scores were similar to those of US men and women, with higher group scores on the Scales entitled Number Checked, Self-Confidence, and Intraception (expressed interest in psychological awareness); lower group scores were obtained on the Succorance Scale (expressed need for assistance):

TABLE 8. Group Scores on the Adjective Check List[a]

#	Name of ACL Scale	Code	Males (II)	Females (II)	Total (II)
1	Number Checked	(No Ckd)	55.00	62.84	61.00
2	Defensiveness	(Def)	51.50	55.30	54.41
3	Favorable Items	(Fav)	56.00	59.38	58.58
4	Unfavorable Items	(Unfav)	45.00	45.84	45.64
5	Self Confidence	(S Cfd)	60.50	59.69	59.88
6	Self Control	(S Cr)	50.50	55.00	53.94
7	Lability	(Lab)	60.00	48.77	51.54
8	Personal Adjustment	(Per Adj)	47.75	54.92	53.23
9	Achievement	(Ach)	59.25	58.54	58.71
10	Dominance	(Dom)	59.00	56.77	57.29
11	Endurance	(End)	54.00	58.38	57.35
12	Order	(Ord)	54.25	59.54	58.30
13	Intraception	(Int)	64.00	58.31	59.65
14	Nurturance	(Nur)	55.25	51.54	52.41
15	Affiliation	(Aff)	52.00	52.69	52.53
16	Heterosexuality	(Het)	41.75	45.23	44.41
17	Exhibition	(Exh)	52.00	52.48	52.37
18	Autonomy	(Aut)	55.00	54.31	54.47
19	Aggression	(Agg)	48.25	48.77	48.65
20	Change	(Cha)	62.50	47.00	50.65
21	Succorance	(Suc)	41.00	41.92	41.70
22	Abasement	(Aba)	46.50	42.92	43.76
23	Deference	(Def)	41.75	46.08	45.06
24	Counseling Readiness	(Crs)	41.75	56.23	53.76
	Number of Participants		4	13	17

a. These obtained scores are based upon standard scores, with an average (mean score) of 50 and a standard deviation (SD) of 10.

TABLE 9. *Group Scores on the SVIB-Male Profiles (Group II)*[a]

Occupational Group	Description of Occupational Group	Scores
I	Biological Sciences and Professional	40.40
II	Physical Sciences	30.00
III	Production and Military Officer	26.40
IV	Technical and Outdoor	18.20
V	Personnel Services	32.20
VI	Esthetic Occupations	39.80
VII	CPA Owner	25.00
VIII	Business Detail and Office Work	15.60
IX	Sales and Business Contact	22.20
X	Verbal Occupations	34.40
SL	Specialization Level	53.40
OL	Occupational Level	64.40
MF	Masculinity-Femininity	39.20
AACH	Academic Achievement	70.00
	Number of Participants	5

a. These obtained scores are based upon standard scores, with an average (mean score) of 50 and a standard deviation (SD) of 10.

Results of the Strong Vocational Interest Blank (SVIB-M) indicated that, as a group, the male participants scored higher on the scales of Group I (Biological Sciences and Professional Interests) and Group IV (Esthetic Occupations), and they scored lower on the scales of Group VIII (Business Detail and Office Work) and Group IV (Technical and Outdoor Occupations). See Table 10 for further information about the Occupational Scale scores. The results of the Basic Interest Scales (SVIB-M) indicated that male participants scored like those men who score significantly high on the scales of Science, Adventure, Medical Service, Social Service, Religious Activities, Teaching, Music, Art, and Writing:

TABLE 10. *Group Scores on the Basic Interest Scales (Group II)*[a]

#	*Name of Basic Interest Scale*	*Scores*
1	Public Speaking	59.0
2	Law/Politics	52.2
3	Business Management	44.0
4	Sales	46.2

TABLE 10. Group Scores on the Basic Interest Scales (Group II)[a]

#	*Name of Basic Interest Scale*	*Scores*
5	Merchandising	42.8
6	Office Practices	40.8
7	Military Activities	46.2
8	Technical Supervision	42.0
9	Mathematics	53.8
10	Science	61.6
11	Mechanical	49.4
12	Nature	56.0
13	Agriculture	49.0
14	Adventure	59.8
15	Recreational Leadership	46.2
16	Medical Service	59.6
17	Social Service	60.2
18	Religious Activities	58.8
19	Teaching	64.2
20	Music	65.?
21	Art	63.6
22	Writing	63.2
	Number of SVIB Profiles	5

a. These obtained scores are based upon standard scores, with an average (mean score) of 50 and a standard deviation (SD) of 10.

The results of the Occupational Scales of the *Strong Vocational Interest Blank* (SVIB-F) indicated that female participants scored highest on Group V (Professional Group, including Psychologist, Librarian, Speech Pathologist, Translator) and lowest on Group VIII (Lawyer and Business Group):

TABLE 11. Group Scores on the SVIB-Female Profiles (Group II)[a]

Group	Description of Occupational Group	Scores
I	Music and Entertainment Occupations	25.71
II	Artistic Occupations	27.21
III	Verbal Occupations	30.35
IV	Social Services	25.21
V	Professional Group	36.28
VI	Medical and Engineering Group	32.50

TABLE 11. Group Scores on the SVIB-Female Profiles (Group II)[a]

Group	Description of Occupational Group	Scores
VII	Military Group	33.71
VIII	Lawyer and Business Group	22.35
IX	Home Economist and Dietician	27.92
X	Therapists and Nurses	32.00
XI	Teacher, Saleswoman, and Operators	25.71
AACH	Academic Achievement	53.60
DIV	Diversity of Interests	47.10
FM	Femininity-Masculinity	49.00
OIE	Occupational Introversion-Extroversion	51.30
	Number of Participants	14

a. These obtained scores are based upon standard scores, with an average (mean score) of 50 and a standard deviation (SD) of 10.

The results of the Basic Interest Scales of the SVIB-F indicated that female participants scored significantly higher than US women on the Physical Science Scale:

TABLE 12. Group Scores on the Basic Interest Scales, SVIB-Female (Group II)[a]

#	*Name of Basic Interest Scale*	*Scores*
1	Public Speaking	49.35
2	Law/Politics	46.92
3	Merchandising	48.92
4	Office Practices	50.28
5	Numbers	52.35
6	Physical Science	60.64
7	Mechanical	56.57
8	Outdoors	54.00
9	Biological Science	53.85
10	Medical Service	54.21
11	Teaching	50.78
12	Social Service	48.64
13	Sports	45.00
14	Homemaking	47.00
15	Religious Activities	49.35

TABLE 12. Group Scores on the Basic Interest Scales, SVIB-Female (Group II)[a]

#	Name of Basic Interest Scale	Scores
16	Music	49.21
17	Art	52.64
18	Performing Arts	51.92
19	Writing	54.35
	Number of Participants	14

a. These obtained scores are based upon standard scores, with an average (mean score) of 50, and a standard deviation (SD) of 10.

The results of the *Sixteen Personality Factors Test* (16 PF) may not be useful, since only 2 males and 5 females have completed the test; perhaps, with other participants, the profile scores can be useful for comparison with adult norms:

TABLE 13. Group Scores on the 16 Personality Factors Test (16 PF) (Group II)[a]

#	Name of 16 PF Scale	Males	Females	Total
A	Reserved: Outgoing	5.0	4.2	4.4
B	Less Intelligent: More Intelligent	9.0	6.4	7.2
C	Affected by Feelings: Emotionally Stable	6.0	5.8	5.9
E	Humble: Assertive	8.0	5.6	6.3
F	Sober: Happy-Go-Lucky	6.0	4.4	4.9
G	Expedient: Conscientious	5.5	5.6	5.6
H	Shy: Venturesome	6.0	5.2	5.4
I	Tough-Minded: Tender-Minded	6.0	7.2	6.0
L	Trusting: Suspicious	5.5	5.2	5.3
M	Practical: Imaginative	8.0	7.2	7.4
N	Forthright: Shrewd	2.0	4.8	4.0
O	Self-Assured: Apprehensive	4.5	4.6	4.6
Q_1	Conservative: Experimenting	9.5	6.4	7.4
Q_2	Group Dependent: Self-Sufficient	6.0	8.2	7.6
Q_3	Undisciplined: Self-Conflict: Controlled	6.0	4.8	5.2
Q_4	Relaxed: Tense	5.0	4.6	4.4
	Number of Participants	2	5	7

a. These obtained scores are based upon standard scores, with an average (mean score) of 5.

The results of the *Minnesota Multiphasic Personality Inventory* (MMPI) indicated that the male participants scored highest on Scale 5 (Masculine-Feminine Interests) and lowest on Scale 0 (Social Introversion); the average profile is similar to that of a man who is seen as having many interests, including artistic and literary (or "feminine" interests), with a high level of ego strength and psychological energy, with an interest in social activities and interpersonal relationships, and a tendency toward critical or rational objectivity and personal sensitivity (a profile of a "creative person"). However, the small number of profiles is a major limitation for any general interpretation of the results. The female participants scored highest on Scale 3 (Hysteria) and Scale 4 (Psychopathic Deviancy) and lowest on Scale 5 (M-F Interests). The average profile is similar to that of a woman with "normal" scores, with a tendency toward psychosomatic complaints and a tendency toward "rational thinking":

TABLE 14. *Group Scores on the Minnesota Multiphasic Personality Inventory (MMPI) (Group II)*[a]

		Males		Females	
#	Name of MMPI Scale	Raw Score (+K)	T Score	Raw Score (+K)	T Scores
?	Number of Unanswered	0.00	--	4.78	--
L	Lie Scale[b]	4.50	52	5.64	56
F	Validity Scale[b]	5.50	57	5.07	56
K	Ego Functioning Scale[b]	14.00	53	17.28	60
1	Hypochondriasis (Hs)	9.00	44	13.93	52
2	Depression (D)	15.25	52	17.35	52
3	Hysteria (Hy)	19.75	56	23.43	61
4	Psychopathic Deviancy	24.25	63	22.92	60
5	Masculine-Feminine	30.25	70	38.85	45
6	Paranoia (Pa)	12.50	64	10.14	56
7	Psychasthenia (Pt)	23.75	52	23.64	52
8	Schizophrenia (Sc)	23.75	53	24.50	53
9	Hypomania (Ma)	23.00	65	19.64	58
0	Social Introversion (Si)	13.75	39	22.71	48
E	Ego Strength (ES)	53.50	65	40.14	50
	Number of MMPI Profiles	5		14	

a. These obtained scores can be compared with standard scores (T scores), with an average (mean score) of 50 and a standard deviation (SD) of 10.

b. Non-clinical Scale

In summary, the results of the vocational interest inventory and psychological inventories indicated that, "on paper," the participants as a group showed no unusual psychological reactions, and higher levels of vocational interests in professional activities than in technical or business detail occupations.

The responses to the questionnaire items indicated that the respondents of Group II claim an average of 14.6 years of education; and a majority (16 of 19) claim to have "some ability" for ESP processes, yet a majority (12 of 19) claim to have "little" interest in formal study of ESP:

TABLE 15. Classification of ESP Interests and Abilities (Group II)

Interests and Abilities	*Males*	*Females*	*Total*
Average Years of Education	15.60	14.49	14.63
Have "no ability" for ESP (telepathy, clairvoyance, precognition, or psychokinesis	0	3	3
Have "some ability" for ESP (telepathy, clairvoyance, precognition, or psychokinesis	5	11	16
Have "high interest" in ESP, including participation in scientific investigation and/or group demonstration	2	5	7
Have "no interest" in ESP, including no participation in scientific investigation or group demonstration of abilities	3	9	12
Total number of participants	5	14	19

The majority of respondents (16 of 19) claimed to have experienced communication with UFO occupants, although the experience may or may not have occurred at the time of a UFO sighting. In some cases, participants claimed that they had not seen UFO occupants and yet they had the distinct impression that they "visited" or were "visited" by UFO occupants and given certain information. See the following two tables for further information on the classification of claims of UFO observations and claims of communications:

TABLE 16. Classifications of Claims of UFO Observations (Group II)

	Self-Description of UFO Observation	Males	Females	Total
A	Has not seen a UFO	0	1	1
B	Has seen "nocturnal wandering light" (V)[a]	0	0	0
C	Has seen "unusual object" moving continuously through sky (V)[a]	0	0	0
D	Has seen "unusual object" stationary or with discontinuous flight (III)[a]	0	0	0
E	Has seen "cloud cigar" in the sky (II)[a]	0	0	0
F	Has seen "unusual object" on or near the ground (I)[a]	2	2	4
G	Has not seen an "unusual object" but has experienced communication with UFO occupants	0	3	3
H	Has seen an "unusual object" and has experienced communication with UFO occupants	3	5	8
I	Has seen UFO occupants and has experienced communication with UFO occupants	0	3	3
J	Has seen UFO, been inside UFO, and has experienced communication with UFO occupants	0	0	0
	Total Number of Participants	5	14	19

a. An attempt was made to classify the statements of UFO observations within the system presented by Vallée, J. and Janine. *Challenge to Science: the UFO Enigma.* New York, N.Y.: *Ace Star Books*, 1966. Pp. 225-226.

TABLE 17. Classifications of Claims of UFO Observations and Communications (Group II)

Classifications of Claim	Males	Females	Total
Has seen a UFO or UFOs	5	10	15
Has not seen a UFO or UFOs	0	4	4
Has experienced communication with UFO occupants	4	12	16
Has not experienced communication with UFO occupants	1	2	3

TABLE 17. Classifications of Claims of UFO Observations and Communications (Group II)

Classifications of Claim	Males	Females	Total
Has seen a UFO but has not experienced communication with UFO occupants	1	2	3
Has seen a UFO and has experienced communication with UFO occupants	4	8	12
Has experienced communication but has not seen a UFO	0	3	3
Has not seen a UFO and has not experienced communication with UFO occupants	0	1	1
Total Number of Participants	5	14	19

As would be expected, the majority of respondents who claimed to experience "mental communication" with UFO occupants also offered statements which were interpreted as "positive," rather than "negative," views of the possible motives of UFO occupants. Most of these respondents claim to receive informations, sometimes on a continuing basis, of the relationship between humankind and a Galactic Federation, or "Space Brothers":

TABLE 18. Classifications of Psychic Impressions of Possible Motives of UFO Occupants (Group II)

Possible Motives of UFO Occupants	Males	Females	Total
A *Hostile*, to invade the Earth or destroy humankind	0	0	0
B *Alien*, unknown extra-dimensional mind	0	0	0
C *Curious*, to study humankind	1	1	1
D *Prevenient*, to prevent destruction of the Earth	0	0	0
E *Nurturant*, to assist development of humankind	0	1	1
F *Hostile* (see above)[a]	0	0	0
G *Alien* (see above)[a]	0	0	0
H *Curious* (see above)[a]	2	3	5
I *Prevenient* (see above)[a]	0	2	2
J *Nurturant* (see above)[a]	2	7	9
Total Number of Participants	5	14	19

a. Has experienced communication with UFO occupants

In some cases, participants received information about impending destruction from earthquakes or floods to the possibility of nuclear war or a natural catastrophe. In some cases, participants received messages which profess a great love for humankind and a desire to assist the development of Earth's civilization.

For example, a respondent, LM, claims to be sixty-five years old; claims to have eleven years of education; claims to have seen UFO, to have seen UFO occupants, and to have received "mental communication from UFO occupants." In response to the question about her "impressions of the possible origins, powers, and purposes of UFO occupants or those who control UFOs," she provided this statement:

> I feel that some UFOs come from other planets in our universe, or galaxy, and some may have bases (not stationary) in submarine-type Mother Ships under the seas, and in very remote areas on our planet and Mother Ships in the higher Earth spectrum.
>
> I sense UFO crews volunteer to come to help us save ourselves from prevalent chaos, and a possible holocaust. I sense their craft operates with natural etherized energy that they use, and "it" is forever recharged. I sense UFO crews are thousands (longer?) of years ahead of Earthman's knowledge in every area.
>
> I think that UFOs monitor Earth inhabitants' collective percentage of evolvement by the degree of "Light" (enlightenment) they evaluate in man's composite body.
>
> I believe there may be a few soul-less UFO crews to try and harm us, but I'm impressed that they are in the minority, and chased out by "Aerial Scout Crews."

The Parnell Study[1]

The Hypotheses. As a good empirical scientist, June Parnell established hypotheses that could be tested. Although she had spoken publicly about her own UFO sighting, she worked on the basic assumption that UFO claims are a form of personal fantasy. She hypothesized that persons who report unusual UFO experiences, such as encounters with Space Beings and their spacecraft, would exhibit personality characteristics that are associated with psychopathology. For example, these persons might show elevated scores on Scale F (Validity Scale, or the frequency of unusual items); Scale 8 (Sc - Schizophrenia Scale); and Scale 9 (Hypomania Scale) on the *Minnesota Multiphasic Personality Scale* (MMPI). And, because UFO encounters are unusual claims, June expected that UFO claimants would respond like persons who score higher than average in such characteristics as unconventionality, greater involvement in fantasy life, and potential for creativity, as measured by Factor M on the 16PF test (*16 Personality Factors Test*).

June established group and subgroup profiles, by category of claimed experience, on all scales of the personality inventories. (Scores on the *Strong Vocational Interest Blank* were omitted from her study.) The reported UFO experiences were categorized in two independent classification schemes.

I. Type of visual UFO experience claimed by participants.

1. No claim of UFO, spacecraft, space being or occupant sighting or encounter. (This is not a control group. These persons decided to claim no UFO experience after completing the questionnaire and inventories.)

2. Claim of UFO observed as light or object in the sky.

3. Claim of UFO observed as a spacecraft.

4. Claim to have seen a space being or a UFO occupant.

5. Claim to have been taken on board a spacecraft.

II. Experience of communication with UFO being.

A. No claim of communication with a space being or UFO occupant.

---

1. The Parnell Study was abstracted in the *Dissertation Abstracts International* (Vol. 47, No. 7, 1987).

B. Claim to have communicated with a space being or UFO occupant.

The primary goal of the Parnell study was to provide a psychological description of the participants. The secondary goal was to test four specific hypotheses, as follows:

H1: Those participants who claim more unusual visual sightings (higher numbered types of experiences) or who claim communication with UFO beings will exhibit greater responses to questions about unusual attitudes, feelings, ideas, and thoughts. (Higher scores on MMPI, Scale F.)

H2: Those participants who claim more unusual visual sightings or communication with UFO beings will exhibit a significantly greater tendency toward divergent thinking, creativity, alienation, and remoteness from their general environment. (Higher scores on MMPI, Scale 8.)

H3: Those participants who claim more unusual visual sightings or communication with UFO beings will exhibit a significantly greater tendency toward elevated but unstable mood, psychomotor excitement, and flight of ideas. (Higher scores on MMPI, Scale 9.)

H4: Those participants who claim more unusual visual sightings or communication with UFO beings will exhibit a significantly greater tendency toward imaginative, absent-minded, or bohemian behaviors. (Higher score on 16PF, Factor M.)

Method. June calculated profiles in terms of standard score means, standard T scores for the MMPI, and standard ten scores (sten) for the 16PF. Ninety-five percent confidence intervals were calculated for these means. Any profile score would be meaningful for inferential purposes when (a) the calculated interval did not include the norm group scale mean on which the MMPI was standardized, and (b) the profile score fell outside the normal range.

The Parnell study involved 225 participants: 83 (37%) males and 142 (63%) females, who had contacted me about their UFO experiences and were invited (or encouraged by other UFO researchers) to participate in the survey. The claimed median age of participants was thirty-seven years (SD=12); claimed average education was 14 years (SD=3). Participants claimed residence in various US regions: 142 (63%) in the West; 34 (15%) Northwest: 25 (11%), South; 11 (5%) Northeast. Thirteen (6%) were from other nations.

Results. Profile scores on the 16PF test indicated that participants could be described as responding like persons who are reserved, more intelligent than average, assertive, experimenting, liberal, free-thinking, self-sufficient, resourceful, and preferring their own decisions. Factor M scores fell within the average range (6.1), indicating that there was a balance between imaginative, bohemian, and absent-minded tendencies versus practical, "down-to-Earth" concerns:

TABLE 19. 16 PF Test Profile Score

Factor	A	B	C	E	F	G	H	I
SS	4.2	6.8	5.9	6.7	5.1	5.5	6.0	6.2
SD	2.0	1.8	2.2	2.0	2.0	2.0	2.1	1.8

Factor	L	M	N	O	Q^1	Q^2	Q^3	Q^4
SS	5.5	6.1	5.1	4.9	6.6	7.2	6.1	5.0
SD	1.9	1.9	1.9	2.1	1.8	1.9	1.9	2.2

Profile scores on the MMPI Validity Scales (L, F, and K) indicate that the participants in the study could be viewed as average in their tendencies between admitting faults and wishing to present a favorable self-image; admitting to a typical number of unusual experiences; defensive, guarded, or independent; and able to deal with everyday problems:

TABLE 20. MMPI Profile Scores: Groups indicating Communication (C) or Non-Communication (NC) with UFO Beings.

	Scales	L	F	K	1	2	3	4	6	7	8	9	0	ES
C	T Score	53	62	55	55	52	58	63	63	55	62	64	50	52
	SD	8	11	9	10	10	8	11	13	9	13	11	9	9
NC	T Score	51	56	58	53	51	59	61	59	55	59	61	50	56
	SD	8	8	9	11	11	8	10	10	10	11	12	9	9

The group mean scores on MMPI Scales 4 (Pd), 6 (Pa), 8 (Sc), and 9 (Ma), are moderately elevated, between 60-63. The scores describe persons who can be viewed as reacting to situational pressures and acting out against their own or other's standards of behavior, or as genuinely concerned about social issues and problems; interpersonally sensitive, overly sensitive to criticism, tending toward personalizing the actions of others toward themselves; thinking differently from others; reflecting creativity, avant garde attitudes, or schizoid processes; having greater than usual psychic energy; engaging in a diversity and multiplicity of thoughts; and engaging in many projects that they usually complete.

On the elevated scales, 8 (Sc) and 9 (Ma) were moderately elevated, while F was just within the normal range. (Data for males and females were grouped, because there were no significant differences between gender scores.)

There was little variation on the MMPI and 16 PF scale scores across the various levels of claimed UFO experiences. The five profiles for each type of experience are more similar than not.

Claims of Communication. The mean F Scale score (62) for those participants claiming communication is moderately elevated, indicating that these persons endorsed more than the typical number of unusual experiences. Scores for Scales 6 (Pa) and 8 (Sc) also were moderately elevated (M=63and 62, respectively) for participants who claimed communication with UFO beings. These participants as a group could be described as scoring somewhat similar to persons who are characterized by interpersonal sensitivity; moral self-righteousness; suspiciousness; and creativity or schizoid processes. Some individuals in the group have scores that are markedly elevated.

The 16 PF test profiles of communicators and non-communicators were similar, differing no more than 1.0 mean sten score on any factor.

Tests of Hypotheses. The tests of hypothesis regarding levels of sighting and communication claims yielded the following results:

Hypothesis 1—regarding responses by participants to questions about unusual attitudes, feelings, ideas, and thoughts—was not upheld on the sighting variable (significance of F =.336). However, this hypothesis received strong statistical support in relation to communication variable (significance of F =.003).

Hypothesis 2—regarding responses by participants to questions concerning a general tendency toward divergent thinking, creativity, alienation, and remoteness from the general environment—received weak statistical support on the sighting variable (F =.112) and cannot be considered to have been upheld. However, the hypothesis of such greater tendencies among those who reported communication with space beings or UFO occupants did receive statistical support (significance of F =.034).

Hypothesis 3—regarding greater tendency toward elevated but unstable mood, psychomotor excitement, and flight of ideas—was not upheld in relation to either experience (significance of F =.447) or communication (significance of F =.146).

Hypothesis 4—regarding a significantly greater tendency toward imaginative, absent-minded, or bohemian behavior—was not upheld. (Sighting: significance of F =.166; Communication: significance of F =.447.)

No significant interactions between the independent variables were found for any of the selected scales relating to the four hypotheses discussed above.

ANOVA data on other scales of the instruments also were examined to see if significant F ratios for either the sighting or communications variable could be found, within the limitation that possibly significant F ratios would not be meaningful for interpretation purposes if mean scores for all levels of the variable fell within the normal range.

Within the limitations of these criteria, there was one finding of interest in addition to the results of the hypotheses discussed above. Respondents reporting communication with UFO beings exhibited a significantly greater tendency toward interpersonal sensitivity and concern about what others thought of them, and tended to be oversensitive to criticism, and to personalize actions of others toward themselves, as these characteristics are measured on Scale 6 (Pa) of the MMPI (significance of $F = .010$).

In summary, those in the study who reported a communication experience not only endorsed a significantly greater number of unusual items and experiences (MMPI, Scale *F*), but also were significantly more likely to exhibit heightened sensitivity or hyper-awareness and creative or schizoid tendencies; these tendencies were not exhibited by those in the study who reported UFOs but did not claim a communication experience (MMPI, Scales 6 and 8).

Discussion and Conclusions. Like the Bloecher, Clamar, and Hopkins[2] study, the results of this study show that claims of UFO experiences are not associated with pathological personality self-reports.

There is no way of knowing if the participants' elevation on Scale 9 (*Ma*) of the MMPI was a prior characteristic or if it was a consequence of the reported UFO experiences. One might assume that persons who have high psychic energy are likely to seek to act upon such an experience and do something about it, such as report it to someone else.

On the other hand, participants' elevation on Scale 4 (*Pd*) of the MMPI might be viewed as caused by the claimed UFO sighting or communication experiences. The experiences themselves, and the difficulty of relating them to a skeptical society and skeptical authorities, could have led to an attitude of questioning authority, and could be said to represent situational pressure and conflict.

The tendency to self-sufficiency, resourcefulness, and preferring their own decisions, as measured by the 16 PF Test, could be described as characteristic of persons who have confidence in the validity of their own experiences, even in the face of adversity. However, a reserved attitude could be expected as reasonable self-protection under the circumstances. Persons of above-average intelligence and assertiveness need a rationale or explanation for their experiences, and are more likely to report them. And persons who are experimenting thinkers might be more likely to describe their experiences as being extraordinary.

---

2. Bloecher, Clamar, and Hopkins 1985.

Participants claiming communication experiences were significantly more elevated on Scales F, 6 (*Pa*) and 8 (*Sc*) of the MMPI, when controlling for sighting experience than those who did not claim communication. Reporting a UFO experience involving communication with UFO occupants, as compared to reports not involving communication, can be regarded as endorsement of a more bizarre experience, and consistent with the Scale F results. The tendency toward suspiciousness and mistrust of others, as indicated by the Scale 6 (*Pa*) results, might be expected in view of the ridicule that individuals sometimes have encountered when reporting these more bizarre experiences.

The greater elevation on Scale 8 (*Sc*) can be viewed positively as indicating creativity, or negatively as indicating possible schizoid tendencies. It could be either a predisposing or a consequential characteristic relating to having and reporting such experiences. Hearing voices is commonly thought to be symptomatic of schizophrenia.[3] However, Posey and Losch[4], using interviews and MMPI results, found that hearing voices is a common phenomenon in a normal (college) population.

Thus, the Parnell study could be interpreted as demonstrating that—as a group—225 participants were "normal" in their responses to personality inventories, regardless of the level of claimed UFO experiences. However, participants claiming communication with UFO beings scored higher on some scales for "unusual experiences" than did participants who did not claim communication with UFO beings. The interested reader who wishes to peruse the tables and figures of the Parnell Study is referred to the Bibliography.[5,6]

---

3. Strauss, & Carpenter, 1981.
4. Posey, & Losch, 1983.
5. Parnell, 1987.
6. Parnell & Sprinkle, 1990.

A Comparison of Studies About UFOErs

The study by Ring and Rosing[1] is among the few empirical studies of the personality characteristics of UFO abductees/contactees/experiencers. Other studies or surveys include those by Bloecher, Clamar, and Hopkins[2]; Bartholomew, Basterfield, and Howard[3]; Bryant and Seebach[4]; Boylan and Boylan[5]; Bullard[6]; Fiore[7]; Hopkins[8]; Jacobs[9]; Parnell[10]; Parnell and Sprinkle[11]; Rerecich[12]; Rodeghier, Goodpaster, and Blatterbauer[13]; and Sprinkle.[14]

In my opinion, the study by Parnell and the study by Bloecher, Clamor, and Hopkins established the observation that most UFOErs are "normal" in their responses to personality inventories and other psychological assessment procedures.

The study by Ring and Rosing, and the study by Rodeghier, Goodpaster, and Blatterbauer, confirmed that general observation.

Bartholomew, Basterfield, and Howard concluded that "fantasy prone personality" is a better explanation than conditions of "psychopathology" for the responses of UFOErs. However, in my opinion, their study is flawed because of the basic assumption that experiences of psychic phenomena are "fantasies."

If a researcher takes the position that, at some level of reality, psychic phenomena (spirit visitation, clairvoyance, telepathy, precognition, psycho-

---

1. Ring and Rosing, 1990.
2. Bloecher, Clamar, and Hopkins, 1985.
3. Bartholomew, Basterfield, and Howard, 1991.
4. Bryant and Seebach, 1991.
5. Boylan and Boylan, 1994.
6. Bullard, 1987.
7. Fiore, 1989.
8. Hopkins, 1981, 1988.
9. Jacobs, 1992.
10. Parnell, 1987.
11. Parnell and Sprinkle, 1990.
12. Rerecich, 1993.
13. Rodeghier, Goodpaster, and Blatterbauer, 1991.
14. Sprinkle, 1976a.

kenesis, etc.) are occurring, then persons who report these events may not necessarily be "fantasy prone" personalities.

Ring and Rosing, Rerecich, and Rodeghier, et al., included "fantasy prone" assessments in their studies. Their results do not support the hypothesis that UFOErs are fantasy prone personalities.

Ring and Rosing suggest the possibility that "abductees" are experiencing alien contacts in the "imaginal" world (between our consensual physical reality and the controversial psychical reality). Rodeghier, et al., imply that UFO abductions are occurring in the consensual reality that we "know" (or claim to know) as the "real world."

Question: Could all three interpretations be correct? Could UFO/ET contacts be occurring at a physical level? At a psychical level? Both levels?

Summary of a Study on Future Forecasting

In 1986, I presented a small study of "future forecasting," based upon the good work of a psychologist, David Loye, Ph.D. Loye (1978, 1983) had developed a brief inventory to assess what he calls the HCP Profile (Hemispheric Consensus Prediction Profile).

Loye learned that both groups of persons, who either are characterized as "left brained" (using analytical and logical processes) or as "right brained" (using intuitive and emotional processes), are successful in predicting possible future events. Further, Loye found that, by pooling results from both groups, their predictions can be even more accurate.

I compared three groups of conference participants: 36 Elder Hostel members (retired persons); 55 UFO investigators (UFO Conference); and 122 counselors and psychologists (ACD: Arizona/Nevada Association for Counseling and Development). The 213 participants were asked to complete the HCP Profile (see Table F-1) and then to respond to three items:

(1) Will there be a nuclear war before 2000 A.D.?

(2) Will President Reagan be re-elected--or complete his term in office?

(3) Imagine a USA (or UN) official announcing public contact with UFOLKs while holding a colored plastic clip. What color is the plastic paper clip? Red? White? Blue? Green?

TABLE 21. Percentages of Group Scores on the HCP Profile

HCP	Percentages of HCP Profile Scores			
Profile Scores	Elder Hostel	UFO Conf	AZ/NV ACD	Totals
1.0	5.6	3.6	1.6	2.8
1.1	2.8		1.6	1.4
1.2	13.9	3.6	4.1	5.6

TABLE 21. Percentages of Group Scores on the HCP Profile

HCP	Percentages of HCP Profile Scores			
Profile Scores	Elder Hostel	UFO Conf	AZ/NV ACD	Totals
1.3	5.6	3.6	6.6	5.6
1.4	16.7	5.5	9.0	9.4
1.5	25.0	9.1	15.6	15.5
1.6	8.3	18.2	18.0	16.4
1.7	19.4	21.8	14.8	17.4
1.8	2.8	14.5	14.8	12.7
1.9	-	9.1	9.8	8.0
2.0	-	10.9	4.1	5.2
M =	14.47	16.55	16.03	15.90
SD =	2.10	2.39	2.25	2.36
Mo =	15.00	17.00	16.00	17.00
Md =	14.47	16.79	16.14	16.00
N =	36	55	122	213
Males =	28%	40%	31%	33%
Females =	72%	60%	69%	67%

Results of the study indicated that there were no significant differences between the responses of groups on the items about nuclear war and President Ronald Reagan:

TABLE 22. Frequency and Percentage of Responses to Items about Possible Future Contacts

		Groups			
Item	Response	Elder Hostel	UFO Conf	AZ/NV ACD	Totals
War?	Yes	3 (8.3)	11 (20.0)	19 (15.6)	33 (15.5)
	No	31 (86.1)	44 (80.0)	101 (82.8)	176 (82.6)
	Blank	2 (5.6)	--	2 (1.6)	4 (1.9)
totals		36 (100.0)	55 (100.0)	122 (100.0)	213 (100.0)
RR?	Yes	29 (80.6)	38 (69.1)	92 (75.4)	159 (74.6)
	No	6 (16.7)	17 (30.9)	28 (23.0)	51 (23.9)
	Blank	1 (2.8)	--	2 (1.6)	3 (1.4)

TABLE 22. Frequency and Percentage of Responses to Items about Possible Future Contacts

Item	Response	Elder Hostel	UFO Conf	AZ/NV ACD	Totals
totals		36 (100.0)	55 (100.0)	122 (100.0)	213 (100.0)
	Red	10 (27.8)	6 (10.9)	27 (22.1)	43 (20.2)
	White	4 (11.1)	10 (18.2)	20 (16.4)	34 (16.0)
UFO?	Blue	6 (16.7)	24 (43.6)	48 (39.3)	78 (36.6)
	Green	8 (22.2)	9 (16.4)	23 (18.9)	40 (18.8)
	Yellow	6 (16.7)	2 (3.6)	3 (2.5)	11 (5.2)
	Blank	2 (5.6)	4 (7.3)	1 (0.8)	7 (3.3)
totals		36 (100.0)	55 (100.0)	122 (100.0)	213 (100.0)

However, the UFO Conference participants and the Counselor Conference participants, who were characterized as more right-brained in their future forecasting processes, responded differently than the retired persons on the item about possible formal contact with UFOLKS. Approximately 40% (rather than the expected 20-25%) of participants at the UFO Conference and Counselor Conference selected the option of a blue plastic paper clip. (Each color was considered to be "encoded" in the mind of the researcher as a time frame of five years: red = 1985 - 1990 A.D.; white = 1990-1995; blue = 1995 - 2000; green = 2000 - 2005.) Thus, if one accepts the methodology and the results, one could speculate that either the right-brained participants were resonating, telepathically, to the mind of the researcher; or else they were sensitive, precognitively, to possible future events about public contact with ETs; or both. Thus, the results could be an indication that some participants are "tuned in" to future events.

However, good left-brained researchers have pointed out some other possible explanations for the results: blue is a very popular color, which may account for the larger number of right-brained participants who selected that color. Also, "red, white, and blue" is a frozen metaphor (e.g., US flag), which may account for higher percentage of participants who selected the color blue.

If a researcher had the money and the motive, then he/she could conduct a similar study, using other (less popular) colors for embedded codes for the years between 1995 and 2005. Or, we can learn if Leo's study was "lucky" as an indicator that 1995-2000 is to be the period that formal contact may be announced.

A Comparison of Possible Other Life Impressions from UFOErs and Non-UFOErs

In 1989, I presented a paper, "A Comparison of Possible Other Life Impressions from UFOErs and Non-UFOErs", at the Second International Conference on Paranormal Research (*Proceedings*, Colorado State University, Fort Collins, CO; June 1-4, 1989. Pp. 655-662).

A total of 123 participants had participated in five reincarnation workshops during 1987. The written impressions of 59 participants at the UFO Conference (UFOErs) were tabulated and compared with the written impressions of 64 participants (non-UFOErs) who attended other reincarnation workshops. The written impressions (see Table G-1) included descriptions of a "light" or "object" or "spacecraft" during episodes of a POL (Possible Other Life) in Trip #1.

TABLE 23. Description of Light or Object in Sky

Group	Ratings of Impressions[a]							Total
	1	2	3	4	5	6	7	
UFOers	17	2	14	0	5	17	4	59
Non UFOers	26	10	6	1	6	20	5	64
Total	43	12	20	1	11	37	9	123

a. Categories of Written Impressions:

1. No Response: participants wrote "none" or left blank in the item about a light or an object in the sky.
2. Natural Phenomenon: participants described impressions of natural events, e.g., "lightning," "meteorite," "fire," "sun."
3. A Light: participants described some kind of light, e.g., "bright light,: "light beam," "circle of light."
4. Object: participants described a human made object, e.g., "explosion of Hindenburg" (dirigible).
5. Unknown Phenomenon: participants described a strange event, e.g., "oval silver light," "strange light," "cone shaped light."
6. Craft: participants described some kind of unusual craft, e.g., "mother ship," "small dome," "bright ship."
7. Space Beings: participants described intelligent entities or beings who were associated with the craft, e.g., "gods," "angel," "Christ-like being," "they helped."

There are no significant differences between the two groups in regard to the proportion of participants who, during POL episodes, claimed to experience lights in the sky or natural events versus those participants who claimed spacecraft and/or spacecraft occupants.

There was one minor difference between the two groups: the estimates of the time period that elapsed during Trip #1:

TABLE 24. Estimates of Elapsed Time in Minutes During Trip No. 1

Group	Ps	Mean	SD	t	df	Prob
UFOers	59	24.75	12.51	-2.51	121	.013
Non UFOers	64	29.92	01.33			

UFOErs, on the average, provided a lower estimate of the 40-45 minute session than did the non-UFOErs. UFOErs estimated the elapsed time as 25 minutes, while non-UFOErs estimated the elapsed time as 30 minutes. (Are UFOErs more susceptible to hypnotic suggestions than non-UFOErs?)

The major difference between the two groups was the proportion of participants who selected various time periods for exploration.

TABLE 25. Comparison of Time Periods Selected by UFOers and Non UFOers

Group	100 AD	1750 AD	1900 AD	2100 AD	2300 AD	Totals
UFOers	18	14	8	7	10	57
Non UFOers	9	22	26	1	5	63
Totals	27	36	34	8	15	120[a]

a. 3 participants did not write any impressions from Trip No. 1.

Chi Square = 20.22; 4 degrees of freedom; P = <.0005

More UFOErs provided written impressions from 100 A.D.; approximately two thirds of non-UFOErs provided impressions from 1750 A.D. and 1900 A.D. UFOErs more often selected future time periods than did non-UFOErs.

The results indicated that more UFOErs explored the distant time periods (past and future) than did non-UFOErs; or that more non-UFOErs explored recent past time periods than did UFOErs; or that both processes occurred. However, no difference was found between UFOErs and Non-UFOErs in the proportion of their impressions about "lights in the sky" versus "spacecraft" and "space beings" during episodes of possible other lives.

Life Reading:
Evaluation of Psychological Resonance Procedures

Participant:_____Date_____

R. Leo Sprinkle, Ph.D.
Counseling Psychologist
105 South 4th Street
Laramie, WY 82070
307/721-5125

Arrangements: Sitting Session or Long Distance (SS LD)

Instructions: Based upon your participation in the audiotaped session, please rate the verbalized impressions in regard to what extent the impressions are similar or dissimilar to *your own views* about the following topics? (Please encircle the appropriate number.)

TABLE 26. Self Views

Topics (Self Views)	Dissimilar - ? - Similar									
Attitudes toward other people?	0	1	2	3	4	5	6	7	8	9
Emotions or feelings about self?	0	1	2	3	4	5	6	7	8	9
Future plans or future hopes?	0	1	2	3	4	5	6	7	8	9
Personality characteristics?	0	1	2	3	4	5	6	7	8	9
Philosophy of life or life style?	0	1	2	3	4	5	6	7	8	9
Relationships with other persons?	0	1	2	3	4	5	6	7	8	9
Spiritual interests or goals?	0	1	2	3	4	5	6	7	8	9
Thoughts of self or self-analysis?	0	1	2	3	4	5	6	7	8	9
Verbal self-expressions?	0	1	2	3	4	5	6	7	8	9
Vocational interests and goals?	0	1	2	3	4	5	6	7	8	9
Overall rating?	0	1	2	3	4	5	6	7	8	9

Comments:

_____

_____

_____

_____

_____

_____

_____

_____

_____

_____

_____

_____

_____

_____

_____

_____

_____

_____

_____

Signature:_____

Date: _____

A Pilot Study on PRIMING Procedures: Life Readings

During an 18 month period, from January 1985 through June 1986, a total of 250 persons participated in a pilot study of PRIMING Procedures (PRIME: an acronym for Psychological Resonance Impressions of Mutual Experiences.[1] There were 124 participants who arranged "sitting sessions" (SS) and 126 participants who arranged "long distance" (LD) procedures. After completing arrangements for fee and appointment (from 1/2 hour to 1 hour), each participant sat quietly while the researcher audiotape-recorded his verbalized impressions of the person, including possible current feelings, possible past life impressions, and possible future goals or activities. Afterward, in SS procedures, each participant discussed reactions and rated the views and impressions as "Similar", "?", or "Dissimilar" to self views and attitudes. (Scale: 9-6 = similar; 5 = ?; 4-0 = Dissimilar.) In LD sessions, the audiotape cassette, plus information about procedures and references to reincarnation, were mailed to each participant, who rated the impressions and returned the rating form. Group ratings were analyzed (with assistance from Dr. Steve Bieber, University of Wyoming) on the basis of gender, location, and 10 items of self-reference, plus the Overall rating of impressions (mean rating on the 10 items). (See Appendix H: Life Reading Evaluation Form.)

The results showed no differences between the group ratings on the basis of gender: 58 males (23%) and 192 females (77%). However, the SS Group rated the verbalized impressions higher, on all of the items, than did the LD Group; 6 of the 11 ratings, including Overall rating, were significantly higher (0.05 level of probability): Emotions or Feelings of Self; Relationships with Others; Thoughts of Self Analysis; Verbal Self Expressions; Vocational Interests and Goals. (See table, following page.)

Only seven participants rated the impressions as "?" or "Dissimilar" to their own views ($\leq$ 5.0 Overall Rating). There was a total of 13 who arranged double sessions (including two participants in triple sessions, and one P in four sessions--both SS and LD). The lowest Group ratings were given to the item called Verbal Self Expressions (SS = 6.75; LD = 6.07); the highest ratings were given to the item called Emotion or Feelings of Self (SS = 7.52; LD = 7.10). The Overall ratings for 250 participants were: SS = 7.19; LD = 6.78.

---

1. Sprinkle, 1986a.

The results tend to support the holographic model of mind, and they tend to support the hypothesis that psychological resonance procedures can be used at a distance to share information.

TABLE 27. LD and SS Groups: Results of Pilot Study

Item	Group	Mean Ratings	SDt	T value	Prob.
1. Attitudes Toward Others	SS	7.33	1.29	1.50	.136
	LD	7.06	1.60		
2. Emotions or Feelings	SS	7.25	1.18	2.33	020
	LD	7.10	1.63		
3. Future Plans or Hopes	SS	6.87	1.60	1.00	.317
	LD	6.63	2.06		
4. Personality Characteristics	SS	7.43	1.28	1.96	.317
	LD	7.06	1.63		
5. Philosophy or Life Style	SS	7.34	1.28	1.70	.091
	LD	6.98	1.79		
6. Relationships with Others	SS	7.32	1.38	2.29	.023
	LD	6.82	2.00		
7. Spiritual Interests	SS	7.37	1.55	1.90	.059
	LD	6.82	1.74		
8. Thoughts or Self Analysis	SS	7.33	1.22	2.59	.010
	LD	6.82	1.85		
9. Verbal Self Expressions	SS	6.75	1.82	2.79	.006
	LD	6.07	2.00		
10. Vocational Interests	SS	6.78	1.91	2.01	.046
	LD	6.25	2.23		
Overall Ratings	SS	7.19	1.02	2.58	011
	LD	6.78	1.45		.

SS = 124 participants; LD = 126 participants; Total = 250 Participants

A Field Study of Life Readings

A field study was conducted between 1985 and 1992 (eight years) in order to test the null hypothesis that Long Distance sessions would not be as effective as Sitting Sessions by participants in PRIMING, or psychological resonance procedures.

Over the years, more and more participants described these sessions as a "life reading", á la Edgar Cayce. Now that I am in private practice, and more influenced by my clients than my colleagues, I also call these sessions Life Readings.

After these sessions, each participant was given an evaluation form, with stamped return envelope, and asked to complete and return the form, with any comment, about the verbalized impressions, or Life Reading. Each session was audiorecorded and the cassette tape was given to the participant. (See Appendix H for copy of evaluation form.)

Percentage of returned forms. One question of interest to any researcher is the response rate of respondents to any survey. From September 1989 through February 1992 (two and one-half years), there were 422 total sessions, including 190 LD (45%) and 232 SS (55%) Life Readings. There were 282 (67%) returned evaluation forms. Thus, during that particular time period, two out of three participants completed and returned evaluation forms.

Descriptive frequencies. Between 1985 and 1992, more than one thousand persons (N = 1,040) returned evaluation forms for LD and SS Life Readings.

Overall rating. The mean or average score of "Overall Rating" was 8.217 on a 9-point scale. Thus, both LD and SS participants rated the verbalized impressions as very similar to their own views about themselves. (The item, Overall Rating, was added to the survey, June 1986, after the completion of the pilot study.)

Location of participants. The majority of participants reported residence in the Rocky Mountain region. There were participants from 40 USA states and three other nations: Australia, Canada, and Spain:

TABLE 28. Location of Participants

Location	Frequency	Percent	Valid Percent
Not USA	4	.4	.5
Hawaii	2	.2	.2
Pacific Coast States	48	4.6	5.6
Rocky Mtn. States	645	62.0	75.6
Southwestern States	64	6.2	75.6
Midwest States	45	4.3	5.3
Southern States	22	2.1	2.6
Middle New England	17	1.6	2.0
New England States	6	.6	2.0
(No location given)	187	18.0	(Probably WY SS)

Frequency of gender. Three out of four participants were females (N = 783, 75%).

Frequency of comments. More than four out of five participants wrote comments (N = 881, 85%), usually about their reactions to the verbalized impressions and the possible personal significance of the Life Reading. The majority of the comments were positive in content, although there were occasional criticisms about the lack of meaningful information.

Average ratings of sessions. Group ratings were analyzed for each of the ten topics:

TABLE 29. Group Ratings of Life Reading Sessions

#	Topic	LD	SS
	N	419	430
1.	Attitudes toward others?	7.7780	7.9395
2.	Emotions about self?	7.7852	7.0140
3.	Future hopes/plans?	7.4224	7.4023
4.	Personality characteristics?	7.7971	7.9395
5.	Philosophy of life?	7.7757	7.0093

TABLE 29. Group Ratings of Life Reading Sessions

#	Topic	LD	SS
6.	Relationship with others?	7.6969	7.7977
7.	Spiritual interests?	7.9403	7.7884
8.	Thoughts about self?	7.6110	7.8000
9.	Verbal self-expressions?	7.0239	7.3302
10.	Vocational interests?	7.2291	7.5465
Total Topics:	Sum of Scores	76.0597	77.5674
	SD	12.463	10.388

Topics were rated by participants in LD and SS groups at similar levels. The lowest ratings for LD participants was "verbal self-expressions" and the highest ratings for LD participants was "spiritual interests." For SS participants, the lowest rating was "philosophy of life"; highest, "personality characteristics." The statistical difference between the two groups on Total Topics (Overall Rating) approaches the 0.05 level of probability; however, in general, the ratings of topics by LD participants are similar to those of SS participants.

Some participants did not rate each topic; usually, I marked a rating of "5" (?) on any unrated topic. The Total Topics or Overall Rating was added, June 1986, after the pilot study was completed; thus, the 1985 evaluation forms (N = 250) did not contain the item, Overall Rating.

The following table presents the combined ratings of both LD and SS groups for their life readings.

TABLE 30. Combined LD and SS Ratings Across Topics

# Topic	Mean	Median	Mode	SD	Valid Cases
1	7.837	8.000	9.000	1.299	1022
2	7.883	8.000	9.000	1.343	1031
3	7.381	8.000	9.000	1.758	1008
4	7.835	8.000	8.000	1.318	1025
5	7.863	8.000	9.000	1.418	1020
6	7.733	8.000	8.000	1.473	1017
7	7.806	8.000	9.000	1.560	1017
8	7.683	8.000	8.000	1.480	1023
9	7.173	8.000	9.000	1.756	988

TABLE 30. Combined LD and SS Ratings Across Topics

# Topic	Mean	Median	Mode	SD	Valid Cases
10	7.353	8.000	9.000	1.841	984
Overall	8.217	9.000	9.000	1.135	783

The reliability coefficient of the ten items (Crombach's alpha) is.9123. Thus, the relationships between the ratings of all topics is very high.

Summary and Conclusion of the Field Study

Approximately 500 LD and approximately 500 SS Life Readings were evaluated by more than one thousand participants. Long Distance sessions were rated, in general, as effective as Sitting Sessions.

The majority of participants were satisfied (and many were pleased) with the personal significance of the verbalized impressions and they rated the comments as similar to their self-perceived characteristics and their spiritual development. However, some participants who participated in both SS and LD sessions said that they preferred the Sitting Session so that they could discuss the significance of the verbalized impressions.

In psychical research studies, the term "cold reading" refers to a session in which one person (a psychic or medium or charlatan) provides information to another person (a client or customer or sucker). The information may focus on significant events in the life of the participant; to personal characteristics; and/or to relationships with other persons.

Accuracy of information, as confirmed by the participant, may be attributed to the psychical intuitiveness of the provider and/or spirit guides, or the accuracy may be attributed to the skill of the provider in noting verbal and non-verbal cues, including body language of the participant.

The skeptical investigator may seek methods of minimizing sensory and perceptual cues in the procedures. Many "believers" (positive) accept the hypothesis that some providers can give accurate information; many "believers" (negative) reject the hypothesis that some providers can give accurate information. Those who are "skeptics" are not sure if some providers can give accurate information. (I remain truly skeptical of my own abilities, so I do not think of these sessions as providing "knowledge"; I call these comments "impressions", and allow the participant to evaluate the significance of the comments.)

If the reader is skeptical about these results, then the reader can consider several hypotheses to explain the results. However, we cannot rely on the hypothesis of "coincidence" or "chance"; there are many participants in the study, and the correlation of agreement is very high. We cannot rely on the hypothesis of sensory cues to explain the results; the Long Distance sessions were conducted without the presence of the participants--and without telephone discussion of the session: no dialogue occurred during the sessions, except between Leo as "Self" and Leo as "Participant".

The only hypotheses that seem to be relevant are: (A) Leo is engaged in a hoax and he is falsifying data; (B) participants in these sessions are very gullible and easily persuaded to accept the verbalized impressions as directly related to their self perceptions; (C) the results are indications that, somehow, Leo and Participant are able to merge psychically and to generate verbalized impressions that are perceived by the Participant as similar to his or her self views.

Hypothesis A (Hoax) could be checked by reviewing data sheets (evaluation forms) and checking for signs of tampering by Leo.

Hypothesis B (participants as gullible) is based on a very cynical view of human nature; however, it probably is the best hypothesis for any scoffer to accept.

Hypothesis C (Resonance between Leo and participant) may be difficult to accept by a skeptical reader, but it seems to fit the procedures and the data.

The only other "reasonable" hypothesis is that Leo is being aided with information about participants from spirit guides. I accept this hypothesis; however, I am unable to describe, adequately, this process.

Scientific Opinion Survey (SOS) and The PACTS Model of Abductee/Contactee Experience

R. Leo Sprinkle, Ph.D.
Counseling Psychologist
105 South 4th Street
Laramie, WY 82070
307/721-5125

Please respond to the following items; then, complete the **SOS** (and the PACTS Model, if appropriate). Thank you very much for your participation in this survey.

Gender: Female _____ Male _____ Age _____

Years of Formal Education _____

Academic Degree _____

Please check, if your consider yourself to be a:

_____ UFO Investigator (reading reports and attending UFO conferences)

_____ UFO Researcher (writing papers and speaking at UFO conferences)

_____ UFO Experiencer (observing UFOs, experiencing encounters, and/or mental communication with UFO entities)

_____ Non-UFO Experiencer

Please encircle the appropriate number.

TABLE 31. Scientific Opinion Survey (SOS)

Please rate your opinion of each statement from Disagree to Agree

1.	Science can be described as a body of knowledge and a method of investigation.	-2	-1	0	+1	+2
2.	The scientific method can be used to study physical matter (Nature), biological organisms (Body), psychosocial behaviors (Mind), and consciousness or spirit (Soul).	-2	-1	0	+1	+2
3.	Both sensing (outer awareness) and intuiting (inner awareness) can be useful in gathering information.	-2	-1	0	+1	+2
4.	Both thinking (thoughts) and feeling (emotions) can be useful in evaluating information.	-2	-1	0	+1	+2
5.	There is credible evidence (acceptable or believable evidence) for the existence of dreams.	-2	-1	0	+1	+2
6.	There is credible evidence for the existence of ESP (clairvoyance, precognition, psycho-kinesis, telepathy).	-2	-1	0	+1	+2
7.	There is credible evidence for the existence of unusual "animals" (Bigfoot, Loch Ness Nellie, etc.).	-2	-1	0	+1	+2
8.	There is credible evidence for the existence of the soul (spirit communication, near-death experience, etc.).	-2	-1	0	+1	+2
9.	There is credible evidence for the reports of healing at a distance (group prayer or meditation).	-2	-1	0	+1	+2
10.	There is credible evidence for the reports of unusual cattle mutilations.	-2	-1	0	+1	+2
11.	There is credible evidence for the reality of UFOs (flying saucers).	-2	-1	0	+1	+2
12.	There is credible evidence for the reality of reincarnation.	-2	-1	0	+1	+2
13.	I have experienced some kind of psychic or ESP event.	-2	-1	0	+1	+2
14.	I have experienced some kind of UFO encounter.	-2	-1	0	+1	+2
15.	My own level of belief in the concept of reincarnation.	-2	-1	0	+1	+2

Instructions: If you have experienced some kind of UFO encounter, please evaluate each level of the PACTS Model as "Dissimilar," "Uncertain," or "Similar" to your own UFO experiences. Thank you.

TABLE 32. The PACTS Model of Abductee/Contactee Experience[a]

	Stage	Experience	Dissimilar... ? ...Similar				
P	Preparation Family & cultural experiences.	Family and/or cultural tradition of ESP and/or spiritual contacts. Childhood visitation by Spiritual Beings (SBs). Lucid dreams or precognitive dreams of possible future events. Psychic experiences (e.g., telepathy, clairvoyance, seeing auras, etc.)	-2	-1	0	+1	+2
A	Abduction Inducted or initiated, involuntarily, by SBs.	UFO sightings and/or UFO abduction experiences. Loss of time experiences or partial amnesic events. Taken aboard spacecraft by SBs or UFO entities. Unexplained body marks, scars, emotional reactions (Why me?). Feeling of being "drafted" for some unexplained purpose.	-2	-1	0	+1	+2
C	Contact Inducted or initiated, voluntarily, by SBs.	Adult visitations (by SBs or spiritual guides). Psychic experiences (telepathy, clairvoyance, PK, healing, etc.). Lucid dreams and/or precognitive dreams of possible future. Emotional reactions of visitations?). Feeling of "volunteering" for a spiritual mission or task.	-2	-1	0	+1	+2
T	Training Instruction for a mission or task.	Obsessive/compulsive behaviors (reading, traveling, visions, etc.). Reading various materials, including "uninteresting" materials. Change in personality; feeling of being monitored; "implanted" knowledge. Review of possible past lives.	-2	-1	0	+1	+2
S	Service Cooperation with SBs.	Channeling verbal and/or written information from SBs. Serving as a "messenger" by conducting research, talking to others, etc. Providing instruction, healing, and/or assistance to others. Working to minimize Planetary difficulties; giving assistance to Humankind. Feeling that one "knows" his/her task or purpose in life.	-2	-1	0	+1	+2

a. Sprinkle, R.L. 1988a.

A Field Study on the Scientific Opinions of UFOErs

(Unpublished study; completed 1993.)

As the reader must know by now, one of my pet peeves is the misuse of the word "scientific". (Especially if the word is overused by someone who is not investigating phenomena but is criticizing someone else who is investigating.) And one of my pet biases is the "fact" (an observation) that UFOErs are experiencing "true" as well as "real" events. Thus, the reader should not be surprised to learn that an attempt has been made to compare the "scientific" opinions of UFOErs and non-UFOErs (Sprinkle, 1993).

Since 1990, I have been collecting some data from interested persons who respond to background items and two brief survey forms: *Scientific Opinion Survey* (SOS) and *PACTS Survey* (based on the *PACTS Model*, Sprinkle, 1988). (See survey forms in Appendix K.)

Between January, 1990 and June, 1992 (two-and-one-half years), data were collected from nine groups of persons who were attending workshops or conferences in California, Colorado, and Wyoming.

Hypothesis.

The research hypothesis is that UFOErs differ from non-UFOErs in their responses to the SOS. (Or, for the traditional researcher, the Null Hypothesis: There is no difference between the responses of UFOErs and non-UFOErs to the items of the SOS.)

Participants.

There were 413 participants, including 122 males (39%) and 190 females (61%). Yes, once again, more females participated than males. Do these majorities of females result from more curiosity, more currency, or more courage? Or all three?

Participants who were willing to provide information about age, education, and academic degree sometimes provided information about residence (N = 135; missing = 278). Twenty different states were represented, with a dozen participants who claimed residence outside the USA.

The range of age was from ten years to 84 years; the mean or average years of age was 46.410 (SD = 11.2). Thus, the majority of participants claimed to be between 35 and 58 years of age.

The types of degrees claimed by participants were as follows:

TABLE 33. The types of degrees claimed by Participants

Degree	#	Degree	#
No degree	11	RN/Nursing	4
GED/HS Diploma	3	BA or BS	43
Assoc. Degree	5	MA or MS	32
HS/Some College	2	MD	1
Business College	1	Ph.D.	14
Other Credential	19		

The average level of claimed years of education was as follows: Mean = 15.992; Mode = 16.000; Median = 16.000; SD = 3.381. Thus, most participants claimed between 13 and 19 years of education.

UFOErs and Non-UFOErs.

Of the 413 participants, 236 (57%) described themselves as non-UFOErs; 177 (43%), as UFOErs. Of those participants who provided information on education and age, the results were as follows:

TABLE 34. Mean Years of Education and Age

Groups	Education	Age
Non-UFOErs	16.1031	46.2400
UFOErs	15.8580	46.5155

The differences in education and age between the two groups are not statistically significant.

Results. UFOErs were compared with non-UFOErs on their responses to each topic of the SOS, including ratings of opinions about various topics of "science" (#1-12); claims of personal experiences in ESP (#13); personal experiences with UFO encounters (#14); and personal belief in reincarnation (#15):

TABLE 35. Differences on the SOS Between UFOErs and Non-UFOErs

| | | Probability | | Mean |
Total	Topic	Level	Signif?	Score
1	Science: Knowledge/method?	.05369	not sig.	4.434
2	Science: also study of consc?	.47860	not sig.	3.785
3	Sensing/Intuiting: gather info?	.00004	sig.	.4.629
4	Thinking/Feeling: eval. info?	.00719	sig.	4.495
5	Credible evidence for dreams?	.11050	not sig.	4.639
6	Credible evidence for ESP?	.00001	sig.	4.570
7	Credible evidence for Bigfoot?	.00012	sig.	3.771
8	Credible evidence for Soul?	.00085	sig.	4.425
9	Credible evidence for healing?	.00000	sig.	4.034
10	Cred. evidence for mutilations?	.00000	sig.	4.394
11	Credible evidence for UFOs?	.00000	sig.	4.490
12	Cred. evid. for reincarnation?	.00000	sig.	3.844
13	I have experienced ESP?	.00000	sig.	4.167
14	I have had a UFOE?	.00000	sig.	3.565
15	Personal belief: reincarnation	.00000	sig.	3.932

The results show that there is no significant difference, statistically, between UFOErs and non-UFOErs in their responses to Topic 1 (Science is both knowledge and method.); Topic 2 (Scientific method can be used to study Nature, Body, Mind *and* Soul.); and Topic 5 (There is credible, or believable, evidence for the existence of dreams.).

One respondent apparently was upset about the item on "dreams": "*Everybody* knows that dreams exist!" However, I noted that a few respondents indicated that they "strongly disagreed" with that statement! The item was included as a possible "baseline" for acceptance by most participants.

In general, we can interpret the ratings as an indication that UFOErs and non-UFOErs differ in their responses to items about "credible evidence" for various phenomena. (Apparently, credibility--like beauty--is in the eye of the beholder!) Also, UFOErs and non-UFOErs differ in their claims about ESP experiences and UFO encounters, and in their level of personal belief in the concept of reincarnation. These UFOErs, as a group, tend to agree with the statements that there is credible evidence for various phenomena of "new science". For example, in a pilot study of 228 participants, there were 122 UFOErs and 106 non-UFOErs. Among the non-UFOErs, there were 35 (33%) who expressed a belief in reincarnation; among UFOErs, 91 (75%). (See Sprinkle, 1991.)

PACTS Survey.

If participants claimed to be UFOErs, then the instructions requested that they also respond to the PACTS *Survey*. Ratings were tallied for each topic: Preparation; Abduction; Contact; Training; and Service. Results from 177 Participants were compared on a 5-point scale from Dissimilar (1 and 2), Uncertain (?), to Similar (4 and 5):

TABLE 36. Ratings by UFOErs of Topics on the PACTS Survey

Topic	Mean	Median	Mode	SD
Preparation	3.940	4.000	5.000	1.238
Abduction	3.546	4.000	5.000	1.336
Contact	4.119	5.000	5.000	1.140
Training	3.874	4.000	5.000	1.257
Service	3.896	4.000	5.000	1.283

The majority of UFOErs indicated that the topics, and related comments, were similar to their own experiences. The results provide some support for the hypothesis that UFOErs perceive themselves as going through an "initiation" or vision quest or shamanic journey, which eventually leads to a mission or duty to serve or assist others.

UFO Researchers who focus primarily on the UFO abduction experience may question whether these other topics are relevant. An interesting study could be conducted on the number of years (and level of maturity?) between "abduction" and "service" for the average UFOEr. When does a UFOEr focus on "abduction" (*being taken away from* Earth) and when does a UFOEr focus on "adduction" (*being taken toward* the Stars)?

Some Models of
Human Behaviors

Premack Principle

Basic Method for Self-Reinforcement:

Attach "good consequences" to one's own behavior.

FIGURE 8. *Premack Principle (Dr. David Premack)[a]*

Any response (A) can reinforce any other response (B), provided that B is made contingent upon the occurrence of A.

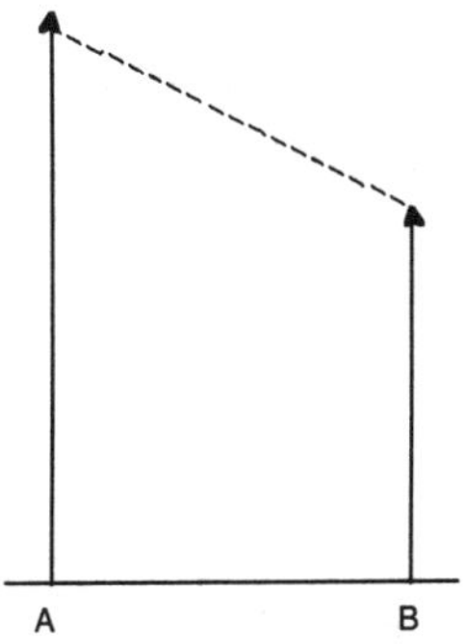

A   B

(In other words, an "if...then" contingency: <u>if</u> B occurs, <u>then</u> A can occur, so that B is reinforced and, thus, occurs more often.)

a. Premack, 1959.

Responses

Based upon his experimental results, Premack[1] concluded: "Reinforcement results when an R of a lower independent rate coincides, within temporal limits, with the stimuli governing the occurrence of an R of a higher independent rate."

1. Premack, 1959, p. 219)

Another way of stating the Premack Principle is: any response (A) can reinforce any other response (B), provided that A is more likely to occur than B, and provided that B is made contingent upon the occurrence of A.

The model of minimizing self pity or self anger is based upon the principle of "waste" or inefficiency. Theme: if one commits an error, or makes a mistake, then it is "natural" to experience some self pity and/or self anger.

FIGURE 9. *Inefficiency from the Effects of Self-Pity and Self-Anger*

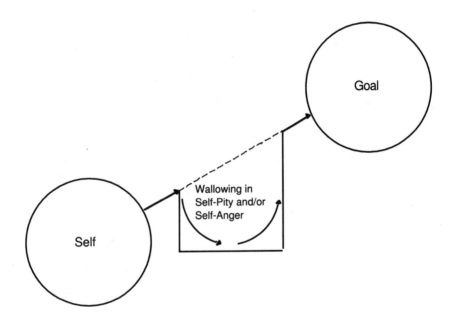

However, if one engages in prolonged self anger, or self-pity, then one's energy is wasted on self-criticism or self-punishment.

A Model of Interpersonal Behaviors

Timothy Leary, Ph.D., provided a model[2] of interpersonal behaviors that is based upon two dimensions: self attitude and attitude toward others. The model can be displayed in several ways, with a variety of labels or names, for behaviors.

2.Adams, 1964.

FIGURE 10. *Leary's Model of Interpersonal Behavior.*

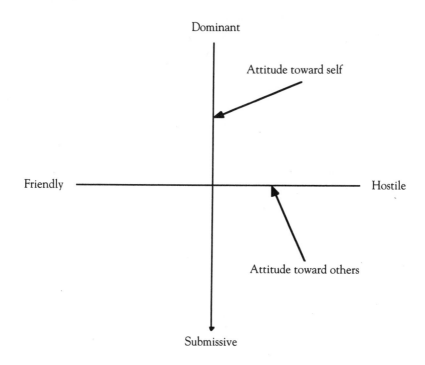

The model indicates that anyone can perceive oneself as "dominant" or as "submissive" (self attitude), and one can perceive other persons as "friendly" or as "hostile" (attitude toward others).

Further, the model indicates that one can predict the patterns of behavior that can occur in various interpersonal interactions; or, if one chooses, one can "control" the patterns of behaviors that occur in interpersonal interactions.

FIGURE 11. *Leary's Model of Predicted Behaviors*

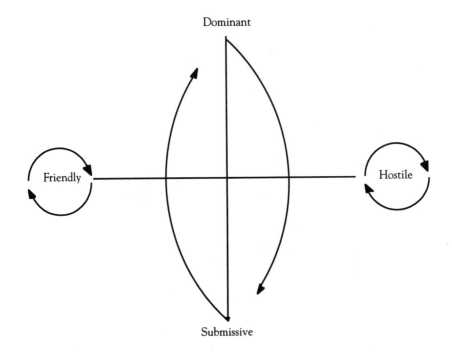

The model indicates that more "dominant" behaviors by one person tend to pull more "submissive" behaviors from another person. Further, "friendly" behavior by one person tends to pull more "friendly" behavior from the other person; "hostile" behavior from one person tends to pull "hostile" behavior from the other person.

Thus, if I exhibit "submissive/friendly" behaviors, then I am more likely to pull "dominant/friendly" behaviors from another person. If I exhibit "dominant/friendly" behaviors, then I am more likely to pull "submissive/friendly" behaviors from another person. If I exhibit "dominant/hostile" behaviors, then I am more likely to pull "submissive/hostile" behaviors from another person. If I exhibit "submissive/hostile" behaviors, then I am more likely to obtain "dominant/hostile" behaviors from another person.

Of course, in any interpersonal interaction, the other person may have a preferred mode of behavior; the person may or may not respond to my manipulations or my pattern of interpersonal interactions. (As psychiatrist Harry Stack Sullivan, M.D., stated: "Nothing makes life difficult except other people and one's own inadequacies for dealing with them.)

Dreikurs' Model of Interpersonal Behaviors. Rudolph Dreikurs, M.D., was a student of Alfred Adler, M.D., and a dynamic person who enjoyed the role of professor and teacher for parents and children.

When I attended a professional meeting in Chicago, 1961-1962, I went early to the room where Professor Dreikurs would be lecturing. I had the opportunity to introduce myself and to tell him that I had learned of his work from one of my graduate students at the University of North Dakota. He peered up at my face and asked, rather brusquely it seemed, "You learn from your graduate students?" Rather hesitantly, I replied, "Well...uh, yes, I do." He smiled and then responded, "Good!"

Dreikurs[3] based his model on the behaviors of children. His model is presented in a book that is rather unusual for a "real" professor: it has only three chapters of theory and seven chapters of practice. Awesome!

Dreikurs categorized the behaviors of children as either active or passive, and as constructive or destructive. Thus, there are four general patterns: active-constructive (AC), passive-constructive (PC), active-destructive (AD), and passive-destructive (PD).

Dreikurs also described four goals of children's behaviors: attention-getting mechanism (AGM); power; revenge; and assumed disability. Thus, his model of children's behaviors shows four goals and four styles of seeking those goals.

When I listened to Dr. Dreikurs, I recognized that his model could be modified for "adult" behavior patterns[4] by adding the model of "neurotic patterns" from psychoanalyst Karen Horney, M.D. The combined model suggests the various patterns of behaviors that adults can use to interact with each other.

3. Dreikurs, R. 1957.
4. Sprinkle, 1976c.

(Moving With Others)? (Non-Neurotic?)

Moving Toward Others

Moving Against Others

Moving Away From Others

TABLE 37. A Model of Adult Behavior Patterns[a]

Active-Constructive	Passive-Constructive	Active-Destructive	Passive-Destructive	Goals
Adult Contribution	Adult Cooperation	Critical (Cynic)	Aloof (Recluse)	Acceptance as Adult (Moving With Others)
Group Leader	Group Follower	Over-Competitive (Climber)	Eccentric (Non-conformist)	Prestige as Adult (Moving Toward Others)
		Wild (Trouble-maker)	Immature (Misfit)	Notoriety as Adult (Moving Against Others)
			Hopeless (Drifter)	Inadequacy as Adult (Moving Away from Others)

a. Sprinkle, 1976d

The MAPS Model of Sciences

FIGURE 13. *MAPS Model: Some Similar Models*

Some Similar Models

Levels of Science (W. Harman)	Levels of Evolution (T. Huxley)	Ancient Model of Reality (Anon.)	ψ Domains (Rychlak)	Psychological Functions (C.J. Jung)
Transpersonal	Spiritual	Soul	Logos	Intuiting
Human	Psycho-social	Mind	Socius	Thinking
Life	Biological	Body	Bios	Feeling
Physical	Physical	Nature	Physikos	Sensing

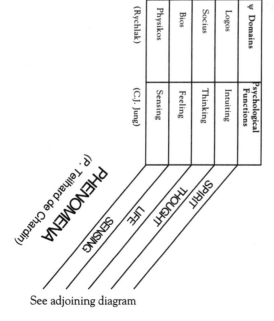

(P. Teilhard de Chardin)
PHENOMENA
SENSING
LIFE
THOUGHT
SPIRIT

See adjoining diagram

FIGURE 14. *MAPS Model: Methods, Phenomena, and Approaches*

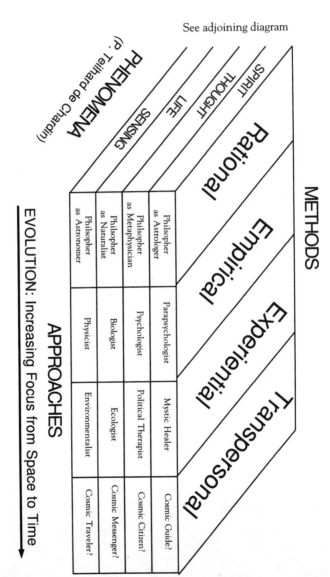

See adjoining diagram

TRANSFORMATION: Increasing Focus from Matter to Light

Some Sources for Further Information

TABLE 38. Some Sources for Further Information

Acronym	Address	Telephone
ACCET	Academy of Clinical Close Encounter Therapists 2826 O Street, Suite 3 Sacramento, CA 95816.	(916/455-0120)
ASPR	American Society for Psychical Research 5 West 73rd Street New York, NY 10023.	(212/799-5050)
CUFOS	J. Allen Hynek Center for UFO Studies 2457 West Peterson Avenue Chicago, IL 60659.	(312/271-3611)
EHE Network	The Exceptional Human Experience Network Rhea White, Director 414 Rockledge Drive New Bern, NC 28562.	(919/636-8734)
Free Spirit	The Newsletter of Spirit Releasement Therapy Center for Human Relations P.O. Box 4061 Enterprise, FL 52725	(407/322-2086)
FSR	FSR Review P.O. Box 162 High Wycombe, Bucks HP 13 5DZ, England	
FUR	Fund for UFO Research P.O. Box 277 Mount Ranier, MMD 20712.	(703/684-6032
IANS	International Association for New Science 1304 South College Avenue Fort Collins, CO 80524.	(970/482-3731)

TABLE 38. Some Sources for Further Information

Acronym	Address	Telephone
IARRT	International Association for Regression Research and Therapies P.O. Box 20151 Riverside, CA 92516.	(909/784-1570)
IF	Intruders Foundation (Budd Hopkins) POB 30233 New York, NY 10011	(242-645-5278)
ISSSEEM	International Society for the Study of Subtle Energies & Energy Medicine 356 Goldco Circle Golden, CO 80403	(303/278-2228)
IFUFOCS	Institute for UFO Contactee Studies 1425 Steele St. Laramie, WY 82070	
IUR	Institute for UFO Research 1304 S. College Fort Collins, CO 80524	(970/493-0312)
MUFON	Mutual UFO Network 103 Oldtowne Road Seguin, TX 78155.	(515/379-9216)
NBP	New Being Project P.O. Box 1657 Guerneville, CA 95446	(707/869-1038)
PEER	Program for Extraordinary Experience Research (John Mack, M.D.) P.O. Box 390707 Cambridge, MA 02139	(617/497-2667)
SES	Society for Scientific Exploration Journal of Scientific Exploration ERL 306 Stanford University Stanford, CA 94305-4055.	(415/593-8581)
UFO	UFO Magazine P.O. Box 6970 Los Angeles, CA 90066-6970.	(310/652-6990)

Some Sources for Further Reading

Almeder, R. (1979). A critique of arguments offered against reincarnation. Journal of Scientific Exploration *Vol. 11, No. 4, pp. 499-526.*

Aronson, V. (1999). *Celestial Healings: Close encounters that cure.* New York: Dutton NAL.

Bowman, C. (1997). *Children's past lives: How past life memories affect your child.* New York: Bantam Books.

Boylan, R.J. (1996). *Project Epihany: Alien emissaries landing or shadow government ambush? Escondido,* CA: The Book Tree.

Brown, C. (1996). *Cosmic Voyage: scientific discovery of Extraterrestrials visiting Earth.* New York: Dutton.

Bryant, A. and L. Seebach. (1997). *Opening to the infinite: Human multidimensional potential.* Mill Spring, NC: Blue Water Publishing.

Cannon, D. (1996). *Legacy from the stars.* P.O. Box 754, Huntsville, AR 72740: Ozark Mountain Publishers.

Corso, P.J. (1997) *The day after Roswell.*New York: Paperback.

Cremo, M.A. and R.L. Thompson. (1994). *The hidden history of the human race.* Badger, CA: Govardhan Hill.

Don, N.S. and G. Moura. (1997). Topographic brain mapping of UFO exeriencers. *Journal of Scientific Exploration, Vol. 11, No. 4, pp. 435-454.*

Emerson, D.A. (1996). *Mars-Earth enigma: A sacred message to mankind.* P.O. Box 460, Lakeville, MN 55044: Galde Press.

Fowler, R.E. (1997). *The Andreasson Legacy.* New York: Marlowe & Co.

Foster, J. (1999). *UFOs: Eminent Discovery on Disc: A lifetime of UFO experiences. 6511 Francis St., Lincoln, NE 68505.*

Griffin, G.E. (1974, 1997). *World without cancer: the story of vitamin B17.* P.O. Box 4646, Westlake Village, CA 91359-1646: American Media.

Hand Clow, B. (1995). *The Pleiadian agenda.* Santa Fe, NM: Bear & Co.

Hawkins, D.R. (1995). *Power vs. Force: The hidden determinants of human behavior.* Sedona, AZ: Veritas Publishing.

Hays, A. (1999). *Voyagers: the sleeping abductees.* Columbus, NC: Granite Publishing.

Hays, A. (1999). *Voyagers: Secrets of Amenti.* Columbus, NC: Granite Publishing.

Hill, P.R. (1995). *Unconventional flying objects: A scientific analysis.* Charlottesville, VA: Hampton Roads.

Hopkins, B. (1996). *Witnessed: The true story of the brooklyn bridge abductions.* New York: Pocket Books.

Howe, L.M. (1996). *Glimpses of other realities, Vol. II: High strangeness.* P.O. Box 300, Jamison, PA 18929: LMH Productions.

Jacobs, D.M. (1998). *The threat: The secret agenda: What the aliens really want...and how they plan to get it.* New York: Simon & Schuster.

Ingerman, S. (1991). *Soul Retrieval: Mending the fragmented self.* San Francisco: Harper.

Lewels, J. 1997). *The God hypothesis: Extraterrestrial life and its implications for science and religion.* Columbus, NC: Granite Publishing.

Mandelker, S. (1995). *From Elsewhere: Being ET in America.* New York: Birch Lane Press.

Manning, J. and N. Begich. (1995). *Angels don't play this HAARP: Advances in Tesla technology.* P.O. Box 201393, Anchorage, AK 99520: Earthpulse Press.

Mannion, M. (1998). *Project Mindshift: The re-education of the american public concerning extraterrestrial life, 1947–present.* New York: M. Evans & Co.

Marrs, J. (1998). *Alien agenda: Investigating the extraterrestrial presence among us.* New York: Harper Collins.

Moorehouse, D. (1996). *Psychic warrior: Inside the CIA's stargate program: the true story of a soldier's espionage and awakening.* New York: St. Martin's Press.

Newton, M. (1994). *Journey of Souls.* St. Paul, MN: Llewellyn.

Novak, P. (1997). *The division of consciousness: The secret afterlife of the psyche.* Charlottesville, VA: Hampton Roads.

Orloff, J. (1996). *Second sight.* New York: Time Warner.

Pratt, B. (1975). *UFO danger zone: Terror and death in Brazil—Where next?* Madison, WI: Horus House Press.

Radin, D. (1997). *The conscious universe.* San Francisco: Harper Edge.

Randles, J. (1995). *Star children: The true story of alien offspring among us.* New York: Sterling.

Schnabel, J. (1997). *Remote viewers: The secret history of America's psychic spies.* New York: Dell.

Sherman, Dan (1998). *Above Black: Project Preserve Dignity.* PO Box 2111, Tualatin, CA 99062: One Team Publishing.

Sitchin, Z. (1996). *Divine encounters: A guide to visions, angels, and other emissaries.* New York: Avon Books.

Stevenson, I. (1997). *Where reincarnation and biology intersect.* Westport, CT: Praeger.

Strieber, W. (1997). *The secret school: Preparation for contact.* New York: Harper Collins.

Strieber, W. (1998). *Confirmation: The hard evidence of aliens among us.* New York: St. Martin's Press.

Taylor, B.J. (In Press). *Love Is a Choice: This is Your Wake-Up Call.*

Teets, B. (1997). *UFOs and mental health. Book One: A briefing of the phenomenon.* PO Box 52, Terra Alta, WV 26764: Headline Books.

Tiller, W.A. (1997). *Science and human transformation.* Walnut Creek, CA: Pavior.

Wesselman, H. (1995). *Spiritwalker: Messages from the future.* New York: Bantam Books.

Wolf, M. (1996). *The Catchers of Heaven: A trilogy.* Pittsburgh, PA: Dorrance.

Woodhouse, M. (1996). *Paradigm wars: World views for a new age.* Berkeley, CA: Frog/North Atlantic.

Bibliography

Adams, H.B. (1964). Mental illness or interpersonal behavior? *American Psychologist*, Vol. 19, No. 3, pp. 191-197.

Adler, A. (1931, 1958). *What life should mean to you*. New York: Capricorn Books.

Alexander, V. (1994(?)). *The Alexander UFO Religious Crisis Survey: The Impact of UFOs and Their Occupants on Religion*. Las Vegas, NV: Bigelow Foundation. Conducted by Victoria Alexander, 1350 Vista Morada, Santa Fe, NM 87501.

Allport, G.W. (1962). Psychological models for guidance. *Harvard Educational Review* Vol. 32, No. 4, pp. 373-381.

Almeder, R. (1992). *Death & personal survival: The evidence for life after death*. Lanham, Maryland: Littlefield, Adams.

Andrews, G.C. (1987). *Extraterrestrials among us*. St. Paul, Minnesota: Llewellyn.

—. (1993). *Extraterrestrial friends and foes*. P.O. Box 2808, Lilbum, Georgia 30226: IllumiNet Press.

Anka, D., & L. Ewing. (1990). *Bashar: Blueprint for change: A message from our future*. Seattle, Washington: New Solutions Publishing.

Aron, E., & A. Aron (1986). *The Maharishi Effect: A revolution through meditation*. Walpole, New Hampshire: Stillpoint.

Ashby, R.H. (1972). *The guidebook for the study of psychical research*. New York: Samuel Weiser.

Bache, Christopher M., Ph.D. (1994). *Lifecycles: Reincarnation and the Web of Life*. New York: Paragon House (paperback).

Baldwin, W.J. (1993). *Spirit releasement therapy*. Falls Church, Virginia: Human Potential Foundation Press.

Bartholemew, R.E., Basterfield, K., & G.S. Howard (1991). UFO abductees and contactees: Psychopathology or fantasy proneness? *Professional Psychology: Research and Practice*, 22, No. 3, 215-222.

Bird, C. (1991). *The persecution and trial of Gaston Naessens: The true story of the efforts to suppress an alternative treatment for cancer, AIDS, and other immunologically based diseases*. Tiburon, California: H.J. Kramer.

Berne, E. (1964) *Games People Play*. New York: Grove Press.

Bloecher, T., Clamar, A., & B. Hopkins. (1985). Summary report on the psychological testing of nine individuals reporting UFO abduction experience. Box 177, Mount Ranier, Maryland 20712: Fund for UFO Research.

Blum, H. (1994) *Out There: The Government's Secret Quest for Extraterrestrials*. New York: Simon and Schuster.

The Book of Urantia (1955). Chicago, IL: The Urantia Foundation.

Boylan, R.J., & L.K. Boylan. (1994). *Close extraterrestrial encounters: Positive experiences with mysterious visitors*. Mill Spring, NC: Blue Water Publishing.

Bramley, W. (1989/1990). *The Gods of Eden: A new look at human history*. 5339 Prospect Road, #300, San Jose, California 95129: Dahlin Family Press.

Broughton, R.S. (1991). *Parapsychology: The controversial science*. New York: Ballantine Books.

Bruhn, A.R. (1989). *The early memories procedures*. 7910 Woodmont Ave., Suite 1300, Bethesda, Maryland 20814: Arnold R. Bruhn Associates.

Bryan, C.D.B. (1995) *Close encounters of the fourth kind: Alien abduction, UFOs, and the conference at M.I.T.* New York: Knopf.

Bryant, A., & L. Seebach. (1991). *Healing shattered reality: Understanding contactee trauma.* Mill Spring, NC: Blue Water Publishing.

Bullard, T.E. (June 1987). *On stolen time: A summary of a comparative study of the UFO abduction mystery*. P.O. Box 277, Mount Ranier, Maryland 20712: Fund for UFO Research.

Bullard, T.E. (1995). *The sympathetic ear: Investigators as variables in UFO abduction reports*. Mount Ranier, Maryland 20712: Fund for UFO Research.

Carey, K. (1991). *Starseed: The third millennium: Living in the posthistoric world*. San Francisco: Harper.

Cerminara, G. (1950) *Many Mansions* New York: Sloan Associates. Reprint 1967 New York: Signet.

Chamberlain, D. (1988). *Babies remember birth*. Los Angeles: Tarcher.

Chapin, T.J., Parnell, J.O., & R.L. Sprinkle. (1986). Hypnosis procedures for exploring memories of UFO experiences. In J.O. Parnell, Ph.D., (Ed.), *Proceedings, Rocky Mountain Conference on UFO Investigation*, 1151 Hidalgo Dr., Laramie, Wyoming 82070; July 17-19, 1986. Pp. 94-111.

Chatelain, M. (1979). *Our ancestors came from outer space*. London: PAN. (Maurice Chatelain, 3976 Kenosha Ave., San Diego, California 92117).

Cheek, D.B., & L.M. LeCron, (1968). *Clinical hypnotherapy*. New York: Grune & Stratton. P. 85.

Clarke, J. (1991). *UFO Encyclopedia, Vols. 1, 2, 3*. Detroit, MI: Omnigraphics.

Clark, R.L. (1995). *Past life therapy: The state of the art*. 22 Pillow Rd., Austin, TX 78745: Rising Star Press.

Condon, E.M. (D.S. Gillmor, Ed.). (1968). *Scientific study of unidentified flying objects*. New York: Bantam.

Cooney, N. (1990-1991). Personal communications.

Couch, A., & K. Keniston. (1960). Yeasayers and naysayers: Agreeing response set as a personality variable. *J. Abnorm. Soc. Psychol.*, 60, No. 2, 1951-174.

Crawford, F. (December 1991). The revealing science of ufology: An anatomy of abduction correlations. *Mufon UFO Journal*, No. 284, 10-15.

Creighton, G. (September 1990). More reports from Russia: XII—A strange encounter in Siberia. *Flying Saucer Review*, 35, No. 3, 17.

Crick, F. (1994). *The astonishing hypothesis: The scientific search for the soul.* New York: Charles Scribner's Sons.

Crystall, E. (1991). *Silent invasion.* New York: Paragon House.

Davenport, M. (1992). *Visitors from time: The secret of the UFOs.* Murfreesboro, TN: Greenleaf Publishing.

Davis, L. (June 1985). How the unidentified flying object experience (UFOE) compares with the near-death experience (NDE) as a vehicle for the evolution of human consciousness. Unpub. Thesis, John F. Kennedy University.

Deardorff, J.W. (1986). Possible extraterrestrial strategy for earth. *Quarterly J. Royal Astronomical Society*, 27, 94-101.

—. (1991). *Celestial teachings: The emergence of the true testament of Jmmanuel (Jesus).* Mill Spring, NC: Blue Water Publishing.

—. (1992). *The problems of the New Testament Gospel origins.* San Francisco: Mellen Research University Press.

—. (1994). *Jesus in India: A reexamination of Jesus' Asian traditions in the light of evidence supporting reincarnation.* San Francisco: International Scholars Publications.

Dossey, L. (1982). *Space, time & medicine.* Boston: Shambhala.

—. (1989). *Recovering the soul: A scientific and spiritual search.* New York: Bantam Books.

—. (1995). How should alternative therapies be evaluated? "Not on the Journey," *Alternative Therapies In Health and Medicine*, 1, No. 2, pp. 6-10-, 79-85.

Downing, B.H. (1968). *The Bible and flying saucers.* New York: Avon.

—. (October 1994). Exodus as a paradigm of UFO strategy. *Mufon UFO Journal*, No. 318, 8-11.

Dreikurs, R. (1957). *Psychology in the classroom.* (new York: Harper & Row).

Druffel, A. (March 1992). Resisting alien abductions: An update. *Mufon UFO Journal*, No. 287, 3-7.

Eisenbud, J. (1967). *The world of Ted Serios.* (Chapter XIV). New York: Wm. Morrow, Pp. 310- 324.

—. *Psi and psychoanalysis.* New York: Grune & Stratton.

Emmons, C.F. (1982). *Chinese ghosts and ESP: A study of paranormal beliefs and experiences.* Metachen, New Jersey: The Scarecrow Press.

Emmons, M.L. (1978). *The inner source: A guide to meditative therapy.* P.O. Box 1094, San Luis Obispo, California 93406: Impact Publishers.

Essene, V., & S. Nidle. (1994). *You are becoming a galactic human.* 1556 Halford Ave., #288, Santa Clara, California 95051: Spiritual Education Endeavors.

Evans, H. (1983). *The evidence of UFOs.* Wellingborough, Northampton: The Aquarian Press.

Ferris, T. (1992). *The mind's sky: Human intelligence in a cosmic context.* New York: Bantam.

Fiore, E. (1978). *You have been here before: A psychologist looks at past lives.* New York: Coward, McCann & Geohegan.

—. (1987). *The unquiet dead: A psychologist treats spirit possession—detecting and removing earthbound spirits.* Garden City, New York: Doubleday.

—. (1989) *Encounters: A psychologist reveals case studies of abductions by extraterrestrials.* New York: Doubleday.

Fowler, R.E. (1974). *UFOs: Interplanetary visitors.* Jericho, New York: Exposition Press.

—. (1979). *The Andreasson affair.* Englewood Cliffs, New Jersey: Prentice-Hall.

—. (1981). *Casebook of a UFO investigator.* Englewood Cliffs, New Jersey: Prentice-Hall.

—. (1990). *The Watchers: The secret design behind UFO abduction.* New York: Bantam.

—. (1992). *The Andreasson Affair, Phase Two.* Englewood Cliffs, New Jersey: Prentice- Hall.

—. (1993). *The Allagash Abductions: Undeniable evidence of alien intervention.* Mill Spring, NC: Blue Water Publishing.

—. (1995). *The Watchers II: Exploring UFOs and the near-death experience.* Mill Spring, NC: Blue Water Publishing.

Freer, N. (1987). *Breaking the godspell: The politics of our evolution.* Los Angeles: Falcon Press.

Friedman, S. (1991). The case for UFOs as alien spacecraft and the government UFO cover-up. (In Michael Lindemann. *UFOs and the alien presence: Six viewpoints.* Santa Barbara, California: The 2020 Group. Pp. 12-60.)

Frieling, R. (1977). *Christianity and reincarnation.* Edinburgh, England: Floris Books.

Fuchs, W.A. (Autumn 1991). *Mysterious holes in Switzerland.* Flying Saucer Review, 36, No. 3, 19- 20.

Fuller, J. (1966). *The interrupted journey.* New York: Dial Press.

Giannone, R. (March 1992). Who are the men in black? *Fate,* 45, No. 3, Issue 504, 46-50.

Ginsburgh, I. (1975). *First, man, then Adam: A scientific interpretation of the Book of Genesis.* New York: Simon and Schuster.

Glum, G.L. (1988). *Calling of an angel.* Los Angeles: Silent Walker Publishing.

Goldberg, B. (1982). *Past lives—future lives:* Accounts of regressions and progressions through hypnosis. North Hollywood, California: Newcastle.

Gordon, J.S. (August 1991). The UFO experience. *The Atlantic*, 268, No. 2, 82-98.

Graeber, M.J. (1976). Dynamic displays: Two case studies. Unpub. manuscript.

—. (1977). Case study No. 2, Bailey. Unpub. manuscript, 52-68.

—. (1978) Dynamic displays, Raefield. Unpub. manuscript, 7-11.

—. (1980). On biorhythmic states in UFO reports. Unpub. manuscript, 1-14.

—. (1990-1991). Personal communications.

Granchi, I. (1992). *UFOs and abductions in Brazil*. Madison, Wisconsin: Horus House Press.

Greer, S.M. (1991-1992). The full spectrum of reality and UFO research. *New Science News*, 1, No. 2, 6-7.

—. (1991). *The CSETI comprehensive assessment of the UFO/ETI phenomenon—2 May 1991*. P.O. Box 15401, Asheville, North Carolina 28813.

—. (1999). *Extraterrestrial Contact: Evidence and Implications*. Afton VA: Crossing Point, Inc.

Grey, A. (1990). *Sacred mirrors: The visionary art of Alex Grey*. Rochester, Vermont: Inner Traditions International.

Grosso, M. (1985). *The final choice: Playing the survival game*. Walepole, New Hampshire: Stillpoint.

—. (1992a). *Frontiers of the soul: Exploring psychic evolution*. Wheaton, Illinois: Wheaton Books.

—. (1992b). *Soulmaker: True stories from the far side of the psyche*. Norfolk, Virginia: Hampton Roads Publ. Co.

Hall, C.S. (1966). *The meaning of dreams*. New York: McGraw-Hill.

Hamilton, J. (1991). (Noah, P.H., Editor.) *Close encounters of the fourth and fifth kind*. Alro Pub. Co. (Jiles Hamilton, 120 Live Oak Lane, Davenport, Florida 33837).

—. (with P. Smith-McMullen, Ed.) (In Press). *Conversations with extraterrestrials*.

Harman, W. (1988). *Global mind change*. Indianapolis, Indiana: Knowledge Systems.

Hastings, A. (1991). *With the tongues of men and angels: A study of channeling*. Fort Worth, Texas: Holt, Rinehart and Winston.

Hawkins, D.R. (1995). *Power vs. Force: The hidden determinants of human behavior*. Sedona, Arizona: Veritas.

Head J., and S.L. Cranston. (1967) *Reincarnation in World Thought*. New York: Julian Press.

Hickman, I. (1983). *Mind probe—hypnosis*. 4 Woodland Lane, Kirksville, Missouri 63501: Hickman Systems.

—. (1994). *Remote depossession*. 4 Woodland Lane, Kirksville, Missouri 63501: Hickman Systems.

Hill, P.R. (1995). *Unconventional flying objects: A scientific analysis*. Charlottesville, VA: Hampton Roads.

Homme, L. E. (1966). May 13, 1966 presentation "Psychotherapy: a special case of behavioral engineering." *Rocky Mountain Psychological Association:* Albuquerque, NM.

Hopkins, B. (1981). *Missing time: A documented study of UFO abductions.* New York: Marek.

—. (1987). *Intruders: The incredible visitation at Copley Woods.* New York: Random House.

Horn, A.D. (1994). *Humanity's extraterrestrial origins: ET influences in humankind's biological and cultural evolution.* P.O. Box 1632, Mount Shasta, California 96067. A. & L. Horn.

Howe, L.M. (1989). *An alien harvest: Further evidence linking animal mutilations and human abductions to alien life forms.* P.O. Box 538, Huntingdon Valley, Pennsylvania 19006: LMH Productions.

Howe, L.M. (1993). *Glimpses of other realities.* P.O. Box 538, Huntingdon Valley, Pennsylvania 19006: LMH Productions.

Hufford, D.J. (1982). *The terror that comes in the night: An experience-centered study of supernatural traditions.* Philadelphia, Pennsylvania: Univ. of Penn. Press.

Hurtak, J.J. (1977). *The Book of Knowledge: The Keys of Enoch.* P.O. Box FE, Los Gatos, CA 95031: The Academy for Future Science.

Huxley, J. (1953). *Evolution in Action.* New York: Mentor Books.

Hynek, J.A. (1972). *The UFO experience: A scientific inquiry.* Chicago: Henry Regnery.

IFUFOCS. (1994). Institute for UFO Contactee Studies, 1425 Steele St., Laramie, Wyoming 82070.

Ingerman, S. (1991). *Soul retrieval: Mending the fragmented self.* San Francisco: Harper.

Intruders Foundation. (1994). P.O. Box 30233, New York, New York 10011.

Jacobs, D.M. (1975). *The UFO controversy in America.* New York: Signet.

—. (1992a). *Secret life: First-hand accounts of UFO abductions.* New York: Simon & Schuster.

—. (1992b). What do sightings mean? *International UFO Reporter, 17,* No. 1, 13-17, 23.

Jacobs, J. (1992). *Systems of survival: A dialogue on the moral foundations of commerce and politics.* New York: Vintage Books.

Jessup, M. K. (1956) *UFOs and the Bible.* London: Citadel Press.

Jung, C.G. (1933) *Modern man in search of a soul.* W.S. Dell, C.F. Baynes, trans. New York: Harcourt, Brace & World.

—. (1959). *Flying Saucers: A modern myth of things seen in the sky.* New York: Harcourt, Brace & Co.

Kannenberg, I.M. (1992). *UFOs and the psychic factor.* Mill Spring, NC: Blue Water Publishing.

—. (1993). *The alien book of truth.* Mill Spring, NC: Blue Water Publishing.

—. (1995). *Project Earth.* Mill Spring, NC: Blue Water Publishing.

Keel, J.A. (1976). *Why UFOs.* New York: Manor.

Kubis, P., & M. Macy. (1995). *Conversations beyond the light*. P.O. Box 11036, Boulder, Colorado 80301: Continuing Life Research.

Kuhn, T. (1970). *Structure of scientific revolutions* (2nd edition). Chicago: Univ. of Chicago Press.

Keul, A.G., & K. Phillips. (1987). Assessing the witnesses: Psychology and the UFO reporter. (In H. Evans & J. Spencer [Eds.] *UFOs, 1947-1987: The 40 year search for an explanation*. London: Fortean Times. Pp. 230-237.)

Kinder, G. (1987). *Light years: An investigation into the extraterrestrial experiences of Eduard Meier*. New York: Atlantic Monthly Press.

Kirsch, I., & S.J. Lynn. (October 1995). The altered state of hypnosis: Changes in the theoretical landscape. *American Psychologist*, 50, No. 10. Pp. 846-858.

Klass, P. (1983). *UFOs: The public deceived*. New York: Prometheus.

Klimo, J. (1987). *Channeling: Investigations on receiving information from paranormal sources*. Los Angeles: J.P. Tarcher.

LeCron, L.M. (1964). *Self hypnosis: The technique and its use in daily living*. New York: Signet.

Leir, R.K. (1999). *The Aliens and the Scalpel: Scientific Proof of Extraterrestrial Implants in Humans*. Columbus, NC: Granite Publishing.

Lewels, J. (April 1995). The holographic universe and the UFO phenomenon. *Mufon UFO Journal*, No. 324. Pp. 4-6.

Little, G.L. (1991). *People of the web*. Memphis, Tennessee: White Buffalo Books.

—. (1994). *Grand illusions*. Memphis, Tennessee: White Buffalo Books.

Loehr, F. (1959). *The power of prayer on plants*. Garden City, New York: Doubleday.

Lorenzen, C.E., & J. Lorenzen. (1967). *Flying saucer occupants*. New York: Signet.

—. (1976). *Encounters with UFO occupants*. New York: Berkeley.

—. (1977). *Abducted! Confrontations with beings from outer space*. New York: Berkeley.

Loye, D.(1978). *The knowable future: A psychology of forecasting and prophecy*. New York; John Wiley & Sons.

—.(1983). *The sphinx and the rainbow: Rain, mind, and future vision*. Boulder, CO: Shambhala/New Science Library.

Luppi, D. (1990). (Co-created by Mission Control and Diana Luppi). *ET 101: The cosmic instruction manual*. P.O. Box 1556, Sedona, Arizona 86336: Intergalactic Council Pub.

Lyons, B. (1987). *The cancer cure that worked! Fifty years of suppression*. P.O. Box 327, Queensville, Ontario, Canada L0G 1R0: Marcus Books.

Macer-Story, E. (1991). *Sorcery and the UFO experience*. Box 741-JAF Bldg., New York, New York 10116: Magick Mirror Comm.

Mack, J.E. (1994). *Abduction: Human encounters with aliens*. New York: Charles Scribner's Sons.

Marciniak, B. (1992). *Bringers of the dawn: Teachings from the Pleiadians*. Santa Fe, New Mexico: Bear & Co.

Maurey, E. (1988). *Exorcism: How to clear at a distance a spirit-possessed person.* 1469 Morstein Rd., West Chester, Pennsylvania 19380: Whitford Press.

McCampbell, J.M. (1973). *Ufology: New insights from science and common sense.* Belmont, California: Jaymac.

McClain, F.W. (1986). *A practical guide to past life regression.* St. Paul, Minnesota: Llewellyn.

McClenon, J. (1991). Social scientific paradigms for investigating anomalous experience. *J. Scientific Exploration, 5*, No. 2, 191-203.

McDaniel, S.V. (1993). *The McDaniel Report: On the failure of executive, congressional and scientific responsibility in investigating possible evidence of artificial structures on the surface of Mars and in setting mission priorities for NASA's Mars Exploration Program.* Berkeley, California: North Atlantic Books.

McGuire, C., & G.D. White. (1955). The measurement of social status. *Research paper in human development,* No. 3 (revised), Dept. of Educ. Psychol., Univ. of Texas.

McNames, L. (SARI).(1980) *Startling Revelations.* 3620 S.E. 84th Ave., Portland, OR 97266: Universariun Foundation.

—. *The Crystal Tower.* 3620 S.E. 84th Ave., Portland, OR 97266: Universariun Foundation.

Meek, G. (1980). *After we die, what then?* Franklin, North Carolina: Meta-Science. (Columbus, Ohio: Ariel Press).

Michel, A. (1974). A letter regarding the programming of the UFO phenomenon. "Mail Bag," *Flying Saucer Review, 20*, No. 3, 29.

Milani, M.M., & B.R. Smith. (1984). *A primer of rotational physics.* Westmoreland, New Hampshire: Fainshaw Press.

Mintz, E.E. (1983). *The psychic thread: Paranormal and transpersonal aspects of psychotherapy.* New York: Human Sciences Press.

Montgomery, R. (1985). *Aliens among us.* New York: Putnam's Sons.

Morehead, A.H., & G. Mott-Smith. (1966). *The complete book of solitaire & patience games.* New York: Bantam.

Motoyama, H. (1993). *Karma and reincarnation.* New York: Avon Books.

Moyer, E. P. (1975). *The day of celestial visitation.* (2nd ed.). Hicksville, New York: Exposition Press.

Murphy, G. (1961). *Challenge of psychical research: A primer of parapsychology.* New York: Harper & Brothers.

Naegeli-Osjord, H. (1988). *Possession & exorcism.* Oregon, Wisconsin: New Frontiers Center.

Netherton, M., & N. Shiffron. (1978). *Past life therapy.* New York: Wm. Morrow.

Newbrough, J.B. (1882) *OAHSPE: A new Bible in the words of Jehovih and his angel embassadors.* New York: OAHSPE Publishing Association.

Newton, M. (1994). *Journey of souls: Case studies of life between lives.* St. Paul, Minnesota: Llewellyn.

O'Leary, B. (1989). *Exploring inner and outer space: A scientists's perspective on personal and planetary transformation.* Berkeley, California: North Atlantic Books.

—. (1992). *The second coming of science: An intimate report on the new science.* Berkeley, California: North Atlantic Books.

—. (1996). *Miracle in the void: Free energy, UFOs and other scientific revelations.* Kihei, Hawaii: Kampua'a Press.

Orcutt, T.L., & J.R. Prell, (1994). *Integrative paradigms of psychotherapy.* Boston: Allyn and Bacon.

Parnell, J.O. (1987). Personality characteristics on the MMPI, 16 PF, and ACL of persons who claim UFO experiences. *Dissertation Abstracts International,* 47, No. 7. (Order No. DA 8623104).

—. & R.L. Sprinkle. (1990). Personality characteristics of persons who claim UFO experiences. *J. UFO Studies* (new series), 2, 45-58.

Pauling, L. (1970). *Vitamin C and the common cold.* San Francisco: W.H. Freeman.

Peebles, C. (1994). *Watch the skies! A chronicle of the flying saucer myth.* Washington, D.C.: Smithsonian Institution Press.

Peterson, J.W. (1987). *The secret life of kids: An exploration into their psychic senses.* Wheaton, Illinois: Theosophical Publishing House/Quest Books.

Posey, T.B., & M.E. Losch. (1983). Auditory Hallucinations of Hearing Voices in 375 Normal Subjects. *Imagination, Cognition and Personality,* Vol. 3, pp. 99-113.

Premack, D. (1959). "Toward Empirical Behavior Laws" *The Psychology Review* Vol. 66, pp. 219-233.

Pritchard, A., D.E. Pritchard, J.E. Mack, P. Kasey, & C. Yapp, (Eds.). (1994). *Alien discussions: Proceedings of the abduction study conference held at M.I.T., Cambridge, Massachusetts; June 13- 17, 1992.* Cambridge, Massachusetts: North Cambridge Press.

Prochaska, J.O., Norcross, J.C., & C.C. DiClemente. (1994). *Changing for good: The revolutionary program that explains the six stages of change and teaches you how to free yourself from bad habits.* New York: Morrow.

Puharich, A. (1974). *Uri: A journal of the mystery of Uri Geller.* Garden City, New York: Doubleday/Anchor.

Pursglove, D. (Ed.)(1995). *Zen in the art of close encounters.* Berkeley, CA: The New Being Project.

Ra, A. (1992). Surviving the infinite wave: Hanging ten on the edge of reality, in the ocean of bliss. Unpub. doctoral dissertation, Union Institute, Cincinnati, Ohio; 11 April 1992.

Rashid, I., & E.A Meier.,Trans. (German); J.H. Ziegler, &B.L. Greene, (English) (1992). *The Talmud of Jmmanuel.* Mill Spring, NC: Blue Water Publishing.

Regnier, E. (1971). *There is a cure for the common cold.* New York: Warner Paperback Library.

Rerecich, R.A., Jr. (1994) *Reports of alien abduction: Prevalence and psychological correlates in a college population.* Unpublished master thesis. Idaho State University.

Ring, K. (1992). *The omega project: Near-death experiences, UFO encounters, and mind at large.* New York: Wm. Morrow.

—., & C.J. Rosing. (1990). The omega project: A psychological survey of persons reporting abductions and other UFO phenomena. *J. UFO Studies* (new series), 2, 59-98.

Rodeghier, M., J. Goodpaster, and S. Blatterbauer. (1991). Psychosocial characteristics of abductees: Results from the CUFOS abduction project. *Journal of UFO Studies.* Vol. 3, pp. 59-90.

Rogo, D.S. (1983). *Leaving the body: A practical guide to astral projection.* Englewood Cliffs, New Jersey: Prentice-Hall.

—. (1985). *The search for yesterday: A critical examination of the evidence for reincarnation.* Englewood Cliffs, New Jersey: Prentice-Hall.

Rockeach, M. (1960). *The Open and Closed Mind.* N.Y.: Basic Books.

Rosenthal, R. (1966). *Experimenter effects in behavioral research.* New York: Appleton-Century- Crofts.

Royal, L., & K. Priest. (1992). *Visitors from within.* P.O. Box 12626, Scottsdale, Arizona 85267: Royal Priest Research.

—. (1993). *Preparing for contact: A metamorphosis of consciousness.* P.O. Box 30973, Phoenix, Arizona 85096: Royal Priest Research.

Russell, P. (1983). *The global brain: Speculations on the evolutionary leap to planetary consciousness.* Los Angeles: J.P. Tarcher.

—. (1992). *The white hole in time.* San Francisco: Harper.

Rutledge, H. (1981). *Project identified: The first scientific field study of UFO phenomena.* Englewood Cliffs, New Jersey: Prentice-Hall.

Salisbury, F. (1974). *The Utah UFO display: A biologist's report.* Old Greenwich, Connecticut: Devin-Adair.

Schwarz, B.E. (1983). *UFO dynamics: Psychiatric and psychic aspects of the UFO syndrome,* I and II. Moore Haven, Florida: Rainbow.

Sheldon, Sidney. (1992). *Doomsday Conspiracy.* New York: Warner Paperback Library. Mass Market Paperback Reprint edition

Sheldrake, R. (1981). *A new science of life: The hypothesis of formative causation.* Los Angeles: J.P. Tarcher.

—. (1988). *The presence of the past: Morphic resonance and the habits of nature.* New York: Times/Random House.

—. (1994). *Seven experiments that could change the world.* London: Fourth Estate.

Simpson, G.R. (1992). *ET corn gods game.* 33 Catalpa Terrace, Darien, Connecticut 06820.

Sitchin, Z. (1990). *Genesis revisited: Is modern science catching up with ancient knowledge?* New York: Avon.

—. (1993). *When Time Began: The First New Age.* New York: Avon.

Spanos, N.P., Cross, P.A., Dickon, K., & S.C. DuBreuil. (1993). Close encounters: An examination of UFO experiences. *J. Abnormal Psychology, 102,* No. 4, 624-632.

—., Burgess, C.A., & M.F. Burgess. (1994). Past life identities, UFO abductions, and Satanic ritual abuse. *Inter. J. Clin. and Experimental Hypnosis*, XLII, No. 4, 433-446.

Sprinkle, R.L. (1961). Permanence of measured vocational interests and socio-economic background. Unpub. diss., University of Missouri, Columbia, Missouri.

— (1962). Scientific attitude survey. (Unpublished attitude inventory).

— (1967). Psychological implications in the investigation of UFO reports. In L.J. & C.E. Lorenzen, *Flying saucer occupants*. New York: Signet. Pp. 160-186.

—. (1968 July 29). Personal statement on investigation of UFO reports. Submitted to J.E. Roush, Chairman, *Symposium on Unidentified Flying Objects*. Hearings before the Committee on Science and Astronautics, United States House of Representatives. 90th Congress, 2nd Session. Pp. 206-210.

—. (June 1969). Personal and scientific attitudes: A study of persons interested in UFO reports. In C. Bowen (Ed.), Beyond Condon, *Flying Saucer Review*, Special Issue, No. 2, 6-10.

—. (1976a). Hypnotic and psychic implications in the investigation of UFO reports. In C.E. and J. Lorenzen, *Encounters with UFO occupants*. New York: Berkeley. Pp. 256-329.

—. (1976b). UFO activity: Cosmic consciousness conditioning? *UFO Phenomena* (EDITECS, Bologna, Italy), *1*, No. 1, 56-62.

—. (1976c). The self improvement program handbook. Unpub. manuscript: University of Wyoming.

—. (1976d). Hypnotic time regression procedures in the investigation of UFO experiences. In C.E., & J. Lorenzen, *Abducted! Confrontation with beings from outer space*. New York: Berkeley. pp. 191-222.

—. (1977). Progress reports: The Kentucky abduction. *International UFO Reporter*, *2*, No. 3, (March) pp. 6-7.

—. (1978/1979). Using the pendulum technique in the investigation of UFO experiences. *UPIAR*. (EDITECS, Bologna, Italy). Vol. III, No. 1, 179-218.

—. (1979). Investigation of the alleged UFO experience of Carl Higdon. In R.F. Haines (Ed.), *UFO phenomena and the behavioral scientist*. Metuchen, New Jersey: Scarecrow Press. Pp. 223-357.

—. (1980). *Proceedings of the Rocky Mountain Conference on UFO Investigations*. May 22, 24, 25, 1980; University of Wyoming, Laramie, Wyoming 82070.

—. (1981). *Proceedings*, Rocky Mountain Conference on UFO Investigation. 1425 Steele St., Laramie, Wyoming 82070.

—. (1982). UFO contactees: Captive collaborators or cosmic citizens? In R.L. Sprinkle (Ed.), *1981 Proceedings*, Rocky Mountain Conference on UFO Investigation. Pp. 227-280.

—. (1985a). *Trance forming yourself: Self hypnosis for stress management and self improvement*. Trans Formations Unlimited, 1425 Steele St., Laramie, Wyoming 82070. (Videotape).

—. (1985b). Psychological resonance: A holographic model of counseling. *J. Counseling and Development*, 64, No. 3, (November) 206-208.

—. (1985c). The significance of UFO experiences. in Pursglove (1995).

—. (1987). A tentative model of abductee/contactee UFO experiences. In J.O. Parnell (Ed.), *Proceedings*, Rocky Mountain Conference on UFO Investigation. (July 17-19, 1986), School of Extended Studies, University of Wyoming, Laramie, Wyoming 82071). Pp. 108-111.

—. (1988a). Psychotherapeutic services for persons who claim UFO experiences. *Psychotherapy in Private Practice*, 6, No. 3, 151-157.

—. (1988b). The changing message of UFO activity: From empirical science to experiential science? In M.L. Albertson, D.S. Ward, & K.P. Freeman (Eds.), *Paranormal Research Proceedings*, Colorado State University, Fort Collins, Colorado: July 7-10, 1988. Pp. 797-815.

—. (1989). "A Comparison of Possible Other Life Impressions from UFOErs and Non-UFOErs" *Proceedings*, Colorado State University, Fort Collins, CO; June 1-4. Pp. 655-662.

—. (1991a). Review of book by Cassirer, M., *Parapsychology and the UFO*. In R. White, (Ed.), *J. of the American Society of Psychical Research*, 85, 87-90.

—. (1991b). Therapeutic reframing of EAT through peer group support. TREAT III Conference, Kansas City, Missouri: March 6-10, 1991. (Fowler Jones, Ed.D., and Rima Laibow, M.D.)

—. (1991c). UFO contactees and new science. in M.L. Albertson, Ph.D. (Ed.) *New Science '91: Proceeding of the International Conference on New Science*; Colorado State University, Fort Collins, CO; Sept 26–29, 1991, pp. 527–539.

—. (1992). Psychical analysis of UFO experiences. *Proceedings*, International Symposium on UFO Research, May 22-25, Denver, CO. Pp. 203-232. (Sponsored by IANS, 1304 S. College Ave., Fort Collins, CO 80524).

—. (1993). A field study on the scientific opinions of UFOErs. Unpublished MS., 105 S. 4th St., Laramie, WY 82070.

—. (1994). UFO Experiences and a possible new experiential science. *Exceptional Human Experience*, Vol. 12, No. 2, pp. 172-184.

—. (1995). A *review*: Anomalous experiences & trauma: Current theoretical, research and clinical perspectives. (*Proceedings* of TREAT II). Edited by Rima E. Laibow, Robert N. Sollod, and John P. Wilson. Dobbs Ferry, New York: Center for Treatment and Research of Experienced Anomalous Trauma. P.O. Box 728, Ardsley, New York 10502. *The J. of the American Society of Psychical Research*, (January 1995), Vol. 89, 84-88.

Snow, C.B. (1989). *Mass dreams of the future*. New York: McGraw-Hill.

Steiger, B., & F. Steiger. (1981). *The Star People*. New York: Beechtree/Wm. Morrow.

Stevenson, I. (1966). *Twenty cases suggestive of reincarnation*. New York: American Society of Psychical Research.

—. (1987). *Children who remember previous lives*. Charlottesville: University Press of Virginia.

Stone, I. (1972). *The healing factor: Vitamin C against disease*. New York: Putnam/Perigee.

Strauss, J.S. & W.T. Carpenter, Jr. (1981). *Schizophrenia*. New York: Plenum.

Strieber, W. (1987). *Communion: A true story*. New York: Beechtree/Wm. Morrow.

—. (1988). *Transformation: The breakthrough*. New York: Beechtree/Wm. Morrow.

—. (1995). *Breakthrough: The next step*. New York: Harper Collins.

Stringfield, L. (1977) *Situation Red: UFO Siege*. Garden City, NY: Doubleday. (Liberty, Kentucky case: pp. 198-211.)

Sturrock, Peter. (1994). "Report on a Survey of the Membership of the American Astronomical Society Concerning the UFO Problem" *The Journal of Scientific Exploration*, Part 1, Vol. 8, No. 1, pp. 1-45; Part 2 Vol. 8, No. 2, pp. 153-195; Part 3, Vol. 8, No. 3, pp. 309-346;

Swann, I. (1975). *To kiss earth good-bye*. New York: Hawthorn Books.

—. (1993). *Your Nostradamas factor: Accessing your innate ability to see into the future*. New York: Fireside/Simon & Schuster.

Teilhard de Chardin, P. (1961) *The Phenomenon of Man*. New York: Mentor Books.

Thompson, K. (1991). *Aliens and angels: UFOs and the mythic imagination*. New York: Addison-Wesley.

Thompson, R.L. (1993). *Alien identities: Ancient insights into modern UFO phenomena*. San Diego, California: Govardhan/Hill Publ.

Timms, M. (1994). *Beyond prophecies and predictions: Everyone's quick guide to the coming changes*. New York: Ballantine Books.

UFOCCI. (1994). UFO Contact Center International, 3001 S. 288th St., #304, Federal Way, Washington 98003.

Vallée, J. (1965). *Anatomy of a phenomenon: Unidentified objects in space—a scientific appraisal*. Chicago: Henry Regnery.

—. (1969). *Passport to Magonia*. Chicago: Henry Regnery.

—. (1975). *The invisible college: What a group of scientists has discovered about UFO influences on the human race*. New York: E.P. Dutton.

—. (1979). *Messengers of deception: UFO contact and cults*. Berkeley, California: And/Or Press.

Van Flandern, T. (1993). *Dark matter, missing planets and new comets: Paradoxes resolved, origins illuminated*. Berkeley, California: North Atlantic Books.

Wambach, H. (1978). *Reliving past lives: The evidence under hypnosis*. New York: Harper & Row.

—. (1979). *Life before life*. New York: Bantam.

Ward, D.S. (1992). Astrology according to the goddess. *Proceedings, International Forum on New Science, 1992*, Fort Collins, Colorado, September 17-20. Pp. 263-271.

Watkins, J.C. (1978). *The therapeutic self: Developing resonance—key to effective relationships*. New York: Human Sciences Press.

Webb, W.N. (1994). *Encounter at Buff Ledge: A UFO case history*. Chicago, Illinois: J. Allen Hynek Center for UFO Studies.

Weiss, B.L. (1988). *Many lives, many masters*. New York: Simon & Schuster/ A Fireside Book.

—. (1993). *Through time into healing.* New York: A Fireside Book.

White, J. (February 1992). Aliens among us: A "religious" conspiracy. *Mufon UFO Journal,* No. 282, 7-13.

White, R.A. (June 1991). Feminist science, postmodern views, and exceptional human experience. *Exceptional Human Experience,* 9, No. 1, 2-11.

—. (December 1993). *Exceptional human experience: Bodegrand Papers,* Vol. II, No. 2. EHE Network, 2 Plane Tree Lane, Dix Hills, New York 11746. "Why write an EHE Autobiography? A Personal Essay," pp. 129-131.

Whitton, J.L., & J. Fisher. (1986). *Life between life: Scientific explorations into the void separating one incarnation from the next.* Garden City, New York: Doubleday/Dolphin.

Williams, T. (Ed.). (1987). *Post-traumatic stress disorder: A handbook for clinicians.* P.O. Box 14301, Cincinnati, Ohio 45214: Disabled American Veterans.

Winters, Randolf. (1994). *The Pleiadian Mission: A Time of Awareness.* Yorba Linda, CA: The Pleiades Project.

Woodhouse, Mark B. (1996) *Paradigm Wars.* Berkeley: Frog Ltd.

Woolger, R.J. (1987). *Other lives, other selves: A Jungian psychotherapist discovers past lives.* New York: Doubleday/Dolphin.

Yogananda, P. (1971) *Autobiography of a Yogi.* Los Angeles, CA: Self-Realization Fellowship, pp. 173-193.

zho-de-Rah and Zon-O-Ray. (1994). *The intergalactic cafe guide to the care and feeding of your light body.* P.O. Box 1124, Sedona, Arizona 86339: InterDimensional Light Infusions.

Index

If you would like to see more
books by

Granite Publishing
or its imprints

Swan•Raven & Co.
or
Agents of Change

Please contact us...

phone: 800.366.0264
fax: 828.894.8454
email: GraniteP@aol.com

- or -

Visit our Web Site at
www.5thworld.com

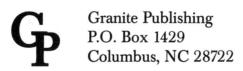

Granite Publishing
P.O. Box 1429
Columbus, NC 28722